Growth versus Security

Growth versus Security

Old and New EU Members' Quest for a New Economic and Social Model

Edited by

Wojciech Bieńkowski
Josef C. Brada
and
Mariusz-Jan Radło

First published 2008 by
PALGRAVE MACMILLAN

Palgrave Macmillan in the UK is an imprint of Macmillan Publishers Limited,
registered in England, company number 785998, of Houndmills, Basingstoke,
Hampshire RG21 6XS.

Palgrave Macmillan in the US is a division of St. Martin's Press LLC,
175 Fifth Avenue, New York, NY 10010.

Palgrave Macmillan is the global academic imprint of the above companies
and has companies and representatives throughout the world.

Palgrave® and Macmillan® are registered trademarks in the United States,
the United Kingdom, Europe and other countries.

ISBN-13: 978-0-230-20053-1
ISBN-10: 0-230-20053-2

This book is printed on paper suitable for recycling and made from fully
managed and sustained forest sources. Logging, pulping and manufacturing
processes are expected to conform to the environmental regulations of the
country of origin.

A catalogue record for this book is available from the British Library.

A catalog record for this book is available from the Library of Congress.

10   9   8   7   6   5   4   3   2   1
17 16 15 14 13 12 11 10 09 08

Printed and bound in Great Britain by
CPI Antony Rowe, Chippenham and Eastbourne

Contents

List of Tables, Figures and Boxes

Tables

Figures

Boxes

Foreword

Angus Maddison divides the last millennium into three distinct epochs of economic growth: the Middle Ages, 1000–1500, when world per capita GDP rose by 0.05% a year; the protocapitalistic epoch, 1500–1820, when it grew by 0.07% a year; and the capitalist epoch, 1820–2000, when the rate of growth was 17 times higher than it was in the preceding epoch. The capitalist epoch was ushered in by the establishment of classical economics in the late eighteenth century. The essence of classical system of economics was liberty in the field of individual choice and liberty in the organization of production and trade. The rule of law was embraced as a means to preserve citizens' liberty and property from encroachments by the state, while at the same time establishing and maintaining law and order. In addition, the general observance of established habits, traditions and moral conventions was considered to be as important as written laws.

Classical liberalism laid the foundation for a flexible system that is compatible with entrepreneurship, innovation and prosperity. While flexible, this system is also orderly.

Growth versus Security is an apt title for a volume of essays that is focused on many of the same issues that engaged classical economists. While dressed in modern attire, the policy prescriptions offered by the authors in this volume have the same look and feel as those proposed by the classical economists.

This leaves us with a problem of benefit-cost calculus that was observed and commented on by Frank Knight in 'Anthropology and Economics' (*Journal of Political Economy*, Vol. 49 No. 2, April 1941): 'The problem of change versus stability presents a major issue of policy on which the study of primitive society might conceivably throw some light. This is the question of the gains and losses involved in individual economic liberty, in comparison with a greater stability which, in theory at least, might be had through a greater emphasis on the folk wisdom presumptively embodied in the traditions of the past, enforced by authority.'

It also leaves us with the problem of public opinion because it is public opinion that determines the benefit-cost calculus and, therefore, the direction of economic policy. As Ludwig von Mises concluded in *Theory and History*: 'A statesman can succeed only insofar as his plans are adjusted to the climate of opinion of his time, that is to the ideas that have got hold of his fellows' minds. He can become a leader only if he is prepared to guide people along the paths they want to walk and toward the goal they want to attain. A statesman who antagonizes public opinion is doomed to failure. No matter whether he is an autocrat or an officer of a democracy, the politician must give the people what they wish to get, very much as a businessman must supply the customers with the things they wish to acquire.'

Hopefully, this volume will enlighten public opinion and tilt the public's benefit-cost calculus towards liberal economic policies that promote economic growth and prosperity.

STEVE H. HANKE
Johns Hopkins University, Baltimore

Preface

The aim of this book is to examine whether the recent economic, social and political developments in the European Union and its member states should lead to a change in our perception that the European ability to compete effectively with the United States and with the emerging economies is the fundamental social and policy question facing Europeans.

European Union member states have always sought to share a common vision of an economic and social model that would be a blueprint for all of them to follow, one that would make Europe both prosperous and different from other parts of the world. For many Europeans, and for many years, the blueprint was what we would call the 'European social model', a system based on a high level of social protection, social dialogue and public services to cover activities vital for social cohesion. Nonetheless, economic and political developments in the 1990s and after 2000 made the blueprint less clear and attractive. The crisis of the Western European welfare state, and the subsequent economic reforms stemming from the crisis, led to changes in the economic and social models of the EU member states and gave rise to a debate about the viability of the European social model. The debate became even more complex and dynamic after successive Eastern enlargements of the Union. These made the Union more diverse, not only in economic terms but also in political terms. The new member states, especially those of Central and Eastern Europe, have come a long and impressive way from communism to the market economy and membership in the EU. However, what they discovered in the Union immediately after their accession were struggles with the inefficiencies of the European market economy model to which they had had to adjust. Only one year after the first Eastern enlargement, a major European project for making the Union the most competitive economy in the world by 2010 had to be scaled down as European ambitions met economic realities.

In this perspective, questions about the economic and social models of the EU member states are fundamental for the future of the Union. This is because almost all of the necessary economic reforms to be implemented in the member states imply fundamental redefinitions of already existing models of social, labour and other economic policies. To shed light on this question, we invited policy experts from member states of the European Union and also from the United States to share their views, observations and the outcomes of their research on this key issue.

Therefore, in this volume the reader will find discussions of such issues as flexicurity as an emerging and popular proposal to revitalize the European social model, an analysis of the Swedish model after its revitalization, and an analysis of intergenerational conflicts and their impact on voting behaviour and growth. Another important development that is analyzed in this volume relates to the question of incorporation of the new EU members. The group of eight post-communist countries plus Cyprus and Malta, despite being underdeveloped for the most part at the start of their membership, have demonstrated the most vigorous growth rates in the enlarged EU and have introduced a number of solutions in the economic policy area that had been previously considered but rarely, or only partially, implemented in old Europe. Low or flat taxes, deregulation of markets and the like are among the hallmarks of these countries' recent policy reforms. As a consequence of the enlargement, the closer examination of the experiences of transition economies such as the Slovak Republic signals an enrichment of the debate rather than its limitation. This is especially true because some of the new EU member countries, despite their relative success, still wonder which socio-economic model will best serve their interests in the long term. They must weigh these potential benefits against the possible need to forego some of the opportunities created by the recent convergence with, and the new membership in, the EU that have contributed greatly to their short-term growth and sparked needed and overdue restructuring and adjustment.

In short, we believe that bringing together expert opinions from old and new member states of the European Union, as well as from the US, to discuss these issues that are so critical to the wellbeing of the new EU will make a positive contribution to the debate on the future of economic and social models in Europe.

WOJCIECH BIEŃKOWSKI
JOSEF C. BRADA
MARIUSZ JAN-RADŁO

Notes on the Contributors

Karl Aiginger is Director at the Austrian Institute of Economic Research, Professor of Economics at the Vienna University of Economics and at the University of Linz and Editor-in-Chief of the *Journal of Industry, Competition and Trade*.

Wojciech Bieńkowski is Professor of Economics and Dean at the Lazarski School of Commerce and Law, as well as Fellow at the Institute for Applied Economics and the Study of Business Enterprise, Johns Hopkins University.

Lajos Bokros is Chief Operating Officer at the Central European University in Budapest. Among other appointments, he served as a director at the World Bank and as Minister of Finance of Hungary (1995–96).

Josef C. Brada is Professor of Economics at the W.P. Carey School of Business, Arizona State University, and Executive Secretary of the Association for Comparative Economic Studies.

Walter D. Connor is Professor of Political Science, Sociology and International Relations at Boston University, as well as Fellow at the Davis Center for Russian and Eurasian Studies, Harvard University.

Karel Dyba served as Minister of Economic Policy and Development of the Czech Republic, 1990–92, and as Minister of Economics, 1992–96.

Ewa Freyberg is Professor of Economics at the Warsaw School of Economics, and has served as Polish Deputy Minister for the Economy.

Stanisław Gomułka is a retired Professor of Economics at the London School of Economics.

Steve H. Hanke is a Professor of Applied Economics and Co-director of the Institute for Applied Economics and the Study of Business Enterprise at Johns Hopkins University in Baltimore, a Senior Fellow at the Cato Institute in Washington, DC, and a columnist at *Forbes* magazine.

Filip Keereman is Head of Unit in the Directorate General for Economic and Financial Affairs of the European Commission.

Per Kongshøj Madsen is Professor and Director of the Centre for Labour Market Research (CARMA), Department of Economics, Politics and Public Administration, University of Aalborg. He is currently the Danish representative within the European Employment Observatory.

Ivan Mikloš is former Deputy Prime Minister and Minister of Finance of the Slovak Republic.

Mariusz-Jan Radło is Associate Professor at the Warsaw School of Economics. In 2004–07, he served as Vice President for Research of the Polish Lisbon Strategy Forum.

Jacek Rostowski is Minister of Finance for the Republic of Poland. He was also Professor of Economics at the Central European University, Budapest, as well as Fellow at the Centre for Economic and Social Analyses (CASE) in Warsaw.

Siegfried Steinlein is Deputy Head of Unit in the Directorate General for Economic and Financial Affairs of the European Commission.

Birgitta Swedenborg is Research Director of the Centre for Business and Policy Studies (SNS) in Stockholm.

Part I

The Creation and Reform of Socio-Economic Systems at the National Level

1
Lessons from Sweden's Welfare State: An American–Swedish Perspective

Birgitta Swedenborg

Introduction

The Swedish welfare state has often been held up as a model for other countries to follow. For a long time, it was seen as a mid-way solution between the state-controlled socialist economies in Eastern Europe and elsewhere, on one hand, and the more unrestrained capitalist economies, often represented by the United States, on the other. Since the demise of socialism in Eastern Europe, Sweden is instead seen as a more social form of a capitalist market economy, one that combines the free play of market forces in large parts of its economy with an extensive social safety net and public provision of welfare services. Although the Swedish model is by no means unique and shares many features with other Nordic welfare states, it remains true that it represents one polar case among capitalist economies and that the United States is at the opposite pole.

In the early 1990s, it was clear that the Swedish economy was heading towards a severe economic crisis and that the causes were, at least to some degree, due to structural problems, including features of Sweden's welfare state. This motivated the Swedish Centre for Business and Policy Studies (SNS) to approach the National Bureau of Economic Research (NBER) in the United States and suggest a joint research project on the Swedish welfare state. The idea was to engage leading American researchers in order to analyze different features of the Swedish economy and to do so with Swedish economists as co-authors. We, at SNS, wanted to obtain in a highly qualified outside perspective on the Swedish economy and welfare state: a fresh perspective that was unencumbered by Swedish policy debate and ingrained sensitivities. We also wanted to see what could be learned from comparing two such diverse economies.

3

We were fortunate in being able to engage some of the most prominent American researchers in the project, which was directed by Richard B. Freeman of Harvard University, Robert Topel of the University of Chicago and myself at SNS. The team included ten American and ten Swedish economists. The participation of the Swedish economists was essential in providing knowledge of institutional context but their contribution went beyond that. The project output was ten separate studies, each authored by an American and a Swede, collected in a volume entitled *The Welfare State in Transition – Reforming the Swedish Model* (1997). A condensed and non-technical version of the report was published in Swedish in 1995 (Freeman *et al.*, 1995).

The project was in many ways unique. Never before had such a distinguished team of American researchers focused their attention on the economic problems of a small foreign country. Never before had researchers been assigned co-authors, who in most cases they did not know before. Still, the project was highly successful in every way. Work on the report coincided with the worst economic crisis that Sweden had experienced since the 1930s, which added a sense of urgency on the part of the research team and also contributed to the immense interest the report met with on its early publication in Sweden.

Ten years later, in 2005, we decided it would be of interest to do a follow-up. The Swedish economy was in a very different state. It had recovered from crisis and was doing well on many counts. But was the Swedish welfare state now alive and well? What had happened to the structural problems and conflicting goals that were the focus of the earlier report? What reforms were made and what reforms remain to be made? What more can we learn with ten years of hindsight?

Most of the researchers in the earlier team agreed to participate in a follow-up study.[1] A preliminary report of their findings was published in Swedish in January 2006 (Freeman *et al.*, 2006a). An academic conference was held in September 2006 and the aim is to submit the conference papers for publication as an NBER conference volume with the working title *Reforming the Welfare State: Recovery and Beyond* in the United States.[2]

In this chapter, I will present some of the findings of the NBER–SNS team in their two research reports on the Swedish welfare state. I believe their analysis and evaluation of the workings of the Swedish welfare state is of interest not only to Sweden and similar welfare states, but also to countries that are considering similar welfare arrangements. At the same time, it is important to note that many welfare state issues involve trade-offs between equity and efficiency, and how that trade-off is

evaluated is ultimately a political question. The NBER–SNS team ana-
lyzes the trade-off but does not take a stand on policy.

In order to set the stage, the chapter begins by giving some background
on the Swedish economy since the early 1990s, going on to describe the
characteristics of the Swedish model and the questions that they raise.
Next, the chapter presents highly condensed summaries of the main
findings of the NBER–SNS reports and the overall conclusions drawn
by the editors, continuing with an account of significant policy reforms
enacted by the centre-right government that came into power in late
2006. The chapter closes with lessons for the transition countries.

Crisis and recovery: the Swedish economy since the early 1990s

In early 1990, Sweden was hit by a severe economic crisis. It coincided
with a sharp international economic downturn, but the Swedish collapse
was more severe than in most other countries. Between 1990 and 1993,
industrial production in Sweden fell by around 18 per cent, comparable
to the decline in the 1930s. Open unemployment rose from 2 to 9 per
cent; total unemployment, which includes persons in labour market
programmes, rose to 14 per cent: levels not experienced since the depression of the 1930s. At the same time, and as part of the problem, inflation
fell from 8 per cent in 1990 to 2 per cent in 1991. Government spending,
already high by international standards, rose to a record 70 per cent of
GDP, as GDP shrank and social spending on the unemployed rose. The
government deficit reached 12 per cent of GDP.

What happened? Why did the Swedish economy suddenly collapse?
The immediate cause of the crisis was the inflationary policy of the
1980s and the attempt to maintain a fixed exchange rate in the face of
a cost crisis. That put an abrupt end to inflation. The defence of the currency also required a sharp rise in interest rates, which at the peak, but
only briefly, were at an incredible 500 per cent. A tax reform in 1991,
limiting tax deductibility of interest payments in combination with rising interest rates abroad and lower inflation, meant that the real rate of
interest after tax rose dramatically. This effectively punctured the real
estate bubble of the late 1980s and led to a real estate and financial crisis,
which threatened several of Sweden's major banks with insolvency.

After the government abandoned the defence of the currency and
allowed the *krona* to float in November 1992, things began to turn
around. The low inflation policy was maintained by setting an inflation
target of 2 per cent for the Central Bank. This policy has been so

successful that Sweden still has a flexible exchange rate and the Central Bank, now independent, still maintains its inflation target of 2 per cent within a band of −1 and +1 per cent. In a referendum in 2003, Swedish voters said 'no' to joining the Euro zone.

With a floating *krona*, a period of strong export-led growth began. The government also embarked on a determined policy to eliminate the budget deficit through a combination of expenditure cuts and tax increases. In the subsequent decade (i.e. 1994–2004), the deficit was eliminated, the debt to GDP ratio was sharply reduced and government spending fell to around 53 per cent of GDP. GDP growth in the period 1994–2004 was higher than the OECD average, 2.9 per cent compared with 2.8 per cent, while growth in GDP per capita at 2.6 per cent was even higher than in the US, where it was 2.1 per cent.

Still, all is not bright. Employment has failed to recover to its earlier low levels. Open unemployment was 5.9 per cent in 2005 and total unemployment, including persons on labour market programmes, hovered at around 8.5 per cent. The duration of unemployment is also considerable, and the Swedish unemployment problem now appears rather like that in the rest of Europe.

Despite rapid growth after the crisis, Sweden has not improved its position in PPP adjusted real per capita income among the OECD countries. Sweden's real per capita income relative to the OECD average has been slipping since the early 1970s, from 14 per cent above the average to 6 per cent below the average in 2004. The improvement since the trough in 1992 has been modest (see Figure 1.1). Sweden has recovered, but it has not recovered fully. Problems remain under the surface. Some of these are long-standing. The 1990s crisis was not only the result of the proximate causes outlined above: poor macro policies and policy mistakes at a time when the international economy was also experiencing a sharp downturn also contributed. The crisis was also the result of structural weaknesses in the Swedish economy, many having to do with the welfare state and its regulated markets.

A commission appointed by the government in December 1992 to diagnose the causes of the crisis and to suggest ways out of it concluded that the economic crisis in Sweden was deep-rooted. In its report in March 1993, the commission, headed by Sweden's leading economist, Assar Lindbeck, emphasized that the economic problems were the result of political decisions and institutional developments in the past. The expansion of the welfare state in the 1970s and 1980s had weakened economic incentives and contributed to public sector deficits. Labour market legislation had favoured short-term job security at the expense of

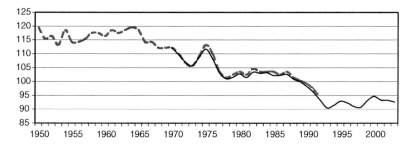

Figure 1.1 PPP-Adjusted GDP per capita in Sweden as a percentage of OECD average, Penn World Tables (1950–92) and OECD Statistics (1970–2004), OECD-23 = 100

Note: The OECD figures (solid line) are for Lindbeck's (1997) '23 Rich OECD countries', which exclude Mexico, Turkey, Poland, South Korea, Hungary and the Czech Republic. The OECD statistics concern current PPPs, while the Penn World Tables (PWT) concern fixed PPPs in 1985 dollars (variable: RGDPCH). The PWT comparison (grid line) has been scaled so that the 1970 level is identical to the level of the OECD series in 1970. Source: Penn World Tables and OECD, National Accounts (online source: OECD), June 2005.
Source: Davis and Henreksson (2006) – see Box 1.1, p. 10

long-term flexibility and dynamism, which hindered adjustment and long-term growth. The system of collective bargaining and an accommodating fiscal policy became inflationary and led to macroeconomic instability. Legislation as well as labour market institutions had focused on distributional outcomes at the expense of incentives and the consideration of efficiency (Lindbeck *et al.*, 1994).

The commission presented a total of 113 reform proposals, addressing both the short-term, acute economic problems and the long-term problems relating to macroeconomic policy; efficiency in labour and product markets, in the social insurance system and the public sector; and economic growth. Many of these reforms have been carried out: some of them major. The government budget process has been strengthened, the Central Bank has been made independent, product markets have been deregulated, competition policy has been strengthened, and the public pension system has been reformed. Other reforms were relatively modest; for example, in the labour market and the social insurance system. Overall, however, the reforms have undoubtedly contributed to the improved performance of the Swedish economy since the crisis.

Despite these reforms, the main features of the Swedish model and welfare state remain intact. The relative success of the Swedish economy prior to and after the economic crisis in the early 1990s therefore continues to puzzle analysts. Does Sweden, along with the other Nordic welfare states, offer an equally successful but more socially responsible model than more market driven economies, as some observers (OECD, 2006) hold? Or are there problems in the Swedish welfare state, as well as in more market driven economies such as the United States, from which both polar opposites can learn? These are some of the questions addressed in both the first and second NBER–SNS reports, where the second was produced against a very different economic backdrop.

Characteristics of the Swedish model and the questions they raise

The defining feature of the Swedish welfare state is its emphasis on egalitarian outcomes. These outcomes are achieved through a generous social insurance system and public provision of social services. The social insurance system covers parental leave, child allowance, unemployment insurance, sick leave insurance, disability benefits and old age pensions. With the exception of child allowance, they are all income related and replace up to 80–90 per cent of an income loss (up to a ceiling) due to unemployment, sickness, and so on. The public provision of social services covers highly subsidized childcare, free education (including tertiary education), healthcare and care of the elderly. Together, they provide security 'from cradle to grave' and allow an egalitarian consumption of social services. The concomitant tax burden, mainly state and local income taxes, payroll taxes and VAT, equalizes incomes further.

The Swedish model in the labour market is characterized by strong labour unions, with union membership of around 80 per cent, cartelized employer organizations and collective bargaining. The labour market is highly regulated, both by legislation and by rules negotiated by collective bargaining. It includes relatively strong job protection laws and generous rights for unions to use broad measures in labour market conflicts, including the right to strike in support of employees in other firms. A complementary feature of Swedish labour market policy includes active labour market programmes (ALMP), intended to facilitate the re-employment of unemployed individuals through training programmes and subsidized employment. Collective bargaining has been credited with the relatively low level of labour market conflict and ALMP with the previously low level of unemployment in Sweden. The Swedish labour market has produced a very compressed wage structure.

Foreign economists looking at the Swedish welfare state confront several puzzling questions. An overriding puzzle is how has it been possible to combine market-distorting social interventions and a very large public sector with one of the highest living standards in the world. Sweden seems to have eliminated poverty while, at least on the surface, maintaining an acceptable rate of growth. Admittedly, economic growth became more sluggish after 1970, when policy interventions accelerated and ended in the 1990s crisis. However, since the crisis, Swedish growth is again above the OECD average. Why have egalitarian outcomes not destroyed work incentives and hindered growth more than they possibly have? To outsiders such as the American economists in the NBER–SNS team, it is remarkable that the Swedish economy has performed as well as it has, and for so long.

A second question is why the policy-induced compression of wages and incomes in Sweden has not created widespread unemployment or non-employment among the least skilled, at least not before 1990. Labour force participation in Sweden is higher than in most other rich countries and unemployment was remarkably low until the early 1990s. But if less skilled Swedes are overpaid relative to the amount they would have received in a more market driven economy, why are, or were, they employed at all? How did Sweden avoid the mass unemployment in other European countries for so long?

A third issue concerns the effects of an unusually high tax burden and the many programmes they finance. The social cost of taxation is estimated to be twice the revenue raised at the margin; that is, every additional *krona* raised in tax revenue costs the private sector 2 *kronor*. Although this represents considerable social waste, how has Sweden kept the negative effect from being even larger? And what about the many public-spending programmes? How efficient are they and can they motivate their costs?

A final question is how the Swedish welfare state can survive in a rapidly changing world, where technological change and globalization calls for flexibility of workers and firms, investment in education and possibly greater income differences. So far, Sweden seems to have lived up to these challenges and ranks high in indices of international competitiveness. How has Sweden achieved this and can it continue?

The NBER–SNS analysis: an American perspective on the Swedish welfare state

The American–Swedish research team focused on different aspects of the Swedish welfare state and produced ten separate research papers in 1997, nine in 2006, each authored jointly by an American and Swedish economist (see Box 1.1). They brought out the achievements of the welfare

Box 1.1 NBER–SNS Reports

The first NBER–SNS report:

Freeman, Richard B., Topel, Robert and Swedenborg, Birgitta (eds) (1997) *The Welfare State in Transition. Reforming the Swedish Model* (University of Chicago Press).

Contents of the Report:

Introduction
Richard B. Freeman, Robert Topel and Birgitta Swedenborg

Generating Equality and Eliminating Poverty, The Swedish Way
Anders Björklund and Richard B. Freeman

Public Employment, Taxes and the Welfare State in Sweden
Sherwin Rosen

Tax Policy in Sweden
Erik Norrman and Charles E. McLure Jr

Wage Policy and Restructuring: The Swedish Labor Market since 1960
Per-Anders Edin and Robert Topel

The Effects of Sweden's Welfare State on Labor Supply Incentives
Thomas Aronsson and James R. Walker

An Evaluation of the Swedish Active Labor Market Policy: New and Received Wisdom
Anders Forslund and Alan B. Krueger

Taxes and Subsidies in Swedish Unemployment
Lars Ljungqvist and Thomas J. Sargent

The Social Costs of Regulation and Lack of Competition in Sweden: A Summary
Stefan Fölster and Sam Peltzman

Industrial Policy, Employer Size, and Economic Performance in Sweden
Steven J. Davis and Magnus Henreksson

A Heckscher–Ohlin View of Sweden Competing in the Global Market Place
Edward E. Leamer and Per Lundborg

The second NBER–SNS report:

Freeman, Richard B., Swedenborg, Birgitta and Topel, Robert (eds) (2006), *Reforming the Welfare State*. Volume based on conference papers presented at NBER–SNS conference in September 2006. Work in progress.

Contents of the Report:

Reforming the Welfare State: Recovery and Beyond
Richard B. Freeman, Birgitta Swedenborg and Robert Topel

Searching for Optimal Inequality / Incentives
Anders Björklund and Richard B. Freeman

Policies Affecting Work Patterns and Labor Income for Women
Ann-Sofie Kolm and Edward Lazear

Wage Determination and Employment in Sweden since the early 1990s – Wage Formation in a New Setting
Peter Fredriksson and Robert Topel

Labor Supply, Tax Base and Public Policy in Sweden
Thomas Aronsson and James R. Walker

Did Active Labor Market Policies Help Sweden Recover from the Depression in the early 1990s?
Anders Forslund and Alan B. Krueger

How Sweden's Unemployment Became More Like Europe's
Lars Ljungqvist and Thomas J. Sargent

Economic Performance and Work Activity in Sweden after the Crisis of the Early 1990s
Steven J. Davis and Magnus Henreksson

Competition and Regulation in Swedish Markets – An Analysis of Remaining Problems
Stefan Fölster and Sam Peltzman

What Have Changes to the Global Markets for Goods and Services Done to the Viability of the Swedish Welfare State?
Edward E. Leamer

state and Sweden's economic policy, as well as problems that the country might want or need to address. Here, I will summarize some of their findings under three broad headings: welfare state policies, the labour market, the welfare state and economic growth. Three papers, two in the 2006 report, fall under the first heading; four papers under the second and three under the third in both reports. Since no condensed summary can do justice to these carefully researched papers, I would refer the interested reader to the full reports.

Welfare state policies

Sweden's far-reaching egalitarianism is striking. Incomes are more equally distributed in Sweden than in other OECD countries, with the exception of neighbouring Finland and Norway. The United States is at the other extreme. The average income of those at the top of the income distribution (90th percentile) in Sweden was 2.96 times higher than the average income of those at the bottom (10th percentile) in 2000. The corresponding ratio for the United States was 5.45.

Björklund and Freeman (1997) showed that Sweden's income equality does not reflect a greater homogeneity among Swedish workers, who do not have markedly smaller differences in productivity than American workers. Instead, it is the result of the Swedish system of wage and income determination. Income equalization has been achieved through a combination of wage setting institutions, policies that encourage labour force participation, compression of the distribution of hours worked, and equalizing taxes and benefits that supplement the incomes of the non-working population. In the 1970s and 1980s, underlying factor incomes became more dispersed, but disparities in disposable income became smaller through taxes and benefits.

How has this been achieved without creating poverty traps for the poor, destroying incentives to work or creating mass unemployment among the less skilled? One answer is that so much of Sweden's welfare benefits are conditional on work. Income replacement in the social insurance system is tied to previous income and subsidized childcare is tied to employment. The system might be called 'workfare', rather than welfare.

Another answer is that the relatively low unemployment in the 1970s and 1980s was partly due to the growth of public sector employment. The public sector did not employ a disproportionate share of the less skilled but it did employ an increasing share of low-skilled workers in this period. A more speculative explanation is that weak incentives for skilled workers to increase their work hours meant an increased demand for less skilled workers, a kind of work sharing. Who pays for this? Taxpayers, of course, pay for the public sector but consumers, too, pay in the form of higher prices for non-tradable private services. Prices in general, and for private services in particular, were, and still are, high in Sweden.

The 1990s saw a slight increase in income dispersion (Björklund and Freeman, 2006). That increase was due to faster income growth of high-income earners, not to declining incomes of low-income earners, whose wages grew and whose incomes were also kept up by income transfers. A new kind of inequality has emerged, instead, in the form of an increase in the dispersion of hours worked, reflecting higher non-employment. Nevertheless, and as noted above, Sweden remains one of the most egalitarian countries in the OECD.

It is interesting to compare American and Swedish attitudes to inequality. Inequality is, of course, a two-sided coin. One side shows that inequality enhances incentives to work and acquire valuable skills. The other side shows that it produces what many see as unfair differences between people. Different people emphasize different sides; economists tend to emphasize the incentive side. International survey data show that Swedes are much less inclined than Americans to view income differences as reward for effort. And even though incomes are much more equally distributed in Sweden, Swedes are much more inclined to want the government to reduce the income inequality that still exists. Whether the Swedish attitude is a cause or an effect of the large welfare state is an open question (Björklund and Freeman, 2006).

Public provision of welfare services is another powerful force for equality. Health and education services, childcare and care of the elderly are available to all on equal terms. The growth of the Swedish welfare state meant growth of public employment. Strikingly, from 1960 until the 1990s crisis, all employment growth in Sweden was in public employment and all was related to women.[3] Restoration of fiscal balance after the crisis forced a reversal of this trend, leading to a decline in public employment and a rise in private sector employment.

Sherwin Rosen (1997) raised the question as to whether public sector growth was welfare enhancing, using subsidized childcare as an example. Subsidized childcare enables women with young children to enter the labour market. It is also motivated by considerations of efficiency, since high taxes distort the women's choice between work in the market and work in the home. Rosen showed that the Swedish level of subsidization (90 per cent of the cost) is excessive, however, and creates new distortions. Both the subsidy and the higher tax that is required to finance it lead to an excessive consumption of the subsidized service, as well as other services produced in non-taxed home production.

Families are overly encouraged to spend more time cooking, cleaning and doing housework rather than working to support their children. Measuring only the monetary aspects of the distortion and using Swedish data, Rosen found that the subsidy created huge welfare losses.

A general conclusion to be drawn from Rosen's analysis is that publicly financed services are not necessarily welfare enhancing when you take account of the distorting effects of taxes and subsidies. The form of the subsidy also plays a role. A monetary transfer – for example, a tax credit to working mothers – is an alternative to subsidized childcare in promoting the economic independence of women but is less distorting (Kolm and Lazear, 2006).

The high taxes required to finance the welfare state create obvious distortions. A major tax reform in 1991 reduced the distortions by establishing a more uniform and broad-based tax system and replacing the earlier progressive taxes with mainly proportional taxes. Still, the efficiency losses are substantial at the margin, since they increase with the square of the tax rate. This means that tax financing should be used only if the social benefit is higher than the social cost, including excess burden.

Proportional taxes, of course, redistribute income among individuals. But, as shown by Norrman and McLure (1997), the redistributive goals of the welfare state are to a large extent achieved not through taxes but, rather, through transfers to specific groups, often redistributing income across age groups rather than across individuals with different lifetime earnings. In this way, redistribution through taxes and transfers substitutes for saving and insurance that the individual could have arranged privately without the deadweight loss of taxes.[4]

The labour market

Swedish wages are highly compressed. In the late 1960s, the Swedish wage structure was similar to that in the US. After that it became increasingly compressed, while in the US it became more dispersed. The Swedish trend is the result of wage policy rather than market forces. The 'solidarity wage policy' of Swedish unions originally meant 'equal pay for equal work' but subsequently came to mean 'equal pay'. Higher than market wages did not lead to unemployment of the less skilled, as could have been expected. Edin and Topel (1997) argue that the reason was that it was 'compensated' by lower than market wages for the skilled, which benefited large skill-intensive firms. It represented a hidden income transfer from skilled to unskilled workers. Edin and Topel warned that the situation was not sustainable and would lead either to a breakdown of central bargaining and increased wage dispersion or to unemployment among the less skilled.

Since the crisis of the 1990s, wage formation has become more decentralized and wage dispersion has increased. The ratio of the 90th to the 10th percentile of gross earnings rose from 2.09 in around 1990 to 2.30 in around 2000. This was less of an increase than in the US, where the ratio rose from 4.23 to 4.64 in the same period. Fredriksson and Topel (2006) suggest that the Swedish increase represents a 'catching up' with market forces.

On the positive side, productivity growth in Sweden has been widely shared, with rising real incomes for all wage earners. In the US, by contrast, only the top income earners (90th percentile) have seen their incomes grow, while those at the bottom (10th percentile) have actually seen their real income fall (see Figure 1.2). Also positive is that increased dispersion in Sweden has raised the return to education and, with it, the enrolment in higher education. Sharply reduced rates of return to education from the late 1960s through to the 1980s had led to lower enrolment rates, but this trend has now been reversed.

On the other hand, the new economic environment post-crisis arguably calls for a greater increase in wage dispersion than we have seen. The Swedish labour market is very different today than it was in 1990, with high joblessness and a much higher share of immigrants (many of whom are low-skilled) from non-OECD countries. At the same time, technological change and global competition calls for increasing wage differences. Although the 1990s' crisis hit all groups, the relative employment prospects have worsened most for low-skilled workers. The employment gap between non-OECD immigrants and Swedish-born was 23 percentage points in 2003. There are several plausible reasons for this. One is that the market for private services is smaller in Sweden than in the US; another is the high minimum wages negotiated by unions. The minimum wage is especially high relative to the median wage (75–80 per cent of the median) in sectors that employ a relatively high proportion of low-skilled workers (hotels and restaurants, retail trade).

In general, minimum wages are higher in countries where they are negotiated than they are in countries where they are legislated. In the US, for example, the minimum wage is 32 per cent of the median wage of manufacturing workers, while the average across industries in Sweden is 60–72 per cent. While wage compression from below reduces the employment opportunities of the low skilled, wage compression from above reduces incentives to invest in education and in a career, to work harder, to change jobs. Both kinds of wage compression are likely to be detrimental to growth.

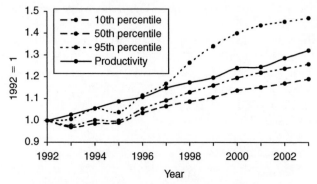

(a) Sweden: growth in average productivity by wage percentile, 1992–2003 (1992 = 1)

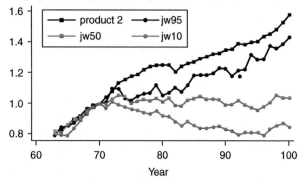

(b) United States: growth in average productivity and wage percentile, 1963–2000 (1970 = 1)

Figure 1.2 Growth in average productivity and wage growth by wage percentile in Sweden (1992–2000) and the United States (1963–2000)
Source: Fredriksson and Topel (2006) – see Box 1.1, p. 11

Taxes and welfare benefits compress incomes further. Aronsson and Walker (1997, 2006) discuss how Swedes have responded in their labour supply decisions to the taxes and benefits of the welfare state. Economists emphasize that incentives matter, but economic theory provides little guidance as to how much people respond. That is an empirical question. The evidence suggests a very weak response when it is based on how the number of contracted hours of work responds to changes in incentives: this is true in all countries, including Sweden. Estimated elasticities in Sweden are around 0.05–0.12. The welfare state provides strong incentives to be in the labour force, but also strong incentives not to work very many hours. Aronsson and Walker observe that Swedes do work relatively few hours, especially compared with Americans, but that their labour supply adjustment occurs in many other dimensions as well. For example, Swedes have more days of absence due to sickness than do people in most other rich countries, despite their good health status. Empirical studies indicate that the generous social insurance system has meant that sickness absence has, to an increasing extent, become a way of flexibly varying working time. An increasing proportion of working-age Swedes is either on sick leave or in early retirement, creating an obvious financial burden on those who work.

When labour supply adjustment is measured as the change in taxable income, rather than contracted hours of work, the response to changes in incentives is much larger. Taxable income captures not only effects on hours of work, but also the effect on quality dimensions such as effort, investment in education and career choice, as well as black economy activity. American studies find elasticities of taxable income with respect to marginal tax rates of around 0.4. Swedish studies find very similar effects, but this research has just started.

In sum, the combined weight of the evidence suggests that the effects on labour supply due to a compressed wage structure, taxes and benefits could be substantial.

A cornerstone of the Swedish model in the labour market is the extensive reliance on active labour market policy (ALMP) to deal with labour market problems. Before the onset of the problems of the 1990s, this policy was credited for Sweden's low unemployment. Forslund and Krueger (1997) found little evidence for that claim. Relief work displaced ordinary jobs, and training programmes were found not to justify their costs. The costs of ALMP were substantial. Total spending on labour market programmes, including unemployment compensation, was 3 per cent of GDP in 1990, with two thirds going to active programmes. In the US, by contrast, total spending was 0.5 per cent of GDP. As unemployment subsequently rose and then declined, total spending followed. However, as shown by Forslund and Krueger (2006), ALMP did little to help Sweden recover from the unemployment crisis of the early 1990s.

The duration of unemployment increased in the 1990s. Official statistics showed that the duration of unemployment was 25 weeks at the peak, but that number underestimates the true duration of jobless spells because open unemployment was interrupted by participation in ALMP. Measuring duration by registration in unemployment insurance offices shows that jobless spells increased throughout the 1990s and reached 110 weeks in length in 2000.

Because participation in ALMP meant that an individual could qualify for another period of unemployment insurance, ALMP reduced the incentive to search for a new job. This is confirmed by several evaluation studies, which conclude that ALMP actually prolonged the duration of unemployment instead of reducing it. Studies also show that training programmes had little or no effect at all on labour market success. The conclusion is that Sweden's celebrated ALMP in this period, as well as in previous periods, at best could not justify its costs and at worst was counterproductive. This is consistent with studies of similar programmes in the US, which also show that ALMP at best has marginal effects on unemployment. In 2000, Sweden made changes in its ALMP policies that could potentially improve its effectiveness. One was that pro- gramme participation would no longer qualify an individual for further unemployment insurance. Another was that individuals were required to be actively engaged in seeking a job or participation in some other programme in order to qualify for continued unemployment insurance. The latter change meant that individuals could no longer use unemploy- ment insurance to finance leisure or supplement black market income.

Sweden's high unemployment in the early 1990s raised concerns that it might become persistent, as it has in many other European countries. Ljungqvist and Sargent (1997) underpinned that concern. They demon- strated, using a simulation model, how high taxes and unemployment benefits might lead to a high unemployment equilibrium once high unem- ployment had arisen. The problem in attributing high unemployment to welfare state benefits is that the European welfare states had lower unem- ployment than capitalist economies such as the US in the 1950s through until the 1970s but higher unemployment thereafter. Why this difference? Welfare state benefits were more generous in Europe in both periods.

The answer given by Ljungqvist and Sargent in subsequent work was that the economic environment had changed. The period after 1980 has been characterized by more economic turbulence, by which they mean economic shocks that alter the value of workers' skills. The increased turbulence is due to technological change, globalization and deregulation in product markets. In such an environment, policies that prolong unemployment spells, such as generous unemployment benefits, lead to a greater loss of skills and make it more difficult for an unemployed individual to become re-employed at his or her earlier wage. Prolonged joblessness means that the individual's skills become more obsolete and the unemployment benefits become increasingly attractive relative to available wage offers. This raises the value of remaining unemployed. In the US, by contrast, the short duration of unemployment benefits, typically six months, makes this outcome less common. This explanation fits the facts, since the increase in European unemployment since the 1980s is mainly due to increased duration of joblessness, not to an increased inflow of unemployed.

Sweden's open unemployment is relatively low, but its rate of jobless-ness, including time on ALMP, is high. Recognizing that sick leave and early retirement at Swedish levels are a form of hidden unemployment, Ljungqvist and Sargent (2006) calculate what part of this should be seen as 'justifiable' and what part should be seen as unemployment. The cal-culation assumes that the rates of sick leave and early retirement in the 1960s and early 1970s were justifiable, since they were unaffected by the subsequent increased generosity of benefits. Adding this hidden unemployment to the official unemployment data raises Swedish unemployment rates and makes Swedish unemployment resemble that of other European countries (see Figure 1.3). Similar adjustments to the

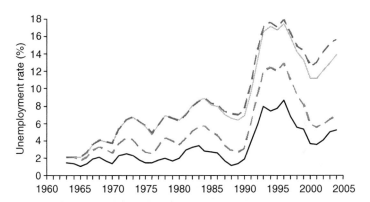

Figure 1.3   Measures of Swedish unemployment

Note: The lower solid line is the official unemployment rate, and the lower dashed line is the unemployment rate after adding participants in labour market programmes. The upper solid line is an adjustment of the latter unemployment rate that includes 'excessive' enrolment in early retirement, defined as early retirees in excess of the fraction of early retirement that pre-vailed in 1963 (that is, 3.5 per cent of the labour force). The upper line is yet another adjust-ment of the unemployment rate that adds the 'excessive' number of long-term sick in excess of the fraction of long-term sickness in 1974 (that is, 0.5 per cent of the labour force.)

Data sources: Open unemployment (yearly average), Labour Force Survey, Statistics Sweden (AKU, CSB); participants in labour market programmes (yearly average), National Labour Market Board (AMS); early retirees and long-term sick (in December), Swedish Social Insur-ance Agency (Försäkringskassan).

Source: Ljungqvist and Sargent (2006) – see Box 1.1, p. 11

European figures would, of course, make them even higher. To reduce unemployment of this sort, it is necessary to reduce the value of being unemployed. This can be done either through lower replacement rates in unemployment insurance, shorter duration of benefits or by a requirement that the unemployed person be engaged in job search full time.

The welfare state and economic growth

Following the turnaround in 1993–94, economic growth in Sweden has been faster than in the 1960s: some of this reflects catching up after the deep crisis, some reflects a global up-turn, some might be the result of economic reforms. On the positive side, and in contrast to the US experience, this has meant rising real incomes for all income earners. On the negative side, Swedish economic growth has not been accompanied by much job creation. Total employment in 2004 was 6 per cent below the 1990 level, despite a population that was 5 per cent higher.

Why have not more jobs been created? What are the characteristics of the jobs that Sweden did not produce, despite high unemployment? Davis and Henrekson (1997, 2006) argue that the 'missing' jobs were those that would be undertaken by less skilled labour and those that compete with household or black market work. They find that low-skill service sectors are smaller in Sweden than in the US and many other countries.

The reasons for this are related to the welfare state. Sweden's high taxes create a huge wedge between what the buyer of a service must earn before tax to purchase the service and what the seller of a service receives net of tax. This tax factor shows how much higher the productivity of the seller must be relative to that of the buyer in order for it to be worthwhile for the buyer to buy the service on the market. At its peak in the late 1970s, the tax factor was 4 for an industrial worker, but subsequent tax reforms brought it down by lowering marginal tax rates. In 2004, the tax factor was 2.5 for an industrial worker and 3.5 for a white-collar worker. In the US, by comparison, the tax factor is 1.3–1.9 for normal incomes. The higher the tax factor the more marginal producers in the market are replaced by low productivity household and black market production. The displacement of work in the market by less productive household work means that official statistics, which do not include household work, overestimate productivity in high-tax societies.

Do-it-yourself activities are widespread in Sweden and so are black market activities. Sweden's statistical office estimates that black market activities make up between 10 and 35 per cent of recorded value added in service sectors such as construction, auto repair, taxi services, freight hauling and hairdressing, and adjusts the official GDP data accordingly.

The extent of do-it-yourself activities can be gleaned from time use surveys that show that although Swedes work much fewer hours than Americans in the market, they work correspondingly more in the home.

Davis and Henrekson argue that there are additional factors that tilt the economy against service sectors (such as wage compression, which raises the wage of the less skilled) and the dominance of the public sector in social service production (which makes it difficult for small service firms to develop). The barriers to private service production, especially low-skill services, are serious in an economy where manufacturing no longer creates more jobs and, thus, all future employment growth must come from the service sector. Reducing these barriers to the growth of the service sector should be helpful in dealing with Sweden's high unemployment.

Other factors that can affect growth performance are the country's competition and regulatory policy. In the early 1990s, Sweden's competition policy was very weak and regulations impeded entry into many markets. Fölster and Peltzman (1997) found that this helped explain Sweden's relatively high prices and slow productivity growth until the early 1990s. Since then, import penetration has increased from 29 to 48 per cent of GDP, competition policy has been strengthened in line with EU law, and many formerly regulated markets have been opened up to competition. Among the deregulated markets are electricity, tele-communications, airlines and railways. Food processing was exposed to increased competition through Sweden's membership in the EU. Deregulation has led to increased productivity and also, in most cases, lower prices (Fölster and Peltzman, 2006).

Sweden's large public sector essentially remains protected from competition, however. Local governments monopolize most of the publicly financed social services such as healthcare, education, childcare and care of the elderly. Although private provision has increased somewhat, it still only makes up 9 per cent of these services. Swedish local governments account for about a quarter of GDP and of total employment, or about twice the corresponding US figures. Fölster and Peltzman (2006) ask: How does the local government affect the local economy, particularly the private sector? How does it affect growth? To answer these questions they use panel data for Sweden's 290 municipalities and various indicators of public policy, including local tax rates and an index of perceived business friendliness based on a survey of business.

Their analysis reveals that municipalities with low tax rates, or municipalities perceived as friendly to business, have higher incomes. It also shows that higher taxes are associated with lower growth, which erodes the tax base and about three quarters of the potential revenue increase from higher tax rates. The estimated effects are remarkably large. Taken at face value, they suggest that Sweden is near the top of the Laffer curve, where further tax increases do not generate more tax revenue. But Fölster and Peltzman caution that, due to data limitations, the analysis is too crude to allow such far-reaching conclusions. Still, the results are sufficiently striking to warrant further analysis of the role of local government policies in economic growth.

A final question concerns how the welfare state manages in an increasingly globalized world. As a small open economy, Sweden has always been extremely dependent on international trade. International trade tends to equalize prices of products and thereby, indirectly, prices of factors of production. Today's increased competition from low-wage countries in Eastern Europe and China therefore poses a potential threat to Sweden's egalitarian wage structure. However, factor price equalization through trade will only happen if countries produce the same products, with the same factor mix. Sweden can avoid the threat of low-wage competition by producing a more skill-intensive product mix. Globalization will then be a great benefit to consumers without any cost to producers. Leamer and Lundborg (1997) found that Sweden's mix of factors of production had become less distinct from that of other countries. They warned that, if Sweden did not invest sufficiently in human and physical capital, it would end up competing directly against low-wage countries in the production of labour-intensive products. Put drastically, Swedish wages would then be set in Beijing instead of in Stockholm. The dilemma of the welfare state, the authors concluded, was that in order to achieve higher incomes and a more equal distribution of incomes in the long run, Sweden might have to accept increased income differences in the short run.

Since then, competition from low-wage countries has become even more intense. Leamer (2006) shows that the correlation between the export product mix of high-income countries and low-income countries in the US and EU markets respectively has increased dramatically. In the late 1980s, capital rich countries were specialized in capital-intensive products, labour rich countries were specialized in labour-intensive products. In the late 1990s, product mixes in all countries had become more similar. Competition between high-wage Sweden and low-wage China has become more direct (see Figure 1.4). Globally, Swedish exports were several times larger than Chinese exports in the late 1980s. Now, Chinese exports are much larger. Moreover, China's phenomenal export growth has, to a large extent, been in Sweden's most important export

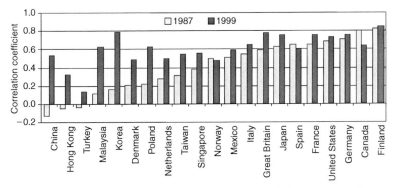

Figure 1.4 Product mix correlation coefficient of Swedish exports to the EU market, 1987 and 1999, 3-digit ISIC
Source: Leamer (2006) – see Box 1.1, p. 11

sectors. Although this suggests an increased risk of wage competition, factor price equalization is probably still some distance off. Within-industry specialization is likely to be sufficiently different for some time yet to insulate Sweden from Chinese wages. Within the electrical machinery industry, for example, China produces relatively labour-intensive products, while those of Sweden are relatively capital-intensive. But the trend is clear. China is rapidly moving up the value-added chain, aided by the technology transfer of multinational companies.

While international trade will put pressure on Sweden's compressed wage structure from below, technological change threatens to do so from above. Leamer (2006) argues that the computer is a powerful force for increased inequality in the post-industrial society, since it eliminates many simple tasks and enhances the opportunities of trained and talented individuals. In the post-industrial society, the manufacturing sector's employment share is falling, while the service sector's is rising. In the US, the finance, insurance and real estate sectors now contribute more to national income than does manufacturing, and these industries display a huge disparity between the 90th and the 10th percentile of wage earners. In Sweden, the disparity is still modest. Perhaps that can last, but at what cost to productivity?

Conclusions

The achievements of the welfare state are clear and hardly controversial. The welfare state produces income security, equal opportunities and highly egalitarian outcomes. It has virtually eliminated poverty. The costs of these policies, aside from their budgetary costs, are less obvious. The authors of the NBER–SNS reports have focused on the structural features that have allowed Sweden to attain these achievements but also on their hidden costs. Their analysis answered some of the questions concerning the Swedish welfare state that had puzzled the American economists at the outset of the project. The answers that emerged from the separate studies in the first report were in the form of some unifying themes, which were developed by the editors in their introductory chapter (Freeman *et al.* 1997). As the Swedish co-author of that chapter, I would like to stress that the outside perspective of the American economists was essential in discerning and developing those themes and also in formulating the conclusions summarized here.

The first theme was that the Swedish welfare state was an interrelated system, where the different parts fit together in a systemic way and reinforced each other in sometimes surprising ways. The separate contributions in the volume analyzed different aspects of the Swedish economy, used different analytical methods and stressed different linkages but together they showed an interrelated whole, which the 1997 report called the logic of the 'welfare state system'.

For example, as argued by Freeman *et al.* (1997), Sweden's highly compressed wages helped explain the lack of growth of private sector employment. That made public sector expansion necessary to maintain full employment, especially in light of the evident policy goal of high labour force participation by women. This growth required high taxes and a public sector that delivered the services that people wanted and would support politically. High taxes, in turn, affected wage determination and made it easier for high-skill workers to accept wage compression by reducing the benefit of wage increases. High taxes also lowered the incentive to work long hours and increased the demand for long vacations, leading to a work sharing of sorts. All of this fed back in the industrial structure, different regulations and the price level. Together, it allowed Sweden to maintain full employment for a prolonged period, though the fragility of such a system when adjustments become necessary is an obvious concern. Changes in the global marketplace and Sweden's structural reforms in the late 1980s and early 1990s called for such adjustments and thus contributed to the subsequent crisis.

Another theme was that the goals and social achievements of the welfare state had high costs, both in budgetary terms and in terms of the more hidden efficiency losses induced by taxes and benefits. The budgetary costs were staggering at the time, as government expenditures reached 70 per cent of GDP. But the hidden costs, too, were substantial. Some of the large expenditure programmes analyzed, such as the Active Labour Market Policy, did not achieve their objectives and, therefore, could not justify their costs. Others, such as subsidized childcare, were excessive and caused huge distortions. The high level of taxes created large excess burdens, affecting incentives to work and to invest, which would reduce productivity and the prospects for long-term economic growth.

The first report concluded that neither the image of Sweden as the ideal welfare state or the United States as the ideal market economy was, or is, true. Both countries have had, and have, big problems. Sweden's achievements are considerable. Most enviable from an American perspective is the elimination of poverty. The costs have been high, but the positive message of the study was that the level of taxes and public spending far exceeded what was required to attain the country's egalitarian goals. The social safety net was so high and some programmes so inefficient that Sweden could reduce its spending on programmes to deal with the fiscal crisis without risking its social goals.

The follow-up study addressed the same questions as the original study but asked what problems have been resolved and what problems, if any, remain. Is the welfare state now alive and well? Is it because of reforms that were consistent with the earlier analysis? Or did improvements occur anyway?

Clearly, important reforms have been made. Fiscal discipline and a much lower level of public spending and public indebtedness are foremost. An independent monetary policy with inflation targeting has contributed to responsible overall wage agreements. Decentralization of wage bargaining has allowed a somewhat more dispersed wage structure. Deregulation of important sectors of the economy has contributed to higher productivity growth. Some reforms were forward looking. Others were justified politically by the fiscal crisis and, though they were efficiency enhancing, proved difficult to maintain when the fiscal situation eased. For example, replacement rates in unemployment and sickness insurance, which were temporarily lowered, were returned to higher levels as soon as government finances permitted.

Many problems remain. Most importantly, unemployment remains high. The fact that some 20 per cent of working-age Swedes are supported by public benefits is a sign that the labour market is not working and that the social insurance system is overly generous. It is hardly a sustainable situation when the ageing population is placing additional stress on social spending.

The findings of the second NBER–SNS study basically confirm those of the earlier report, implying that the earlier analyses were pretty much on target. The renewed analysis also resolved some of the earlier puzzles. Not least of these was the puzzling fact that Sweden's wage and income compression had not created mass unemployment among the less skilled and more of an incentive crisis. The current high rate of joblessness, much of which reflects the fact that the rewards for working are low relative to benefit levels, suggests that there is now an incentive crisis. It represents a failure in what in the earlier report was called 'workfare' as opposed to 'welfare', because of those aspects of Sweden's welfare system that encouraged work. The high rate of joblessness also represents a failure of Sweden's egalitarian policies. It has created a new form of inequality: inequality between those who hold jobs and those that do not. This inequality has both economic and social dimensions, which can undermine the social cohesion that was created by the previously egalitarian work effort.

The findings also re-emphasize concerns about long-term economic growth. Although growth has been exceptionally high since the deep crisis, much of it probably represents recovery from the crisis, some of it is due to structural reforms and some simply reflects higher growth in other countries. How sustainable is it? The report's editors see a serious conflict between egalitarian policies and long-term growth. Sweden's egalitarian outcomes are achieved in ways that limit incentives to work, to invest in skills and to seek out productive activities. Since productivity growth is the source of growth in economic wellbeing, egalitarian policies could reduce living standards for all (Freeman *et al.* 2006).

Politically, it may be harder to undertake structural reform when the economy is doing well, as it is today. But Freeman *et al.* admonish that Sweden would be well advised to do so, in order to avoid future crises and to provide for future prosperity. The welfare state institutions are so pervasive in Sweden that they must work well. In Sweden, economic and social policy needs to be more judicious than similar policies in other countries, where government policies are less important and where individuals face greater incentives to adjust more flexibly. To ensure stability, it is essential to identify potential problems before they erupt.

The follow-up report emphasizes three problem areas: the high social costs of some social welfare programmes, problems caused by the compression of wages, and disincentives and distortions caused by high taxes.

High social costs of some social welfare programmes   Equity-efficiency trade-offs need to be considered in all such programmes, but some Swedish programmes are costly without achieving much that is positive. These can be reduced with little or no loss of equity. ALMP, which continues to absorb large resources despite the programme's failures, is an example. Other programmes have unintended effects and disproportionate social costs. Sickness insurance is an example. The increasing numbers of Swedes absent from work for reasons of health cannot be attributed to increased sickness of the workforce or worsened work conditions. Rather, it reflects abuse of the system due to overly liberal benefits. Similarly, high replacement rates in unemployment insurance exacerbate joblessness rather than merely mitigating the effects of joblessness. By reducing the 'moral hazard' in these programmes, social costs would be lowered.

Problems caused by the compression of wages In a market setting, wages reflect productivities. In Sweden, wages reflect the egalitarian goals of labour unions. International trade, technical and structural changes have generated greater wage inequality in modern economies than was true twenty or thirty years ago. That means that Sweden's compressed wage structure deviates more from underlying economic conditions now than before. It also means that the social costs of Sweden's egalitarian wage structure are much higher today than they were thirty years ago. Although wages are not a policy variable, wage determination is indirectly affected by policy; for example, labour laws and unemployment insurance.

Disincentives and distortions caused by high taxes These create large wedges between an individual's productivity and take-home pay. They mean that Swedes work less in the market and more, and less productively, in the home or in grey market activities. They make it less worthwhile to invest in education and in a more productive career. They also make it difficult for small firms in the private service sector to develop and provide jobs for the less skilled, including Sweden's growing immigrant population.

The problems identified are all solvable. Moreover, the follow-up report reiterates, they are solvable without threatening Sweden's welfare state. From an American perspective, Sweden has built such a strong social safety net and so much shared prosperity that the danger is not that Sweden will lose equity but rather that it will lose prosperity. Sweden's position is very different from that of the US, where policies are less egalitarian and market forces play more of a role in determining the distribution of income. In the US, a little more redistribution would have a very large effect on equity, but would cost very little in terms of efficiency. In Sweden, the opposite is true. A little more efficiency would not sacrifice much equity.

The NBER economists offer their analysis and outside perspective on the Swedish economy. They make no recommendations. They are sensitive to the fact that, ultimately, the choice of what to do is a political one.

A new government, new policies

The welfare state has widespread support in Sweden, having been built during decades of Social Democratic dominance of Swedish politics. In September 2006, a coalition of centre-right parties was voted into office for the first time since 1991, and only the fourth time since 1932. The incoming government was elected on a platform that promised to deal with the high level of joblessness in Sweden. It pledged support for the welfare state but claimed that the welfare state could not survive unless joblessness was decreased and benefit dependency was reduced.

The policy reforms that the new government is now enacting are consistent with the analyses in the NBER–SNS reports insofar as they reduce the benefits of being unemployed and strengthen the incentives to work. The reforms reduce replacement rates in unemployment insurance from 80 to 70 per cent after 200 days, to 65 per cent after 300 days, refrain from raising the ceiling on benefits and limit the duration of benefits; after 300 days a 'job guarantee' becomes effective. They also require union members to pay a larger share of the cost of unemployment through higher membership fees. Simultaneously, they increase the return to work by introducing an earned-income tax credit (in-work benefits), which primarily benefits low-income earners. A number of other reforms are designed to make it more attractive to employ hard-to-employ workers.

The reforms represent a balanced policy package that should reduce unemployment without being too onerous for the currently unemployed. By concentrating the tax credit on low-income earners, it is hoped that the policy will counteract the high thresholds created by reduced benefits-cum-taxes poverty traps that low earners face in going from unemployment to employment. The fact that the policy reforms are introduced during an economic upswing with a tightening labour market should increase the probability of success.

The new policy is in the same direction as the welfare reform enacted in the US during the Clinton administration. The US reform expanded the earned-income tax credit and put time limits on welfare benefits, thereby requiring welfare recipients to go out and find work. It had the effect of increasing the employment rate of low-skilled unmarried women with children from 30 to 50 per cent in the 1990s. In doing so, it greatly reduced poverty. The economic boom helped, but the reform was important. This conclusion was not changed by a return of poverty in the subsequent recession, as some thought it would. Poverty did not increase more than it had in previous recessions. The Clinton reforms were tougher than the ones now carried out by the new Swedish government. But they demonstrated that incentives matter, and that policies that appear hard on the poor and unfortunate can actually reduce poverty and improve life prospects when they are combined with benefits targeted to those who work, especially low earners. The Swedish policy reform is currently meeting intense opposition from unions. If it survives, Sweden has taken another significant step in reforming the Swedish model in a direction that could strengthen its egalitarian achievements in the long run.

Lessons

What can we learn? Does the Swedish model represent an equally successful but more humane economic and social model than that offered by more unrestrained capitalist economies? Is it a model that other European countries – in particular, transition economies – can emulate?

In its recent Jobs Report, the OECD took what some saw as a more balanced view of how countries might successfully deal with high rates of joblessness and other labour market problems. They emphasized that there might be different roads to success: one is represented by market-reliant countries such as the US and most other Anglo-Saxon countries plus Japan and Korea, and the other by 'other successful performers' including Austria, Denmark, the Netherlands, Norway and Sweden. Success was measured as average employment rates, which for both groups were higher than in other OECD countries. The successful performers had stable macro economic policies and deregulated product markets in common, but differed in tax levels and labour market policies. The market-reliant countries had low taxes and flexible labour markets with relatively wide income disparities. The 'other successful performers' were welfare states, characterized by collective bargaining, generous welfare benefits, ALMP, low-income disparities but high taxes. The choice between the two models reflects different social preferences and traditions. But it is not clear that they are equally successful: it depends on which measure of success one uses. Using labour force participation, open unemployment, and recent rates of economic growth, Sweden and the United States, for example, appear equally successful. Similarly, Sweden and the Nordic welfare states rank at the top of the

World Economic Forum's list of global competitiveness, along with the United States.

But, as shown by the NBER–SNS analyses, the employment measures used by the OECD neglect the hidden unemployment in Sweden. One fifth of working-age Swedes are supported by public benefits and most of this is related to joblessness. Many of those not working are included in the labour force, which means that high labour force participation is not the same thing as many hours of work. Also, the high rate of economic growth in Sweden might not be sustainable since, to a large extent, it reflects recovery from severe crisis. Real income per capita, adjusted for purchasing power, is still below the OECD average. Income equality and distorted incentives could well be a serious hindrance to future growth. Finally, and contrary to OECD claims, ALMP is not a cure for a inadequately working labour market.[5] These problems need to be addressed in Sweden, if the country wishes to prosper. On the other hand, the American model also has its shortcomings: widespread poverty, huge income differences, crime, and a large fraction of the least skilled in prison. As emphasized by the NBER–SNS team, each model has its shortcomings and both can learn from each other. Different models allow institutional competition and allow us to learn from, and emulate, more successful solutions.

Sweden will undoubtedly undertake more reforms in the future, as underlying economic realities put pressure on current institutions. Many of these reforms are likely to make Sweden a more market-reliant welfare state. Sweden has often proved itself a pragmatic reformer. At the same time, one should not underestimate how market-reliant Sweden already is, and has been for a long time. One of the most important reasons for Sweden's successful performance in the past has been its openness to international trade and acceptance of globalization. As a small economy Sweden has always recognized the benefits of international specialization and competition, and Swedish firms and workers alike are committed to free trade. This commitment has coexisted with the more regulated labour market and welfare state, and helps explain why Sweden has done as well as it has. This is one positive lesson other countries can learn from the Swedish experience.

What other lessons can the transition countries, in particular, draw from the Swedish experience? Let me suggest three cautionary lessons. One is that the welfare state easily overshoots what is sustainable in the long run. That happened in Sweden in the 1960s and 1970s, and led to slower growth and, eventually, a deep crisis. Overshooting occurs because the social costs of welfare arrangements are not immediately obvious and, furthermore, grow over time as economic agents adjust, and social norms with them. The erosion of social norms, so visible in Sweden, means that it becomes socially acceptable to overuse welfare state benefits and evade taxes by working, and buying services, in the grey market. Norm changes reinforce the effects of existing incentives against work (Lindbeck, 2006).

Another lesson is that it is difficult to retrench the welfare state. The welfare state creates very visible benefits but diffuse costs, which means that there is strong resistance to reduced entitlements from affected interest groups. This is the case also in the labour market, where existing arrangements favour 'insiders', those who have jobs, at the expense of 'outsiders', those without jobs. Insiders in the labour market have the power, both as voters and as union members, to block reforms that would help outsiders. Reforms become possible only in a serious crisis, as in Sweden in the early 1990s, or when the social costs become very visible, as in the recent Swedish election when high joblessness came into focus and was perceived as a threat to the welfare state.

A final lesson is that there is a trade-off between the egalitarian goals of the welfare state and the social costs they create. True social costs include the deadweight losses of both benefits and taxes. The more generous the welfare state, the higher the social costs. In fact, the social costs increase more than proportionately with the high taxes required to finance benefits. While rich countries can afford to sacrifice some prosperity for greater equality, poor countries cannot as easily afford such luxury. Countries that hope to grow and increase their prosperity cannot afford to neglect incentives. This is perhaps the most important lesson for the transition countries.

Notes

1 One of the most prominent members of the original team, Sherwin Rosen, had died: Edward Lazear replaced him on the new team. A couple of the Swedish economists were also replaced. A full list of authors in both studies is given at the end of the chapter.
2 The research effort in both projects was financed by a number of Swedish research foundations, among which the main contributor was Handelsbankens forskningsstiftelser.
3 Tax reform in 1970 lowered the marginal tax rate faced by married women by making their income tax independent of the income of their spouses. This made women enter the labour market in large numbers.
4 This is the only chapter that was not followed up in the 2006 report.
5 Simple cross-country comparisons such as the ones made by the OECD Jobs Study can be deceptive. Lindbeck (2006) shows that when ALMP activities

are related to total unemployment, which includes persons on ALMP, rather than just open unemployment, the association between ALMP and unemployment is positive rather than negative. In other words, more ALMP is associated with higher unemployment. The line of causation is, of course, arguable; but this caveat is not heeded by those who infer from similar cross-country comparisons that ALMP leads to lower open unemployment.

References

Freeman, R.B., Swedenborg, B. and Topel, R. (1995) *NBER-rapporten: Välfärdsstat i omvandling – Amerikanskt perspektiv på den svenska modellen* (Stockholm: SNS Förlag).

Freeman, R.B., Swedenborg, B. and Topel, R. (2006a) *NBER-rapporten II: Att reformera välfärdsstaten – Amerikanskt perspektiv på den svenska modellen* (Stockholm: SNS Förlag).

Lindbeck, A. (2006) 'Market Reforms, Welfare Arrangements and Stabilization Policy – A Triple Interaction in Employment Policy', Paper presented at the OECD Minister Conference, 15–16 June, Toronto.

Lindbeck, A., Molander, P., Persson, T., Petersson, O., Sandmo, A., Swedenborg, B. and Thygesen, N. (1994) *Turning Sweden Around* (Cambridge, Mass.: MIT Press).

OECD (2006) 'Boosting Jobs and Incomes – Policy Lessons from Reassessing the OECD Jobs Strategy', OECD Jobs Report (Paris: OECD).

2
Flexicurity in Denmark: A Model for Labour Market Reforms in the EU?

Per Kongshøj Madsen

The concept of flexicurity

The fundamental idea behind the concept of flexicurity is that flexibility and security are not contradictory to one another, but in many situations can be mutually supportive. Flexibility is not the monopoly of the employers, just as security is not the monopoly of the employees. In modern labour markets, many employers are beginning to realize that they might have an interest in stable employment relations and in retaining employees who are loyal and well qualified. On their part, many employees have realized that to be able to adjust their work life to more individual preferences, they, too, have an interest in more flexible ways of organizing work; for example, to balance work and family life. So, the foundation is there for a new interaction between flexibility and security that stresses the potential for win–win outcomes in situations that are traditionally conceived as characterized by conflicting interests.

This idea of virtuous circles between flexibility and security has now moved to the very centre of European policy-making. Thus, the Presidency's conclusions from the European Council in Brussels in March 2006 stated that:

> In this context, the European Council asks Member States to direct special attention to the key challenge of 'flexicurity' (balancing flexibility and security): Europe has to exploit the positive interdependencies between competitiveness, employment and social security ... The Commission, jointly with Member States and social partners, will explore the development of a set of common principles on flexicurity.

One purpose in this article is to discuss the potential for developing such common principles. However, before addressing this mainly normative issue, the following sections briefly present some of the main elements of the flexicurity concept and take a look at the Danish version of flexicurity, which is often taken to be a major source of inspiration for the European discourse.

Flexicurity as a strategy, a state of affairs or an analytical tool?

The Dutch scholar Ton Wilthagen (1998) defined flexicurity as a policy strategy, more precisely as:

> A policy strategy that attempts, synchronically and in a deliberate way, to enhance the flexibility of labour markets, work organization and labour relations on the one hand, and to enhance security – employment security and social security – notably for weaker groups in and outside the labour market, on the other hand.

The popularity of flexicurity as a political strategy is not surprising, given its promise of creating win–win situations for both employers and employees.

However, in some cases, a state of flexicurity has, over the years, not been reached through implementing a deliberate political strategy, but through a gradual process of political struggle and compromise with a strong element of path dependency. In such cases, flexicurity can be conceived thus:

> Flexicurity is (1) a degree of job, employment, income and 'combination' security that facilitates the labour market careers and biographies of workers with a relatively weak position and allows for enduring and high quality labour market participation and social inclusion, while at the same time providing (2) a degree of numerical (both external and internal), functional and wage flexibility that allows for labour markets' (and individual companies') timely and adequate adjustment to changing conditions in order to enhance competitiveness and productivity (Wilthagen and Tros, 2004).

In this later definition, also developed by Ton Wilthagen, flexicurity is no longer a deliberate policy strategy, which makes the definition more relevant in a comparative context and in analyzing, for instance, the Danish case, where flexicurity is the outcome of a long historical development and not a specific political blueprint.

The third and final understanding of flexicurity is as an analytical frame that can be used to analyze developments in flexibility and security, and compare national labour market systems. It is this analytical frame that we are going to use to show a number of national combinations of flexibility and security. As an analytical frame, flexicurity is closely related to another popular labour market concept: the idea of transitional labour markets (TLMs).[1] The basic assumption in the TLM approach is that the boundaries between the labour market and various social systems (such as the educational system, the unemployment system, pension system, private households) must become more open towards transitional states between paid employment and activities outside the market.

Forms of flexicurity

Both flexibility and security are multi-dimensional concepts that come in a variety of shapes. Using Atkinson's well-known model of the flexible enterprise as a starting point, it is possible to distinguish between four different forms of flexibility: numerical flexibility, working time flexibility, functional flexibility, and wage flexibility (Atkinson 1984).

A groundbreaking aspect of the flexicurity concept is the linking of these four forms of flexibility with four forms of security. First, job security, which means the security of being able to stay in the same job and which can be expressed via employment protection and tenure with the same employer. Second, employment security, which means the security of staying employed, though not necessarily in the same job; here the general employment situation, active labour market, training and education polices play a key role. Third, there is income security, which relates to having secure income in case of unemployment, sickness or accidents, and is expressed through the public transfer income systems, such as unemployment and cash benefit systems. And finally, combination security, the possibilities available for combining working and private life; for example, through retirement schemes, maternity leave, voluntary sector unpaid work and so on.

As illustrated in Figure 2.1, there are sixteen potential combinations of flexibility and security. This matrix is a heuristic tool that is applicable, for instance, in characterizing different flexicurity policies or combinations of flexibility and security in certain schemes, or to describe stylized

	Job security	Employment security	Income security	Combination security
Numerical flexibility				
Working time flexibility				
Functional flexibility				
Wage flexibility				

Figure 2.1   Configurations of flexibility and security

relationships between flexibility and security in different national labour market regimes.

Some of the combinations in Figure 2.1 represent trade-offs in the sense that a higher level of, for instance, job security will imply less numerical flexibility and vice versa. In most other cases, the interplay between the various aspects of flexibility and security is more complex. There is therefore some debate concerning the interpretation of the matrix above. Wilthagen and Tros (2004) mainly discuss it as an illustration of different trade-offs between forms of security and flexibility, where the term 'trade-off' signifies that something must be traded for something else. Thus, more numerical flexibility can be balanced by providing some form of security instead; for instance, increased income security. However, as stated by Leschke *et al.* (2006: 3), the situation is more complex:

> First, there is not only a trade-off between flexibility and security. The flexibility gains of employers do not necessarily mean a loss of security among employees; similarly, security gains of employees do not necessarily have to go along with flexibility losses among employers. Therefore, the talk about a balance between flexibility and security – usually thought of as a compromise between employers and employees – does unduly simplify the nexus.

Therefore the flexibility–security nexus can also reflect a mutually supportive or complementary relationship. Among examples of such interrelations could be:

- More combination security, such as maternity leave and childcare, can lead to a greater numerical flexibility for women in transitions into and out of the workforce
- Job security can induce employees to be loyal to the employer and to invest in firm-specific human capital, thereby increasing internal functional flexibility
- More income security could stimulate numerical flexibility by making it less risky for employees to attempt a job shift
- More numerical flexibility can facilitate structural change and thereby job growth, which provides more job opportunities and thus more employment security.

In other situations, the nexus might lead to vicious relationships where, for instance, more numerical flexibility could induce employers to invest less in employee training and thereby reduce the employment security of the employees. Also, more job insecurity leads to overall insecurity, lower investments in human capital and, in the longer run, perhaps to lower fertility. The exact character of the interplay between security and flexibility will thus depend on the specific circumstances.

Level, regulation and national forms of flexicurity arrangements

The complexity in the debates about flexicurity is further increased by the fact that flexicurity arrangements might vary according to the level at which they function, leading to different outcomes at the national, regional, local or industry/firm-level. Furthermore, they might vary according to the actors involved (whether the government, social partners, individual firms or employees) and to the regulative tools applied (such as laws, collective agreements, individual contracts and so on).

Although, in general, countries will provide examples of most of the possible forms of flexicurity configurations, the comparative country studies often point to certain forms of flexicurity as prevailing in specific countries. In Germany and Belgium, for instance, the emphasis is on more traditional forms of flexibility (such as working time flexibility and functional flexibility in the internal labour market) whereas the focus, for instance, in Denmark is to a greater extent on numerical flexibility in the external labour market.

The same goes for the security aspect, where Germany and Belgium still tend to focus on income and job security, even though the Hartz reforms in Germany can be seen as attempts to introduce more focus on employment security. There are, of course, also general tendencies observable across countries, such as an increased focus on wage flexibility, functional flexibility and elements of combination security. Some countries are, in fact, impossible to place within this matrix, as there is no synchronous attention to flexibility and security aspects. This is true, for example, of the US, where numerical flexibility and wage flexibility are of greater importance than elements of security, or Spain, where the labour market is split into an insecure and flexible labour market for atypical workers and a secure, inflexible market for the full-time permanently employed.

The Danish case

In the flexicurity literature, the Danish employment system is often referred to as a prime example of a labour market with a flexicurity arrangement that functions well, even to such a degree that the Danish model and flexicurity are seen as almost identical. An important consequence of the broad perception of flexicurity outlined above is, of course, that flexicurity is much more than just a single national model. However, the specific interplay between the welfare state and the labour market in Denmark can be interpreted as a remarkable hybrid between the flexible, free-market welfare states characterized by high numerical flexibility, with liberal hiring-and-firing rules, and the generous Scandinavian welfare regimes of high social security through relatively high benefit levels. Therefore Denmark is an outstanding case regularly mentioned in the literature.[2]

The Danish labour market model is often described as a golden triangle of flexicurity (see Figure 2.2). The model combines high mobility between jobs with a comprehensive social safety net for the unemployed and an active labour market policy. In fact, the mobility as measured by job mobility, job creation, job destruction and average tenure, is remarkably high by international standards (Madsen 2006). The high degree of worker mobility between jobs is definitely linked to the relatively modest level of job protection in the Danish labour market. Another reason could also be a higher willingness by workers to take risk due to the

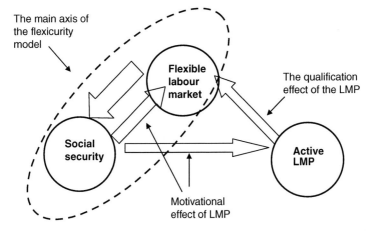

Figure 2.2 The Danish 'flexicurity model'
Source: Madsen (2006)

comprehensive social safety net and probably also the low stigmatizing effects of social security in Denmark.

Despite one of the lowest levels of job protection among OECD-countries (OECD 2003b, ch. 5), Danish workers have a feeling of high job security among all subgroups of workers (Auer and Cazes 2003). Also, a recent Eurobarometer reported that a majority of more than 70 per cent of the Danes found it beneficial to change jobs every few years. This can be contrasted to a level of below 30 per cent in countries such as Austria, Germany and Poland (Eurobarometer 2006: 6).

The arrows between the corners of the triangle in Figure 2.2 illustrate flows of people. Even if the unemployment rate is low from an international perspective, Denmark has almost the highest European level of the percentage of the employed who are affected each year by unemployment and receive unemployment benefits or social assistance, around 20 per cent. But the majority of these unemployed persons manage to find their own way back into a new job. As an indication, the incidence of long-term unemployment (longer than 6 months and longer than 12 months) as a percentage of total unemployment was in 2004, respectively, 45 per cent and 22.6 per cent in Denmark compared with 60.4 per cent and 42.4 per cent in the EU-15. Those who become long-term unemployed end up in the target group for the active labour market policy, which, ideally, helps them to find employment again. The model illustrates two of the most important effects in this connection. On the one hand, as a result of the active measures, the participants in various programmes (for example, job training and education) are upgraded and therefore improve their chances of getting a job. This is the effect of active labour market policies (ALMP) on levels of qualification.

On the other hand, these measures can have a motivational or threatening effect in that unemployed persons who are approaching the time when they are due for participation in ALMP might intensify their search for ordinary jobs, in case they consider participation in ALMP a negative prospect. Thus, one effect of labour market policy will be to influence the flow from unemployment benefits back to work this also applies to those unemployed who do not actually participate in the active measures. An econometric study has concluded that this motivational effect accounts for the major part of the macro-effect of ALMP in Denmark (Rosholm and Svarer 2004).

Finally, it is important to note that the Danish model of flexicurity is not the result of a well-defined grand scheme, but the outcome of a long historical development with strong elements of path-dependency. Thus, the high level of worker mobility supported by a low level of employment protection is a long-standing feature of the Danish labour market dating back to the General Agreement between the social partners that was the outcome of a general strike in 1899. Similarly, when it comes to income security, the present version of the system for economic support for the unemployed dates back to the last large reform of the unemployment benefit system in 1970, where the state took over the responsibility for financing the extra costs of unemployment benefits that were caused by increases in unemployment, the principle of public financing at the margin.

The third element in the triangle, active labour market policy, is also the outcome of a long tradition of interventions into the functioning of the labour market. Labour market policy in Denmark has a long political legacy, although it only developed into a distinct policy area in the mid-1950s. Also reforms of labour market policy in the 1990s were the outcome of a carefully prepared compromise that was struck in the early 1990s in a special tri-partite committee. Therefore, corporatist structures play an important role in explaining the development and robustness of the particular Danish version of flexicurity (Jørgensen 2002).

Both in the international as well as in the Danish debate there has, from time to time, been a tendency to jump to the conclusion that the success of the last decade is a result of the flexicurity model just described. It is, however, essential to point out that the positive developments in the Danish labour market since the early 1990s are not attributable exclusively to the Danish flexicurity model. Without a successful balancing of the macroeconomic policy and the trends in the international business cycle, growth in employment and falling unemployment would not have been possible. The coincidence of low inflation and a halving of the registered unemployment rate is also a by-product of a new agenda for collective bargaining and wage formation which helped the labour market adjust to the shift from high unemployment to full employment while keeping wage increases at a moderate level and not departing from the international trend towards low inflation. This agenda developed gradually during the 1980s and was formalized by a joint declaration of the social partners in 1987, when they stated that they would take the international competitiveness and macro-economic balance of the Danish economy into account during wage negotiations.

Learning from the neighbours?

Given the political attractiveness of flexicurity as a strategy and the accomplishments of the countries where flexicurity is found as a widespread state of the employment system, it is not surprising that there is a great interest in learning from the more successful neighbours. However, due to the complexity of many flexicurity arrangements and their specific historical, social and political roots, simple transfers of institutions or policies are rarely feasible.

The booming literature on policy transfer and Europeanization illustrates the options for, but also the barriers to, policy learning either directly from neighbours or from policies advocated by supranational bodies such as the European Union (Dolowitz and Marsh 2000; Olsen 2001). Inspired by Schmidt (2002), one can list a number of factors that determine the transferability of policies into a given country. These include its economic vulnerability, exemplified by the presence or absence of economic crisis, and the political institutional capacity, which is inherent in the principal policy actor's ability to impose or negotiate change. Important factors are also policy legacies and preferences, which determine the fit of potential policies with long-standing policies and institutions and with existing preferences. Related to the latter is the flexibility or robustness of the national policy discourse, determining the ability to change preferences by altering perceptions of, for instance, economic vulnerabilities and policy legacies. With direct reference to the transferability of flexicurity policies, Wilthagen (2005: 265) has also stressed the importance of political institutional capacity in the form of mutual trust between the social partners and the government when it comes to developing flexicurity policies. Adequate central and de-centralized level platforms and channels for coordination, consult-ation and negotiation are also highly important.

The importance of these points is, of course, related to the core of the flexicurity concept: moving from one configuration of levels of flexibil-ity and security to another will often necessitate one of the parties, typ-ically the employees, accepting some form of increased flexibility, and thus uncertainty, in their working life in order to receive compensation in the form of improved security arrangements provided by the employ-ers or the state. For the employees, this obviously implies the risk of being cheated by accepting more flexibility, but never getting the reward in the form of increased security. Trust created by historical experiences with bargaining processes, and perhaps supported by some form of state guarantee, is necessary. The French experience in the spring of 2006, with the government's attempt to increase flexibility without having either negotiated a compromise with the social partners or presented clear compensation for the increase in flexibility, is an illustration of this point.

Figure 2.3 provides a simple picture of the crucial role of the distribu-tion of losses and gains for different actors over time in the creation of a new balance between security and flexibility. In the example, trade unions are persuaded to accept a lower level of job security to create a more dynamic labour market and therefore a rise in employment over time. However, the new jobs will not come overnight. Even when they come, it will take a while before the benefits of the new balance is

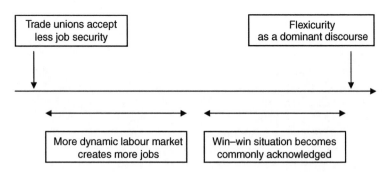

Figure 2.3 Timing and the acceptance of a flexicurity arrangement

created. Therefore, the chance of the example becoming reality will depend on:

- The realism of the causal interrelation between lower job protection and the creation of new jobs; is it empirically true that a lower level of EPL will lead to a growth in overall employment?
- Security arrangements, especially in the transition period, provided by employers and government; since some groups of workers will be worse off due to more rapid restructuring, security arrangements in the form of income security and employment security must be in place and perceived to be trustworthy
- Finally, the political institutions must have the flexibility to adapt to the new discourse.

The issue of economic vulnerability enters the bargaining process around flexicurity arrangements as a double-edged sword. On the one hand, economic crisis can be the factor that changes political preferences and puts the need for labour market reform high on the political agenda. On the other hand, an economic crisis is rarely a situation where economic resources for improving workers' security are abundant. Higher public spending on income security or policies providing more employment security will, for instance, be hampered by fear of increasing deficits in the government budget. Such worries can be offset by pointing to the fact that this public spending must be conceived of as investments and that it will be repaid through the longer-term growth created by a more flexible labour market. However, as illustrated by the recent German experience, the rules of the EMU could inhibit increased spending for security arrangements and thus transform flexicurity policies into pure policies of flexibilization. Finally, one can point to the fact that the pre-existence of a certain institutional infrastructure will facilitate specific flexicurity arrangements. A well-developed system of industrial relations with established patterns of negations between the social partners at different levels and also between the social partners and government will, of course, facilitate the sort of bargaining and compromising that is important in creating and sustaining flexicurity arrangements.

Also, institutions supported by the public sector can be important. For example, a comprehensive public system for adult education and training will make it easier to develop flexicurity arrangements that involve employment security through the upgrading of the skills of unemployed workers or workers at risk of unemployment. A well-developed system of childcare is indispensable for creating security for working parents and, thus, for a flexible supply of younger women on the labour market.

However, the aim of this chapter is not to provide detailed prescriptions on how to implement flexicurity policies in specific national contexts. This is a complex task better left to national analysts and policy-makers in the respective countries. In this process, supranational actors such as the European Union will, of course, play an important role by creating mechanisms for, and facilitating the exchange of, policy lessons and good practices between countries. Here, a better comprehension of best practices with respect to flexicurity policies from other countries, including Denmark, can act as an important source of inspiration and can lay the ground for shifts in national discourses that, over time, may lead to a 'subtle transformation of states' (Jacobsson 2004). The main attraction of Denmark in this context is therefore its uniqueness as a European country having implemented an encompassing version of a specific form of flexicurity. And, as any teacher will know, one real-life example tells more than a torrent of abstractions.

Criteria for 'good flexicurity practices'?

As mentioned above, the Presidency's Conclusions from the Brussels Summit in March 2006 have called for the development of a set of common principles on flexicurity. Fortunately, the development of such principles will not have to start from scratch. When looking at the rapidly expanding literature on flexicurity and related subjects, one can find a number of more or less general recommendations offered by the various authors. One such example can be found in the work of Schmid and Gazier (2002), who present four major criteria for transitional labour markets:

- Empowerment: empower individuals to cope with the new risks of social life
- Sustainable employment and income: make transitions pay!
- Flexible coordination: establish a new balance between centralized regulation and self-organization; allocate more power to local levels
- Cooperation: stimulate local networks and public–private partnerships; the linking of resources.

In a more recent study discussing the Hartz reforms in Germany, Leschke *et al.* (2006: 5) list the criteria they would apply in order to assess the reforms in terms of efficient and equitable flexicurity criteria:

First, we ask to what extent flexibility, especially internal and external numerical flexibility has been strengthened by the latest labour market reforms. To assess the security dimension, we ask whether the measures provide minimum income security to the atypically employed. As state-run labour market policies do not aim anymore at improving job security, we further concentrate on the question if the measures enable transitions into standard employment, as an expression of enhanced employability. Lastly, we try to assess if option security among the atypically employed is improved. Thereby the particular needs of the schemes' target groups are taken into account. Concerning unemployment, we adopt a broad definition, which includes illegal employment and discouraged workers.

Along a similar vein, Wilthagen and Houwerzijl (2005) have searched for a policy checklist that could act as a tool for assessing the extent to which labour market flexibility was reconciled with social cohesion. This was done in the context of the so-called 'tree model' from the Council of Europe's methodological guide. Their draft checklist consists of three parts: flexibilization, employment and income. It is expanded into a rather complex set of tables with indicators that are to be applied in order to assess the overall coherence between flexibility and security in different situations.

Towards a set of common principles?

As is evident from the literature, the design of a common set of principles of flexicurity is by no means an easy task. This is due, in the first place, to the multidimensional character of the concept itself. As described above, flexicurity arrangements might combine different forms of flexibility and security, both along the flexibility and the security dimension, and thus lead to a multitude of possible configurations. To cover these by a common set of principles is not a simple assignment. Furthermore, complications stem from the diverse national, regional and local contexts within which flexicurity arrangements are to be designed and implemented. When drafting such principles, two pitfalls are therefore obvious. One will be that drafting the principles at such a high level of generality will severely limit their value for practical policy deliberation and evaluation. The other risk is that the set of common principles will inflate into a very detailed manual with guidelines for all kinds of specific situations, thus losing sight of the comprehensive character of the principles. The approach taken here in discussing a set of common principles in the following paragraphs is to begin the outline at the highest level of abstraction and then allow this to be developed into more specific guidelines that can be applicable for specific arrangements and contexts. Two observations can be made before the attempt to identify the common principles at the most general level. First, in the present context, flexicurity should be conceived as a political strategy rather than as a state of affairs or an analytical tool. This is also the perspective taken by Wilthagen in his early definition of flexicurity (Wilthagen, 1998). Following this observation, one might give a few thoughts to the question of what the *differentia specifica* should be for common principles related to a flexicurity strategy compared with principles or guidelines for political strategies in general. Here, three observations can be made:

- Flexicurity policies will normally imply the integration of different policy areas that call for increased emphasis on interactions between policy elements
- Flexicurity policies will be exceedingly loaded with conflicting interests, since they will almost always imply winners and losers, especially in the short run, and therefore deliberations about compensating mechanisms
- While one can argue that some, but not all, configurations of flexibility and security will eventually manifest themselves as win–win situations, the gains and losses may be unevenly distributed over time; one might also find that certain subgroups (for instance, among the employed with a very high level of job security) could come out as losers in the longer run.

These preconditions will influence the focus of the common principles that are outlined below.

Second, principles can be related to different aspects of a flexicurity strategy. Based on the standard concepts of policy analysis, one can distinguish between three aspects of a policy: (1) the policy context; (2) the political process and policy implementation; and (3) policy outcomes. In case of political strategies aimed at creating some form of flexicurity arrangements, one can the assign one overarching principle to each of these three aspects and, therefore, at the most general level one can identify three common principles for all flexicurity arrangements.

When it comes to content of the policy in question, the basic criterion must be the principle of integrating flexibility and security. Policies will not fulfil this condition if they solely imply changes in either some form of flexibility or security. At the core of the concept of flexicurity is the idea that some form of flexibility is combined with some form of security arrangement that reduces the actual or potential costs either for the employees or for the employers of the flexibility in question. Here, the flexicurity aspect will imply demands on individuals or employers to adapt to changing situations and also, in a more proactive manner, to take more risks within a given environment. The safety net might be in the form of income security or one of the other forms of security spelled out above.

A second general standard for flexicurity is related to policy implementation and could be labelled the principle of legitimate negotiations. In democratic societies, flexicurity arrangements will be designed, implemented and changed through a political process. Furthermore, one might, as stressed by Leschke *et al.* (2006), imagine situations where no trade-offs are present, at least not in the longer run. Such flexicurity arrangements can be conceived as positive-sum games with a positive net gain. But even positive-sum games could have some participants who face the risk of not experiencing net gains, or who have to wait for their rewards until later. Thus, moving from one configuration of levels of flexibility and security to another will involve situations where one of the parties (typically the employees) must accept some form of increased flexibility, and thus uncertainty in their working life, in order to receive compensation in the form of improved security arrangements provided by the employers or the state. For this new situation to be sustainable calls for a high degree of legitimacy, which again must be based on some form of negotiated agreement between actors that have a mutual trust and share some form of common understanding.

Based on the flexicurity literature, one can finally point to a third general principle, which relates to the policy outcome with respect to forming the basis for sustainable employment, both in general and with respect to the situation of weak groups on the labour market or in society as a whole. Such ideas are also inherent in all the examples of policy guidelines or assessments cited in the previous section and lead to the inclusion of a principle of sustainable employment and social cohesion in the set of common principles as they are defined at the most general level.

Based on these three general principles, one can, at a lower level of abstraction, identify a set of guidelines or a checklist that could be applied in assessing the design and implementation of flexicurity arrangements within a specific context.

Thus, based on the principle of integrating the two elements in the flexicurity concept, one can develop a set of guidelines that has the following main elements:

- First, both the flexicurity and security elements of the flexicurity strategy must be well defined with respect to the concrete arrangements and the instruments involved
- The interaction between the flexibility and the security elements must be unambiguous with respect to trade-off(s), positive interactions and vicious circles
- The distributional aspects of the flexicurity strategy should be analyzed
- Mechanisms of compensation for potential gains and losses for different groups must be included in the strategy.
- Second, along a similar vein, one may develop the principle of legitimate negotiations into a set of common guidelines for the *political and social process* that shapes the flexicurity arrangements:
  - All relevant stakeholders, including those at the local level, should take part in the process of decision-making
  - The process must be transparent with respect to the distribution of gains and losses from the flexicurity strategy
  - The political process should include political guarantees that ensure the implementation of the flexicurity strategy over time
  - The flexicurity strategy should mobilize and link resources from different actors.
- Third, one may specify a more detailed set of criteria for the *outcome* of the flexicurity strategy with respect to sustainable employment and integration of weaker groups:
  - Ex ante policy evaluations should be made to uncover long-term and societal consequences of the flexicurity strategy as a whole, including its effect on institutional competitiveness
  - The flexicurity strategy should, in the long run, improve the employment options and the quality of employment for all groups on the labour market
  - The flexicurity strategy should have an advantageous effect on the distribution of welfare and living conditions in general
  - The flexicurity strategy should empower weak groups to cope with their situation both as individuals and in cooperation with others.
- Finally, at a third and even more practical level, one can specify a set of principles in the form of good flexicurity practices with respect to

all three general principles as they are laid out in the guidelines. A few examples could be:
- Income security can support labour mobility and structural change by increasing willingness to take risks and thus increase numerical flexibility
- Employment security: institutions for adult vocational training can provide skills that are transferable and improve both functional and numerical mobility
- Combining security in the form of public child-care institutions and maternity leave can support mobility of women into work
- Arrangements supporting the flexible retirement of older workers through part-time pensions and similar schemes could increase the integration of older workers into the labour market
- Including the trade unions in the process of policy formation at the local level will increase the willingness of workers to enter into flexicurity arrangements that trade more flexibility of working time or pay for more job or employment security
- Active labour market programmes could support the (re)integration of long-term unemployed onto work and thus provide employment security for this group.

Where is the European Union actually moving?

As mentioned above, flexicurity is now a top issue on the European policy agenda. Initially, it was given a prominent role under the Austrian presidency in the spring of 2006, also reflected in the call for a set of common principles by the European Council in March 2006. From the perspective of the Commission, flexicurity is to be interpreted as having four elements (Spidla 2006):

- First, contractual arrangements that are modern and that allow a sufficiently flexible organization of work while at the same time containing segmentation of the labour market and reducing undeclared work
- Second, active labour market policies that help people to adjust to rapid changes, to situations of unemployment and switches to new jobs
- Third, life-long learning systems that keep abreast of the requirements of a constantly changing configuration of work organization
- Finally, social security systems that combine the need to make labour market mobility easier with the provision of appropriate supplementary income.

It is thus evident that the Commission is developing a general view on flexicurity that is close to 'going Danish' with less emphasis on the broader perspective on flexicurity that is included in the scientific literature as described earlier in this chapter.

A probable outcome of this process could be a soft version of common principles that highlights the various options or pathways that are open to specific groups of member states, but without having the form of strict common guidelines known from the European Employment Strategy, or, in the words of the Commission's report on Employment in Europe from November 2006:

> The main aim . . . is to present a preliminary characterization of the balance between flexibility and security across Member States – to reflect their current institutional setting – and, on that basis, to propose a taxonomy of countries in a reduced number of 'flexicurity' systems. This should be seen as preliminary work leading to the Commission's report on flexicurity scheduled for the end of 2007, which, in addition to describing the current situation, will also present a number of 'typical' pathways built around the above-mentioned four principles, that Member States could select in order to improve their balance between flexibility and security (European Commission 2006: 76).

With respect to the policy process, the report stresses the need for the policy focus to be shifted from individual policy tools to reform packages that encompass several approaches simultaneously in order to, on the one hand, exploit well-documented policy interactions that enhance the benefits of reforms on labour market performance, and, on the other hand, to make policy change more acceptable politically and socially. Whether the national capacity for policy reforms in the member states can put this ambitious vision of comprehensive reform packages into reality is the main challenge for European employment policy in the coming years.

Conclusion: learning from Denmark?

The general message of this chapter is that the positive international attention lavished on Denmark in recent years is, in fact, justified. Measured on a number of different dimensions, the Danish labour market does, indeed, demonstrate a high degree of flexibility. Above all, the extraordinary Danish combination of high mobility between jobs, low job security and high rates of unemployment benefit deserves attention and makes it possible to interpret the Danish labour market model as a unique variety of flexicurity. On top of this comes a highly developed active labour market policy and, in general, a well-developed continuous educational system. These add an element of employment security by strengthening the labour market competences of both the unemployed and people in employment.

When this unique flexicurity model is taken as a source of inspiration, it must be realized that it makes certain demands on the social partners and the political decision-makers. The trade unions must accept employment security rather than job security. That can be difficult, particularly in times of increasing employment insecurity due to, for instance, offshoring of jobs. The best response in this situation is not increased job protection, but improved employment security for exposed or vulnerable groups; for example, massive investments in adult vocational education and training.

For their part, the employers must come to terms with the fact that a precondition for the low degree of job protection not to result in increasing employment insecurity is a well-functioning, generous and relatively expensive unemployment and social assistance system. As a continuation of this, the political decision-makers must realize that substantial changes at any of the corners of the flexicurity triangle are not possible without serious repercussions for the other corners of the triangle. Any political intervention in the labour market must therefore be based on a holistic understanding.

These lessons to be learned, and mutually recognized, are vital to preserve a flexible and secure labour market. They also demonstrate how difficult it will be to export this model to other European countries. One transferable lesson, however, is that a generous welfare state is not incompatible with a dynamic and well functioning labour market that functions well. This lesson extends beyond the correlation between a labour market characterized by low job protection, generous unemployment benefits and active labour market policy.

The high degree of flexibility on the Danish labour market is furthermore supported more indirectly through a number of welfare state services – such as a comprehensive educational system (including adult vocational training and education), a well-developed childcare system, a relatively well-functioning and publicly financed health care system and so on. From a labour market perspective, many of these welfare schemes can be viewed as investments in structures that function well rather than as costs. It is this lesson from the Danish experiences that can serve as inspiration for the development of the European social model.

Notes

1 See for instance, Schmid and Gazier (2002).
2 For more detailed expositions of the Danish employment system and the lessons that can be learned from it, reference can be made to Madsen (2006, 2007) and to Bredgaard *et al.* (2005, 2006).

References

Atkinson, J. (1984) 'Flexibility, Uncertainty and Manpower Management', IMS Report 89 (Brighton: Institute of Manpower Studies).

Auer, P. and Cazes, S. (2003) *Employment Stability in an Age of Flexibility. Evidence from Industrialized Countries* (Geneva: International Labour Organization).

Bredgaard, T., Larsen, F. and Madsen, P.K. (2006) 'Opportunities and Challenges for Flexicurity – The Danish Example', *Transfer – European Review of Labour and Research*, 12(1): 61–8.

Bredgaard, T., Larsen, F. and Madsen, P.K. (2005) 'The Flexible Danish Labour Market – A Review', CARMA Research Papers 1:2005 (Aalborg University: CARMA).

Dolowitz, D.P. and Marsh, D. (2000) 'Learning from Abroad: The Role of Policy Transfer in Contemporary Policy-Making', *Governance*, 13(1): 5–24.

Eurobarometer (2006) 'Survey on Europeans and Mobility' (Luxemborg: Eurobarometer).

European Commission (2006) *Employment in Europe 2006* (Luxembourg: European Commission).

Jacobsson, K. (2004) 'Soft Regulation and the Subtle Transformation of States: The Case of EU Employment Policy', *Journal of European Social Policy*, 14(4): 355–70.

Jørgensen, H. (2002) *Consensus, Cooperation and Conflict – The Policy-Making Process in Denmark* (Cheltenham: Edward Elgar).

Leschke, J., Schmid, G. and Griga, D. (2006) 'On the Marriage of Flexibility and Security: Lessons from the Hartz-reforms in Germany', Discussion Paper SP 2006–108, (Berlin: Wissenschaftzentrum).

Madsen, Per Kongshøj (2007) 'Distribution of Responsibility for Social Security and Labour Market Policy. Country Report: Denmark', AIAS Working Paper 2007-51 (Amsterdam: Amsterdam Institute for Advanced Labour Studies, University of Amsterdam).

Madsen, Per Kongshøj (2006) 'How Can It Possibly Fly? The Paradox of a Dynamic Labour Market in a Scandinavian Welfare State', in John A. Campbell, John A. Hall and Ove, K. Pedersen (eds), *National Identity and the Varieties of Capitalism: The Danish Experience* (Montreal: McGill-Queen's University Press): 321–55.

OECD (2003) *OECD Economic Outlook*, Volume 2003/1, No.73, June(Paris: OECD).

Olsen, J.P. (2001) 'The Many Faces of Europeanization', ARENA Working Paper 01/2.

Rosholm, M. and Svarer, M. (2004) 'Estimating the Threat Effect of Active Labour Market Programmes', IZA Discussion Paper 1300.

Schmid, G. and Gazier, B. (2002) *The Dynamics of Full Employment: Social Integration through Transitional Labour Markets* (Cheltenham: Edward Elgar).

Schmidt, V. (2002) 'Europeanization and the Mechanics of Economic Policy Adjustment', *Journal of European Public Policy*, 9(6): 894–912.

Spidla, V. (2006) 'Opening address' for the seminar 'Labour Mobility in the EU and China: Trends and Challenges Ahead', 13 October 2006.

Wilthagen, T. (2005) 'Striking a Balance? Flexibility and Security in European Labour Markets', in Thomas Bredgaard and Flemming Larsen (eds), *Employment Policy from Different Angles* (Copenhagen: DJØF Publishing): 253–67.

Wilthagen, T. (1998) *Flexicurity – A New Paradigm for Labour Market Policy Reform?* WZB Discussion Paper, FSI, 98–202 (Berlin: WZB).

Wilthagen, T. and Houwerzijl, M. (2005) 'Reconciling Labour Market Flexibility and Social Cohesion: A Methodological Tool proposed by the Council of Europe', Paper presented at Forum 2005, Council of Europe.

Wilthagen, T. and Tros, F. (2004) 'The Concept of "Flexicurity": A New Approach to Regulating Employment and Labour Markets', *Transfer – European Review of Labour and Research*, 10(2): 166–87.

3
Slovakia: A Story of Reforms

Ivan Mikloš

Introduction

Since the fall of communism in 1989, Slovakia has experienced the exciting story of a new democracy and a newly independent country that went through very turbulent and often almost contradictory periods. Between 1993–98, its first six years of existence as an independent state, Slovakia languished in international isolation, considered by many to be the 'European black hole'[1] due to its illiberal democracy[2] and the international inexperience of Vladimir Meciar's government. It was excluded from the process of international integration that brought other transition economies into the framework of the OECD, NATO and the EU. Even worse, Meciar's government implemented an economic policy that by 1998 had the country on the brink of collapse.

The Meciar era was followed by two governments led by Mikulas Dzurinda in the years 1998–2006. Economic stabilization, catching up with the integration deficit, and deep structural reforms that made the country one of the reform and economic leaders in region were the outcomes of that period. After the 2006 elections, a new government led by Robert Fico took power, and the programme of the dominant coalition party included cancellation of all the reforms that had been implemented by the Dzurinda government. However, reality has differed from expectations, and, except for healthcare reform, the previous reforms have remained in force even though the fate of some of them is still uncertain. The objective of this chapter is to show how economic policy and reforms in the 1998–2006 period made such fundamental changes in the socio-economic model in Slovakia and what the outcomes of these changes are.

Slovakia is a small open economy. With 5.4 million inhabitants, it is the smallest of the so-called Visegrad Four countries: Poland, the Czech Republic, Hungary, Slovakia. In terms of per capita incomes, Slovakia is approximately at the same level as Hungary, behind the Czech Republic and ahead of Poland. The private sector accounts for 91.3 per cent of GDP, and the openness of the country to international trade and investment is evident from the fact that the ratio of foreign trade to GDP is greater than 1.

Economic and political development up to 1998 under Meciar

Slovakia, as an independent country, was formed after the split of Czechoslovakia on 1 January 1993. The lack of experience in state governance and the incompetence of the populist politicians who led the country to its independence in an imprecise and purposeless way hampered early progress, as did the illiberal democracy[3] that defined the country's early political life and the international inexperience of the Meciar government. Over the course of six years, these policies resulted in a complicated and unfavourable international political and economic situation. In the mid-1990s, the other Visegrad countries joined the OECD, but Slovakia was denied membership. A similar setback marked the discussions about joining NATO. The EU Summit of December 1997 agreed to start accession talks with nine new member states, among which Slovakia was, again, not to be found. From the economic point of view, the situation was unfavourable as well. The economy achieved relatively high growth rates, averaging 5.4 per cent over the period 1994–98, but this growth was achieved by unsustainable means. The current account deficit over 1996–98 averaged 9 per cent of GDP, and the government budget deficit was almost 6 per cent. This expansionary fiscal policy had to be neutralized by the restrictive monetary policy of the Central Bank, which had luckily kept its independence from the government. This monetary policy resulted in a sharp rise in interest rates, with negative impacts on the economy, investment and business development, and the government's debt service costs.

The government did not combat the principal problem of corruption: on the contrary, it was exacerbated by the non-transparent privatization that benefited people loyal to the country's political rulers[4] and through looting and asset stripping at companies and banks remaining in state ownership. Companies usually were not restructured so as to become motivated by profits but, rather, were encouraged to persist in rent-seeking behaviour and to maintain over-employment. This situation existed not only in state-owned companies, but also in companies privatized for symbolic prices by people, usually the communist era managers, who were aligned with the government.

Implementation of such domestic and foreign policies isolated Slovakia not only politically, but also economically. Direct foreign investments 1993–98 were only $6.6 billion, which was 1.6 per cent of GDP, compared with Hungary, where it was 5.4 per cent, and the Czech Republic, where it was 3.1 per cent of GDP for the same period.

The Dzurinda reforms of 1998–2006

The situation changed after the 1998 elections, when the first government of Mikulas Dzurinda took over. This government brought together a broad coalition of three centre-right and one centre-left, reformed, communist political parties whose policy objective was to speed up reforms, to accelerate Slovakia's integration into international institutions and into the EU, and to stabilize the endangered economy. The government successfully completed these objectives. Slovakia joined the OECD in 2000, NATO in 2004 and the EU, together with the rest of the Visegrad countries, in May 2004. The government also fulfilled its priorities in the economic area. Restructuring, recovery and the privatization of the banking sector took place. The economic reforms were a challenging and costly operation. The three major state-owned banks, which held almost 50 per cent of all bank assets, were on the verge of collapse in 1998–99. Their recovery through the cleansing of bad debts by a state agency cost the state budget almost 12 per cent of GDP. Subsequently, international tenders from foreign investors in Austria, Germany and Italy privatized the refinanced banks.

The entry of strategic investors into other so-called strategic sectors such as telecommunications, energy distribution and the gas company and, later, during the second Dzurinda government, into power plants, was realized as well. The government also raised regulated prices that had been, until then, held at artificially low levels and established an independent regulatory office for network industries that has set the prices of these commodities independently of the government since 2002.[5] A new law on bankruptcy and compensation was adopted to strengthen the rights of creditors to increase financial discipline and to create pressure for the restructuring of the business sector.

Public finances were partially revitalized; a set of fiscally restrictive measures that led to a more sustainable government's budget was adopted in May 1999. The business environment improved, inflows of foreign investments increased, and the restructuring of the business sector began. However, the easing of pressure on firms to over-employ workers along with demographic developments led to an increase in unemployment.[6] The unemployment rate increased from 12.6 per cent in 1998 to 19.2 per cent in 2001, when it peaked, giving Slovakia the highest unemployment rate in Europe.

The second Dzurinda government

The 2002 elections, to the surprise of many observers, resulted in the creation of a second government led by Mikulas Dzurinda. Compared to the first Dzurinda government, this one was more homogeneous in its ideas and programmes, and, thus, it was able to enact an ambitious reform programme. The government consisted of four centre-right parties, and it was characterized by a high degree of programme compatibility in the economic area. The coalition partners agreed to the pressing need to implement an economic policy that would create conditions for high and sustainable economic growth. Such an outcome was to be reached through an increased level of economic freedom, a revitalized macroeconomic framework centred on the long-term sustainability of public finances, an improved business environment, and deep structural reforms, as well as an increase in foreign investments and admission to the EU and, eventually, to the Euro zone. These aims were included in the government programme declaration and, in principle, were fulfilled, with some exceptions.[7]

The main areas of significant change were:[8]

- Macroeconomic framework and public finance reform
- Tax reform
- Pension reform
- Healthcare reform
- Social reform and labour market reform
- Public administration reform and fiscal decentralization
- Business environment improvements.

A fundamentally important area of policy development was the MINERVA programme, adopted by the government in 2005, which sought to provide the basis for the future development of the knowledge economy in Slovakia.

The macroeconomic framework and public finance reform

One of the key conditions for high and sustainable economic growth in the long run is a healthy macroeconomic environment with sustainable public finances. Moreover, our deep conviction was that by increasing economic freedom and promoting the effective functioning of institutions, mainly institutions of the public sector, we could make a major contribution to growth. The coordination of, and interactions between, these forces are important as well.

The need for mutual and synchronous harmonization of the following objectives appeared to be a challenging task because of their political consequences and risks:

- Increasing the level of economic freedom by decreasing taxes and redistribution
- Decreasing the budget deficit and setting it on a long-term sustainable path
- Realizing deep reforms that would have an uncertain short-term impact on public finances
- Improving the business environment.

This was why the coordination of individual reforms, mainly by the Ministry of Finance, was so important. The relationship between the macroeconomic framework and reforms is mutually supportive. Without reforms, for example in the social or healthcare area, it would not have been possible to decrease public expenditures, and, without creating macroeconomic space for them, reforms would have foundered for lack of resources. From this point of view, the fiscal perspective is not only a key indicator, but also a tool for setting in motion the implementation of necessary changes.

Table 3.1 shows that the ambitious goal of decreasing redistributive government policies while bringing the government budget under control was successfully realized.

Hypothetically, if the level of redistribution that had existed in 1998 had continued during the time span of the two Dzurinda governments, some 400 billion SKK more would have been required to pay for them. This comparison testifies to the enormous growth of economic freedom together with public finance reform in Slovakia. This was a very reasonable investment from an economic standpoint, but a relatively risky investment into faster economic growth and development from a political standpoint.

Table 3.1 Redistributive government policies in Slovakia (GDP in %)

	1998	1999	2000	2001	2002	2003	2004	2005
Public expenditures	45.3	47.2	51.7	43.3	43.3	39.4	38.9	37.1
Tax quota II	35.7	34.3	33.0	31.6	32.0	31.1	30.0	29.5
Balance of public finances*	−4.8	−6.4	−11.8	−6.5	−7.7	−3.7	−3.0	−3.1
Gross public debt	34.0	47.2	49.9	49.2	43.3	42.7	41.6	34.5

Note: * In 2005 without costs of implementing the second pillar in the pension system.
Source: Eurostat

Table 3.2 Economic performance of Slovakia, 2003–04 (in %)

	2002	2003	2004	2005	2006
GDP growth	4.1	4,2	5.4	6.0	8,3
Inflation	3.3	8.5	7.5	2.7	4.5
Unemployment rate	18.5	17.4	18.1	16.2	13.3
Employment growth	0.2	1.8	0.3	2.1	3.8
Real labour productivity growth	4.7	2.3	5.8	4.7	6.0
Current account*	−7.9	−0.9	−3.4	−8.5	−8.2

Note: The high deficit in 2005–06 was mainly the result of high imports of investment goods, the effects of which are currently reflected in the increase of exports and also in the lower current account deficit. In January 2007, exports already exceeded imports.
Source: Eurostat and Statistical Office of the Slovak Republic, Ministry of Finance of the Slovak Republic

A big question mark was the reaction of the economy to restrictive fiscal policy in 2003, and the secondary impacts of increases in regulated prices and indirect taxes in 2003–04. As evident from Table 3.2, despite fiscal restraint in 2003–04, the economy was performing well. This confirms the experience of other countries that fiscal restraint, if combined with structural reforms and improvement in the business environment, does not necessarily have to hinder economic growth.

Growth in the years 2006–07[9] obviously mirrors the direct and indirect effects of the reforms. It was crucial that that high economic growth be reached without significant inflationary pressures or unsustainable deficits in the current account. It is clear that the mix of fiscal, monetary and structural policy was chosen relatively well. The results garnered international attention, including that of the independent credit rating agencies. While in 2000 Slovakia had definitely the worst rating among all Visegrad countries, currently Slovakia ranks first in the region.

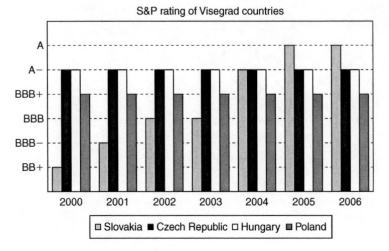

Figure 3.1   Long-term ratings at year end by S&P

The reform of public finance brought, from the medium-term viewpoint, significant cost savings in public expenditures. The main objectives of public finance reform in 2002–03 were:

- Transparency of public finance
- Programme budgeting and budgets for longer budgetary horizons
- Improvement of macroeconomic and fiscal analyses and forecasts
- New budget regulations restricting the use of public resources
- Concentrating liquidity into the state treasury and professionalizing debt and liquidity management.

Implementation of the methodology of ESA 95 was the key factor in increasing the transparency of public finance because this methodology makes it easier to spot cover-ups and shifts in deficit reports, which had been common before 2002.[10] ESA 95 methodology, which facilitates international comparisons of fiscal outcomes and is embedded in the new law on budget regulations and which highlights the deficit of total public finance on an accrual basis rather than on a cash basis, was crucial. The fact that the government stopped offering state credit guarantees and eliminated almost all state funds for support of firms contributed to increased transparency and the implementation of tough budget restrictions.

Programme budgeting and budgeting for, currently, three years into the future have strengthened strategic planning and facilitated effective control of public resource use. Tough budget restrictions were significantly strengthened as well. In the past, uncontrolled indebtedness was common in some public institutions, especially in healthcare, regional education, railroads, and radio and television broadcasting.[11]

Significant improvement of macro economical analyses and forecasts was achieved by strengthening the analytical capacities of the Ministry of Finance, specifically by improving internal staff skills, but also by involving external capacities. The capacity of the Institute of Financial Policy (IFP) of the Ministry of Finance, which became the central analytical resource of the government, was strengthened as well. Two committees, the Committee for Macroeconomic Forecasts and the Committee for Tax Forecasts, were founded. Their members are reputable economists and analysts from the private and public sectors.

These committees discuss periodic forecasts of the IFP three times a year even before they are published, and the committees' members publish them together with commentaries. Thanks to these changes, implemented in 2002–06, it was possible to persuade all parliamentary political parties, the opposition included, that forecasting of the state budget and public revenue is a professional matter and that the size of the deficit or surplus should be the only topics for political discussion.

Since 2005, all the financial flows of public administration, with the exception of local governments, are concentrated in the state treasury. This creates direct and indirect savings for the state budget. Direct savings stem from the lower interest margin between paid and received interest, which had been collected by banks in the past, and lower expenses for state debt management. Indirect savings result from the strengthening of the state's position on the financial market thanks to the concentration of resources in the state treasury and thanks to the creation of an agency for debt and liquidity management. This agency is responsible for the operational aspects of state debt management, while the strategic management of debt is still the responsibility of the Ministry of Finance.

Organizational and process changes at the Ministry of Finance also contributed to the overall improvement of public finance management. During 2003, an organizational, functional, process and information audit was undertaken at the Ministry, and the outcome was process reorganization of all activities, a new organizational structure and a decrease of a job positions by 30 per cent from 849 to 599. In the biggest section of the Ministry alone, this represented a decrease from 147 to 88 job positions, while a new Department of Budget Analyses was created. In 2004–06, the Ministry continued to improve management by implementing a managerial quality system. Since 1 January 2005, the Ministry of Finance of the Slovak Republic has been a member of the European Foundation of Quality Management (EFQM). In October 2005 the Ministry was the first ministry in Europe to be awarded the first-level award from EFQM, the 'Committed to Excellence' award: in May 2006, it was acknowledged with the higher-level, 'Recognized for Excellence' award. The main objective of EFQM implementation was the strengthening of motivation and the creation of pressure for an ongoing process of quality management that would survive changes in the political appointees leading the Ministry. Audits and increased quality management in the Ministry of Finance showed that huge deficiencies and inefficiencies also existed at many other levels of the state administration, because it was generally acknowledged that, even before the introduction of these improvements at the Ministry, it was already one of the most efficient government units.

Tax reform

Principles and foundations of tax reform   Tax reform is definitely the best known, and also most discussed, Slovak reform. There are two reasons for this. First, the new tax system was introduced in January 2004, shortly before EU accession, and that is why it received broad attention and positive evaluations from entrepreneurs and economists, However, there were also negative reactions, mainly from politicians in the countries that are, because of market rigidities and the inefficiency of their institutions and economic models, tax systems included, unable to cope with the consequences of global competition. It is no coincidence that Slovak tax reform had the strongest responses, both positive and negative, in countries such as Germany and France.

The second reason for interest in the Slovak tax reform is its uniqueness. This stems not from the implementation of a flat tax, since such a tax had already been implemented in Estonia, Ukraine and Russia, and later in Romania. Rather, the Slovak feature of note was the distinctive transparency and simplicity of the system, the result of:

- Elimination of almost all exceptions to the tax regime
- Elimination of all special rates and special regimes
- Elimination of almost all deductible items
- Elimination of double taxation where possible (for example, the elimination of the dividend tax, the inheritance tax, the gift tax and the real estate transfer tax)
- Elimination of deforming components in tax policy that had been used for other than fiscal objectives.

There was no explicit promise to implement a flat tax in Slovakia in the 2002 programme of the government, only a statement of its willingness to consider its implementation:

> The government will enforce the increase of tax and contribution collection effectiveness. Simplification of tax legislation and especially updates of those parts of tax legislation that enabled ambiguous interpretation will contribute to increase in tax collection. The government will consider the possibility of the unification of income tax rates ... The tax burden will be transferred from direct to indirect taxes ... The government will unify VAT rates before joining the EU.[12]

Based on this declaration, the objective was to transform the Slovak tax system into one of the most competitive systems in the EU and the OECD.

The lack of relevant analyses and quantifications of the fiscal impacts of the implementation of various flat tax rate combinations and indirect taxes, mainly VAT, was the reason for the very careful tone of the government's statements about its willingness to implement the flat tax in its programme declaration.

The tax reform was based on principles of justice, neutrality, simplicity, exactness, effectiveness and the elimination of double taxation. Thus, it is based on principles that are highlighted in every tax theory textbook but rarely applied in any country.

Horizontal justice is protected by unified taxation of equal subjects of taxation. Vertical justice ensures that subjects with higher income, property or consumption pay higher taxes but with proportionality maintained, which means that taxation should not increase with an increased tax base.[13] The neutrality principle ensures that taxation only minimally distorts economic processes and the economic decision-making of subjects. In terms of simplicity and exactness, the tax rules include only the inevitable minimum of clearly conceived norms that do not allow conflicting interpretations. An effective tax does not allow legal tax avoidance, does not facilitate illegal tax evasion and does not indirectly motivate subjects to tax evasion by inefficient taxation. Elimination of double taxation results from taxing income only once, at the point of transfer from production to consumption or reinvestment, which relates especially to property taxes and dividend income taxes.

After the programme declaration of the government was passed, a new working team for preparing the tax reform, led by the Minister of Finance, was created at the Ministry of Finance. The team prepared calculations and forecasts of fiscal impacts in several variations of two basic alternatives: with flat tax implementation and without flat tax implementation. The decision to implement the flat tax was the outcome of this deliberative process, mainly because a flat tax facilitated a more effective and exact fulfilment of those objectives and principles listed above that were included in the programme declaration. The risks connected to the tax reform variant without the implementation of flat tax were higher uncertainty in forecasting the fiscal impact and the higher political risk of unavoidable VAT unification at a higher level.

In January 2004, the new tax system became effective in Slovakia. The system is based on five key measures:

- Implementation of a flat personal and corporate income tax rate at the level of 19 per cent, replacing the old tax with five tax brackets from 10 per cent to 38 per cent for individuals and 25 per cent for legal entities and a huge number of exceptions and special rates[14]
- Unification of VAT rates at the level of 19 per cent, replacing the old rates of 14 per cent and 20 per cent
- Elimination of dividend tax
- Elimination of gift tax, inheritance tax and real estate transfer tax
- Elimination of almost all exceptions, deductible items, special regimes and special rates.

The tax burden on high-income groups would have decreased because the rate for the highest income groups was cut in half, from 38 per cent to 19 per cent, and the burden on the lowest income groups, where the rates increased from 10 per cent to 19 per cent, would have increased. To make the flat tax politically palatable, the exempt level of income was increased by a factor of almost two-and-a-half and was also indexed.[15] As a result, the real effective tax burden decreased on groups with low incomes, and the effective rate is therefore still progressive. People with low incomes do not pay anything, while high incomes are taxed almost at 19 per cent.

Figure 3.2 shows that, in the first year of the new tax system, people with incomes up to 42.6 per cent of the average income did not pay any income tax, and, from this level up, their effective tax rate continuously rose from zero per cent to 19 per cent.

Indirect taxes were increased, which of course was neither popular nor simple. Increased consumption taxes were inevitable in order to reach the minimum EU level that Slovakia was required to attain as part of

Changes in income tax rates		
(in %)	2003	2004
Personal income tax	2; 2,25; 2,5; 2,75; 10; 20; 28; 35; 38	19
Corporate income tax	15; 18; 25	19
Allowance tax	1; 5; 10; 15; 20; 25	19

Figure 3.2   Comparison of the old and new tax systems

its EU accession package. The unification of VAT rates at 19 per cent was the most delicate area because sensitive commodities such as food, pharmaceuticals, books, health aids and newspapers were in the lower 14 per cent rate before the reform. The unification of VAT rates not only had important fiscal objectives, but also was objectively reasonable because it eliminated economic deformations connected with the different taxation of various goods.

Evaluating the results of tax reform after the first three years   The government assumed that the tax reform would contribute to an improved business environment, higher motivation to work and more business start-ups and investment, as well as increased foreign investment and a decrease in tax evasion. Today, after more than three years implementation, we can conclude that these expectations were fulfilled and that, in some areas, developments even exceeded expectations. Tax reform became an important marketing asset for Slovakia and played an important role in attracting foreign investors. This resulted not only from the tax's simplicity and low level, but also from the fact that overall taxation of capital in Slovakia is the lowest among all EU countries due to the elimination of dividend tax (see Figure 3.3).

Fiscal outcomes of the tax reform are positive as well. The Ministry of Finance was very careful when conceiving the reform because its objective was not only to create tax competitiveness, but also macroeconomic stability and to decrease the budget deficit.

The level of uncertainty in forecasting the fiscal impacts of tax changes in the first year of implementation was high due to the magnitude of the

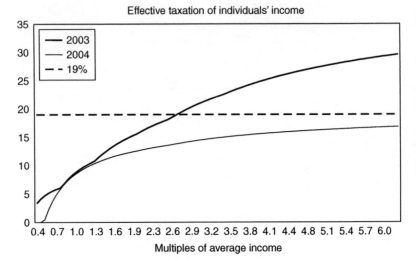

Figure 3.3   Effective tax rates, 2003 and 2004

changes and because it was the first step of our EU membership, which brought other uncertainties, mainly in connection with the new regime of VAT enforcement implemented after joining the EU.

The high level of uncertainty was also evident from the significant differences in the forecasts of the fiscal impacts of the tax reform that had been prepared by the Ministry and other external institutions, including international institutions. Results of the first year of the reform showed that the Ministry's forecast was relatively correct. The forecast for direct taxation, which decreased, was lower than actually occurred and, for indirect taxation, which increased, it was the opposite. Overall, the tax reform in its first year of functioning was fiscally rather neutral.

It is obvious that the forecast of the Ministry of Finance for the years 2006 and 2007 was too conservative. Definite numbers for 2006 and significantly higher economic growth overall show that reality was far more favourable for all important taxes. Overall the yields were exceeded by more than 20 bn SKK (or 1.2% of GDP) in 2006. Depite these facts, the trend of a decreasing tax burden relative to GDP will continue because GDP growth is higher than expected.

Tax reform and its foreign critics   Slovak tax reform evoked a strong response in foreign countries. It was predominantly positive, but some

Table 3.3 Tax income in 2003–07, as a percentage of GDP, ESA 95

(ESA95)	2003	2004	2005	2006	2007
Direct taxes	6.7	5.5	5.6	5.7	5.7
Income tax – individuals	3.3	2.6	2.7	2.6	2.5
Income tax – corporate	2.6	2.4	2.7	2.8	2.8
Tax collected through withholding	0.8	0.4	0.3	0.3	0.3
Indirect taxes	11.2	12.2	12.6	11.5	11.4
VAT	6.6	7.7	8.0	7.7	7.4
Consumption taxes	3.3	3.3	3.7	2.9	3.2
Property taxes	0.1	0.2	0.0	0.0	0.0
Local taxes	0.7	0.7	0.9	0.8	0.7
Other taxes	0.5	0.3	0.1	0.1	0.0
Total tax income	17.9	17.7	18.3	17.2	17.0

Table 3.4 Tax income in 2003–07, in thousands of SKK, ESA 95

(ESA95)	2003	2004	2005	2006	2007
Direct taxes	80,839	73,961	82,703	92,913	102,336
Income tax – individuals	39,680	35,122	39,310	42,215	46,046
Income tax – corporate	32,016	33,164	39,538	45,839	51,268
Tax collected through with holding	9,143	5,675	3,855	4,859	5,022
Indirect taxes	136,378	165,919	185,981	188,126	205,708
VAT	80,455	104,859	117,332	126,018	134,599
Consumption taxes	40,527	44,596	54,466	48,265	57,115
Property taxes	1,489	2,734	0	0	0
Local taxes	8,420	9,119	12,692	12,878	13,250
Other taxes	5,487	4,611	1,491	965	744
Total tax income	217,217	239,880	268,684	281,039	308,044

Notes: Data for 2003, 2004 and 2005 are actual; data for 2006 and 2007 are the forecast of the Ministry of Finance of the Slovak Republic.

critical evaluations pointing at alleged tax dumping or unfair tax competition appeared from some West European politicians.[16] They claimed that low taxes led to missing tax revenues that would have to be compensated by EU subsidies, which would have to be financed by wealthier countries. These countries would suffer from the fact that investors would therefore leave the old member countries and relocate to the new member countries thanks to alleged tax dumping. Such reasoning is incorrect and clearly politically motivated. As shown by the fiscal results of the Slovak tax reform above, the reform was, in

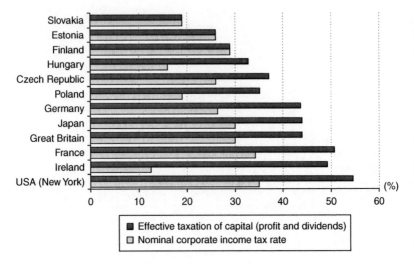

Figure 3.4   Income tax of individuals and dividend tax in EU countries

principle, fiscally neutral. Total tax income in the first year, 2004, was 22 billion SKK higher than in 2003 (239.9 billion SKK as opposed to 217.2 billion SKK). The slight decrease in the tax burden, as measured by the ratio of tax revenues to GDP from 17.9 per cent to 17.7 per cent, was caused by economic growth.

Not even profit tax, which is the object of criticism connected to tax dumping or alleged unfair tax competition, decreased. While in 2003 we collected at the 25 per cent rate 32.016 billion SKK from this tax at the 25 per cent rate, in 2004, at the 19 per cent rate, collections were 33.164 billion SKK, which means 1.1 billion SKK more. In 2005, the increase in tax revenues was even higher. Where, then, are the missing revenues?

Moreover, we cannot draw any conclusions by only comparing the rates of direct taxes. Real revenue from these taxes, mainly corporate income tax, depends also on the width of the tax base and the exceptions and opportunities for tax evasion. The best example is the comparison of percentage profit tax rates and their collection as a proportion of GDP in Germany, Ireland and Slovakia.

As is evident from Figure 3.5, the higher the rate is, the lower the tax collection as a share of GDP and vice versa. In Slovakia, the development over the period 2002–06, shown in Figure 3.5, is also interesting.

The comparison of revenues and corporate income tax rates in Slovakia before and after the reform leads to the same conclusion as

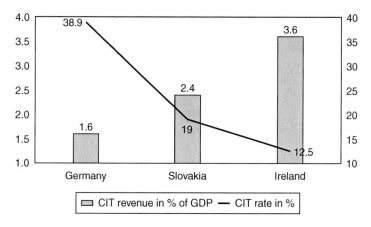

Figure 3.5 Corporate income tax rates and tax revenue in selected EU countries

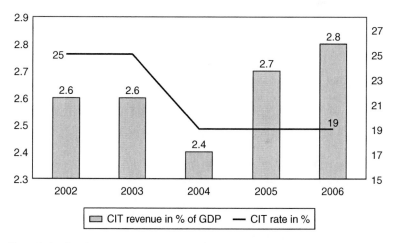

Figure 3.6 Corporate income tax rate and revenue in Slovakia

from the comparison of Ireland, Slovakia and Germany: the lower the rate, the higher the revenue.

Arguments about the need to compensate for so-called missing income – which, as shown, was not missing – with funds from other EU members are unfair also from the other side. Thanks to reforms, including tax reform, net EU contributors will pay to the new countries, the net receivers, less than they would have to otherwise. This is evident from the obvious fact that reforms lead to faster economic growth, which leads to an earlier graduation of the new members from the position of being net receivers of EU funds.

The efforts of some countries to restrict tax competition by the harmonization of tax rates should be considered harmful. Tax competition leads to higher pressure for the realization of inevitable changes and reforms, to greater market flexibility, to increased efficiency of public administration, and to pressure for the realization of necessary structural reforms.[17] And it is exactly here that the source of the problems of many Western European countries is to be found. Tax and other competition from new EU member countries only highlight the structural and policy shortcomings in the preparedness of many of the old EU member countries to face severe global competition.

The European commission currently does not mandate harmonization of income tax rates, but it has started an initiative for unification of the income tax base. The Commission reasons that it would simplify business conditions and decrease transaction costs of companies that have their business activities in several member countries, and that it would also lead to a decrease of court trials emerging from the existing differences. These effects would probably really appear, but Slovakia, together with the Baltic States, Ireland and Great Britain, is and will continue to be fundamentally against it for two reasons. First, there is a potential risk that this would be just the first step on the way to the harmonization of rates, which we strongly reject, because rate harmonization cannot be realized without base harmonization. Second, an even more important reason is that a harmonization of tax bases that would not harm Slovakia; that is, one that would not narrow the tax base, or implement various exceptions, or allow special regimes and deductible items or reduce the transparency, simplicity, exactness and neutrality of our tax system, is, in practice, absolutely impossible. Moreover, a narrower base would mean the inevitability of a rate increase.[18]

The effect of the tax reform on living standards was one of the important political questions, prior to the introduction of the reform and also after its implementation. We will deal with this question later in the context of the tax reform and all the other changes realized recently.

Pension reform

The reform objective is to halt the demographically conditioned increase of the debt of the continuously funded pension system and to increase the involvement of citizens in their living standards in retirement.[19]

Achievement of these objectives was realized with the help of the so-called three-pillar pension system. While the first pillar is formed by the continuous or 'pay-as-you-go' system, the second, new, capitalization pillar is based on pension savings and is obligatory for everybody who entered the labour market after 30 June 2005 for the first time, and for those who already were working and voluntarily chose to enter the second pillar before that date. The third pillar lies in various forms of voluntary pension savings and insurance.

There were five key measurements in the pension reform: implementation of a strong capitalization pillar; strengthening the merit principle in the first, continuous pillar; implementation of a new valorization mechanism, increase of retirement age, and enlargement of tax advantages in the third pillar.

Implementation of a strong capitalization pillar   Payments to retirees reflect their contributions, which means that the amount of the pension is not known in advance and will depend on contributions and their appreciation under the management of the pension fund management companies (PFMCs). The level of contributions into the second pillar is 9 per cent of the assessment base, which is the individual's salary. These funds are the property of the individual, and they are transferred to personal pension accounts of savers in their PFMC. They are not subject to taxation and are inheritable by the owner's survivors. There exist strict rules of state supervision, risk transfer from the side of the state and PFMC, and risk diversification and payment regulation. Interest in entering the second pillar was enormous; more than 1.5 million people entered before 30 June 2006, while the original forecast was 200,000–300,000. Six PFMCs received a license to manage accounts fulfilling legal conditions.

Strengthening the merit principle in the first, continuous pillar   The new system ensures direct ties between contributions and pension payments. The system is set up to ensure that a participant earning an average income for 40 years will receive a pension equal to 50 per cent of average income.

Implementation of the new valorization mechanism   In contrast to the former annual political decision on the level of pension, a so-called Swiss valorization mechanism was implemented that ensures an annual increase of pensions by the average of last year's inflation and nominal income growth.

Increase of retirement age   The original retirement age for men of 60 and 53–57 for women, based on the number of children, was increased to 62 years of age. This increase is realized at the rate of 9 months per year.

Enlargement of tax advantages in the third pillar   Participants can deduct up to up to 12,000 SKK annually from their income tax base. This is the only exception in the tax system, and the objective was to motivate people to opt for long-term pension savings. Another change was in taxation of the income from these savings. The rate was raised from 10 per cent of the total pension payment to 19 per cent, but this higher rate applies only to investment gains rather than to the original contribution.

The impact on the long-term sustainability of public finances is an important part of pension reform. Thanks to the reform, the implicit liability should decrease from the original 400 per cent of GDP in 2003 to approximately 170 per cent in 2080.[20] Positive fiscal impacts of the implementation of the second pillar will appear in the long term as well. In forthcoming years, the reform will decrease public finance revenues by approximately 2 per cent of GDP annually.

Healthcare reform

This was probably the most complicated reform from both a technical and political viewpoint. Before reform, the system did not function well, and it was characterized by poor services, dissatisfaction of all participants, a high level of corruption, new debts, soft budget restrictions, waste and ineffective functioning as a result of both excess demand for some services and redundant and ineffectively used capacities in other areas. Another problem was that the state did not act as an effective regulator; neither was it an active participant in the healthcare system.

Our reform objective was to eliminate these imperfections with the help of these measures:

- Healthcare debt reduction
- Implementation of fees for services connected to healthcare
- Transformation of health insurance companies into joint stock companies, transformation of healthcare institutions into non-profits or joint stock companies
- Implementation of strict budget restrictions for all subjects in the system
- Clear separation of a so-called basic package of healthcare funded from the system of public insurance and healthcare exceeding this package funded by additional insurance or cash payments.

The reform was implemented in two basic phases. The first, and mainly symbolic, phase decreased excessive demand by implementing token co-payments for services such as visits to a doctor, prescriptions, ambulance transport and hospital stays. This contributed to a decrease in demand for unnecessary visits to the doctor and excessive use of pharmaceuticals, less corruption and a greater sense of responsibility of patients for their health. A process of healthcare debt discharge was activated as well.

In the second phase, healthcare supervision was established as an independent activity, independent of the government. Strict budget restrictions were put in place for all healthcare providers; public insurance companies were transformed into joint stock companies. A basic package of healthcare was developed. These measures led economic pressures and incentives to decrease excess capacities in the system and to increase its effectiveness. These measures stabilized the finances of the system, and by the end of the mandate of the second Dzurinda government, the indebtedness of the system had decreased significantly.[21]

Social system reform and labour market reform

A high unemployment rate, at times the highest in Europe, and low motivation for people to solve their living situation on their own were the most significant motives for implementation of these reforms. Reforms were implemented under the motto 'Working will pay off' and had to ensure that active job seeking would really pay off. Moreover, the reforms should also eliminate the obstacles that limited employment and employers, ensure effective help and support in job-seeking activities for long-term unemployed people and limit misuse of the system. The main tools of change were:

- Flexible labour code and labour market
- Implementation of activation benefits and activity support system
- Decrease of the tax and social payment burdens on employment
- Transfer of sick-benefits during the first ten days of sickness from the state to employer together with a decrease of benefits
- Transfer of part of the child allowance claimable for each child so that it can be claimed only by those who have taxable income
- Increase directness of assistance to the disabled.

A principle of income differentiation between those who work and those who do not and also between those who want to work and be active and those who do not was a significant part of the reform.

The labour market did not, and still does not, create enough working opportunities, especially for long-term unemployed people with low education, even though significant improvements were obtained in this regard. Therefore, activation benefits were implemented in the area of social care, and these benefits could be claimed only by those who actively participated in active labour market policy projects, in public works, in re-qualification projects and so on.

Various new direct social benefits that were aimed at solving specific problems related to long-term unemployment, low-income families with small children, and support of school attendance were implemented as well. These had a positive impact on the solution of specific problems but, on the other hand, they further complicated an already complicated social system.

Flexibility of the labour market was connected to the following areas:

* Deregulation of working time adjustment, increase of mandatory overtime limits and overtimes agreed with employer
* Simplification of layoffs in case of economic problems of employer or his dissatisfaction with the work of the employee
* Simplification of hiring and work status
* Elimination of all restrictions on working pensioners.

Data in Table 3.5 clearly show that developments in the areas of employment and unemployment were significantly positive in 2002–06, which is partially the result of social system reform and labour market reform.[22]

Public administration reform and fiscal decentralization

Dzurinda's governments achieved very important reforms in public administration in 1998–2006. The main objective was to adjust the relationship between the central government, the regional authorities, and community governments in public administration in order to better reflect the principle of subsidiarity. The territorial structure of the country was changed through the implementation of a three-level model of public administration, local and regional communities were strengthened, and competencies connected to offering local and regional public services

Table 3.5 Unemployment development and employment growth in Slovakia, 1998–2006 (in %)

	1998	1999	2000	2001	2002	2003	2004	2005	2006
Unemployment rate	12.6	16.4	18.8	19.2	18.5	17.4	18.1	16.2	13.3
Employment growth	−0.4	−2.7	−1.8	0.6	0.2	1.8	0.3	2.1	3.8

were transferred to local and regional authorities. The final phase of public administration reform that was realized was fiscal decentralization, which had been prepared in 2003–04 and implemented from 2005 onward under the sponsorship of the Ministry of Finance.

Fiscal decentralization brought a significant strengthening of the independence and predictability of local and regional government funding. The fundamental principle of the reform was the change from a system of inter-governmental negotiations about budget transfers to local governments to a system that gave local governments a share of income tax revenues that was mandated by law.

Communities receive 70.3 per cent of personal income tax revenue and self-governing regions receive 23.5 per cent annually. These funds are then divided among individual units based on criteria that are set by government order, are agreed with self-governmental units and are related to their competencies and the volume of services they are to deliver measured by criteria such as the number of children and elderly, area of the region, size, temperature and climatic zone and so on.[23]

Improvement of the business environment

All the above reforms directly or indirectly improved the business environment. Probably the most important effects were those of the tax reform, labour market reform, macroeconomic stabilization and public finance reform. In addition, the government also implemented some other measures, such as improving the administration of justice, simplifying legislation, speeding up the process of registering businesses and updating the land cadastre. Inefficient law enforcement, ineffective public administration, and excessive bureaucracy remain the biggest weak points of the Slovak business environment.

Changes in the socio-economic model

During the past eight to ten years, as a result of the changes described above, Slovakia has undergone a major revision of the way in which society and the economy function. Simply said, Slovakia, of the eight post-communist countries that joined the EU in the first enlargement, is the only country that had fully achieved the transition from a predominantly continental socio-economic model to a predominantly Anglo-Saxon economic model.[24] While the Baltic countries had, from the beginning, sought to build their system more or less on Anglo-Saxon principles, Poland, the Czech Republic, Hungary, Slovakia and Slovenia had thought to build their system more in line with the model of

Germany and Austria, which means that they were inspired by the European continental model. In part, this was the result of their historical heritage and of their geographic neighbourhood.

With respect to data in Table 3.6 and the current economic results that already reflect the direct and indirect effects of our reforms, Slovakia achieved a major turnaround in its performance.[25] As a result, Slovakia became one of the fastest growing economies in Europe. Gross domestic product grew at 8.3 per cent in 2006 and 9.7 per cent in the second half of that year. Employment growth reached 3.8 per cent in 2006. The number of unemployed decreased by 20 per cent over the year while, at the same time, labour productivity growth exceeded real income growth. Forecasts for 2007 predicted further acceleration of economic growth and indeed it reached over 10 per cent in real terms (10.4%). This growth is based on a healthy foundation, supported by a decreasing fiscal deficit and an improving current account.[26] It is not a coincidence

Table 3.6   Comparison of groups of countries

	GDP growth	Employment growth	Portion of R&D on GDP	Tax quota II	Soc. Exp./ DP	ALMP/ GDP	ALMP/ Unemp. Exp.
Germany	0.9	−0.3	46.8	40.2	29.5	0.85	24.7
France	1.6	0.3	53.8	45.8	31.2	0.73	27.0
Belgium	1.9	0.4	49.9	47.7	29.3	0.92	25.9
Austria	1.9	0.1	49.9	43.6	29.1	0.43	21.6
Average	**1.6**	**0.1**	**50.1**	**44.3**	**29.8**	**0.73**	**24.8**
Poland	4.0	−0.2	43.3	34.2	20.0		
Czech Republic	4.4	0.3	44.1	36.3	19.6	0.13	25.8
Hungary	4.3	0.2	49.9	38.6	20.7	0.21	30.1
Slovenia	4.0	0.5	47.2	40.7	24.3		
Average	**4.2**	**0.2**	**46.1**	**37.5**	**21.2**	**0.17**	**28.0**
Great Britain	2.5	0.9	44.7	38.5	26.3	0.16	20.0
Ireland	5.1	2.9	34.1	32.2	17.0	0.49	30.9
Average	**3.5**	**1.4**	**39.4**	**35.4**	**21.7**	**0.36**	**33.2**
Estonia	9.0	1.2	33.2	31.0	13.4	0.04	17.2
Latvia	7.9	1.9	33.6	29.2	13.3	0.15	50.2
Lithuania	9.0	1.5	36.0	29.6	12.6		
Average	**8.6**	**1.5**	**34.3**	**29.9**	**13.1**	**0.10**	**33.7**
Slovakia	5.6	1.1	37.1	29.5	17.2	0.07	15.2

Note: GDP growth = average 2002 to 2006; employment growth = average 2002 to 2005; R&D and tax quota for 2005; social expenditures and ALMP for 2004.
Source: Eurostat

that Ireland and the new EU countries that apply the Anglo-Saxon economic model are the fastest growing economies in Europe. It is precisely because these countries significantly increased the level of economic freedom and realized structural reforms that they are able to enjoy the benefits of an improved business environment and dynamic investment and growth.

Impact of reforms on living standard

The politics of reform is one of the key problems of the reform process in each country. The problem lies mainly in the fact that reform means change, and people are afraid of and resist change. This is true everywhere in the world, even though evident to a greater or lesser degree. Change by itself means uncertainty created by new conditions regardless of the real impacts of the change. Moreover, reforms are very often connected to higher expenditures than revenues in the short term. This leads to the rejection of reforms and to a situation where the effects of reforms, especially social effects, are perceived to be more negative than they really are. Slovakia's recent experience is proof of this.

In the opinion of the majority of Slovaks, the reforms, even though necessary and in many areas correctly applied, were socially unacceptable. According to a majority of the population, the reforms were an enormous burden for people and negatively influenced mainly the lower income groups. Public opinion polls confirm these views, and the evidence was also apparent in the outcome of the parliamentary elections in June 2006, when the party of the current Prime Minister, Robert Fico, which built its agenda on a strict and detailed critique of the reforms and on their total rejection, won the election.[27]

What has been the resulting reality? ... Significantly different.

Let's look at how the transformation process, as described in this text, has influenced living standards based on real income development.

As is evident from Table 3.7, Slovakia experienced two decreases in real income in the last ten years. The first, by 7.9 per cent, occurred between 1999–2000 and the second, by 2.0 per cent, in 2003. The first is related to

Table 3.7 Pace of real income growth in national economy, 1993–2006

In %	1994	1995	1996	1997	1998	1999	2000	2001	2002	2003	2004	2005	2006
Pace of real income growth	3.2	4.0	7.1	6.6	2.7	−3.1	−4.9	1.0	5.8	−2.0	2.5	6.3	3.3

coping with the heritage of 'Meciarism' in the economy and the second to the solution to the impacts of budget liberalization in the election year 2002 and reform of public finance management and transfer to strict budget restrictions.[28] The years 1999–2000 were even more difficult, because the decrease of real income by 7.9 per cent was accompanied by a decrease of employment by 4.4 per cent while, in 2003, the 2.0 per cent decrease of real income was already connected to an increase of employment by 1.8 per cent.

The majority of the reforms were implemented at the beginning of 2004 and, even though the deterioration of living standards is generally connected to the reforms, the data in Table 3.8 show that it is not true. The temporary deterioration of living standards was not caused by reforms but by the inevitable macroeconomic stabilization, together with steps that were necessary for the elimination of previous economic policies.

Consider the development of the real income of individual income groups in 2004, which was crucial from the viewpoint of implementation of almost all reforms. Note that January 2004 also marked the last important phase of price deregulation of energy, gas, transportation costs, water rates and rents.[29] At the same time, tax reform was commenced, which decreased direct taxes, but the public was much more sensitive to the increase in consumption taxes and the unification of VAT. From a psychological point of view, the unpopular part of the tax reform was more visible because it was reflected in an increase of prices that was immediately noticeable after 1 January, while the decrease in direct taxes was evident only in pay cheques, less visibly and with a delay.

Despite these facts, already in the first year of reforms, even though connected to the last phase of price deregulation, the majority of employed people did not experience a decrease in their living standard. On the contrary, increased prices due to deregulation and increased indirect taxes were more than offset in all income level groups, mainly by decreased direct taxes and the growth of nominal income, but also by decreased grocery prices after Slovakia joined the EU on 1 May 2004.[30]

The following Figure shows the development of real income of income level groups in 2004.

Figure 3.7 shows that in the first year of tax reform, even though there was price deregulation, real incomes of all income level groups having incomes from working activities improved. Data from the graphs are evidence that the change of net income depended on two factors: the level of income and the number of children. Higher-income and low-income groups noted the highest increase of net income; people with income close to the average figure benefited the least. High-income earners gained

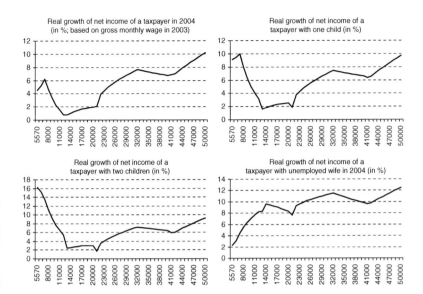

Figure 3.7 Development of real income of income level groups, 2004
Source: Ministry of Finance of the Slovak Republic (2006)

from the lower tax rate of 19 per cent; low-income households gained from the increased range of deductible items. Middle-income tax payers were, relatively, the worst off because the decrease in the rate of tax was minimal and the impact of increases in exempt income was relatively low. The effect of the number of children comes from the bonus for children.

While average real income in the national economy increased by 2.5 per cent in 2004, real net income of an employee with minimum income increased by 3.1 per cent, of an employee with average income by 1.0, and of an employee with triple the average income by 8.3 per cent.

An employed couple, both working for the minimum wage and with two children, improved by 9 per cent; a couple working for average wage with two children by 5.9 per cent. The situation for pensioners did not worsen in 2004, their real income increased by 0.4 per cent.[31] Left out of the analysis are the unemployed, social assistance cases and so on. In their situation, a change in overall philosophy occurred, when new mechanisms stimulating activity and participation were applied, and the result was differentiation of income based on activity and per- sonal effort. It is assumed that mainly passive, unemployed people, and those who abused the system by using it as an additional source of income, experienced a decrease of real income from public sources.

In the following years, the influence of tax and other reforms on living standards is positive, even in more significant ways than in 2004. The evidence lies in the rise of real wages by 6.3 per cent and an increase of employment by 2.1 per cent in 2005, as well as 3.3 per cent rise of real wages and 3.8 per cent increase in employment in 2006.

The European Union measures and compares the so-called risk of poverty, which is estimated by the percentage of inhabitants that have an income, after social transfers, lower than 60 per cent of the median income. The name for this indicator is quite deceptive because, more than poverty, it expresses income differentiation.[32] Based on currently published data for 2005 (Eurostat), Slovakia has its risk of poverty at a level of 13 per cent, which is a lower poverty rate than in the majority of EU countries. According to Eurostat, the situation is as follows:

  9 per cent Sweden
10 per cent Czech Republic
11 per cent Netherlands
12 per cent Denmark, Finland, Austria
13 per cent France, Luxembourg, Hungary, Germany, Slovakia
15 per cent Belgium, Malta
16 per cent Cyprus
18 per cent Estonia
19 per cent Latvia, Italy, Great Britain
20 per cent Greece, Ireland, Portugal, Spain
21 per cent Lithuania, Poland.

Data showing that 13 per cent of Slovak inhabitants have an income, after social transfers, lower than 60 per cent of the median already includes the impact of reforms because it reflects the reality of 2004. Therefore, these data already reflect all the changes, tax and social reform included. This proves that the deep structural reforms realized in Slovakia during 2002–06 did not lead to a significant increase of income differentiation. On the contrary, they led to higher dynamics in the economy and to the creation of conditions for higher income growth, living standards and employment.

Fico's era (2006–?)

After Meciar's (1993–98) and Dzurinda's (1998–2006) terms in office, Fico's era began after the 2006 elections in Slovakia. How long will it last and what possible consequences for the fate of the reforms might it have? The political party Smer, whose chairman Robert Fico also became the Prime Minister, won the 2006 elections. Smer created a new government together with HZDS, whose chairman remains Vladimir Meciar, and SNS. Both of these coalition partners, with the same party chairmen, were members of the coalition during Meciar's era. They did not make any significant movement forward in terms of values and intellect. Their position in the government is only minor, and the programme focus of the government is determined by the strongest party, Smer. Smer based its entire election campaign on strident criticism of the previous government and its policies, especially of the reforms described in this chapter. Smer essentially rejected these reforms and promised to repeal all of them. After the first nine months of being in power, the government's willingness or ability to undertake such a total dismantling of the reforms is unclear. In principle, health reform has been distorted, even destroyed. Fees have been eliminated, weak budget restrictions are being implemented, the independence of the Healthcare Surveillance Authority has been restricted, and obligatory insurance for state policyholders in the state insurance companies is being prepared. The consequences are already visible. The system is unavoidably heading towards problems that the reform had resolved: new debt, insolvency, inefficiency and corruption are increasing. Even though public resources are added to the system, no real effect is evident.

The tax reform has been left unchanged, even though it was the main target of Smer's election campaign. Only cosmetic changes have been made. At higher incomes, approximately from three times the average wage, the non-taxable base is being gradually decreased to zero from approximately five times the average wage. Besides that, a reduced VAT rate for pharmaceuticals and sanitary goods was implemented. Pressure was also put on the second pillar of the pension reform, the new system's essential part. The Prime Minister announced his intent to decrease contributions to the second pillar by one third from 9 per cent to 6 per cent. The reason he gave is that such a reduction would result in lowering fiscal costs by approximately 7 billion SKK, approximately 0.5 per cent of GDP. Under pressure from the public, he decided to postpone his plan.[33]

Another reform whose destiny is still unclear is the labour market reform. The government has submitted a new labour code, which was created in the headquarters of the labour unions and which significantly decreases the flexibility of the labour market and provides various privileges for labour union officials.[34] This has resulted in a serious fight between employers and the labour unions, as well as between Smer and the opposition. The result is still uncertain because the other coalition partners, HZDS and SNS, have expressed their unwillingness to support this legislation.

A very important constraint on the government that forces it to keep to reasonable fiscal limits is the commitment to join the Euro zone. During Dzurinda's government, in November 2005, Slovakia entered the ERMII system with the goal of adopting the Euro in 2009. Fico hesitated at the beginning, but under the pressure of depreciation of the Slovak crown after the creation of his coalition in July 2006, he decided to stick to the Euro goal, and this objective became a part of the governmental programme. Therefore, the Maastricht criteria serve as an effective protection against a fiscally irresponsible increase of public expenditures spent on the fulfilment of unrealistic campaign promises, some of which became a part of the governmental programme.

The question related to the post-election situation in Slovakia is not whether Slovakia is going to grow in the next three or four years. It will, and it will grow rapidly, regardless of what the government does. The economy is strong, and the persistence of the past economic trends is a positive factor. The question is whether this positive development is sustainable in the long run. If Slovakia takes a chance on the right social and economic model, it will grow even more rapidly than its neighbours in the long term, and it will reach or even overtake more developed, so-called 'old' EU member states. It is possible, and Slovakia has created good initial conditions to reach such a goal. The question is whether Slovakia will use this opportunity.

The example of Ireland could serve as an inspiration. When Ireland entered the EU in 1973, its per capita DP was 50 per cent of the EU average, as in Slovakia in 2004. Now, Ireland's GDP per capita is 140 per cent of the EU average, and it is the second most developed EU country after Luxemburg. Estonia is on a good path to follow this success. While at the beginning of the 1990s Estonia was only at 50 per cent of the economic level of the Czech Republic, in 2010 it will reach the same level. For a better illustration, if the Czech Republic were to be growing as fast as Estonia, it would reach the level of Austria in 2010, because the Czech Republic was at 50 per cent of the level of Austria's economy in the early 1990s. Since it is not growing that swiftly, the Czech Republic will reach 'only' 75 per cent of the Austrian per capita GDP in 2010.

So, what then are the necessary conditions for Slovakia to be able to perform in the same way as Ireland and Estonia? It depends on three conditions. First, macroeconomic stability should be maintained and the reforms should not be distorted or cancelled because they contribute significantly to rapid growth. This does not mean that they cannot be modified or improved. The healthcare reform is being cancelled, with a negative impact on public finance and the business environment; the destiny of labour market and pension reforms is still unclear. In the area of tax reform, there have been only minor, cosmetic changes made; however, these are not in the right direction. It will be also very important not to surrender to the pressure of certain other EU countries to harmonize direct taxes through the harmonization of rates or the tax base. Unfortunately, there might be some change in the standpoint of Slovakia in this area as well.[35]

Second, the government should focus on solving problems in those areas that are the biggest weak points in our future competitiveness. Key tasks in this regard are improving law enforcement and the effectiveness of state and public administration, decreasing corruption, and reducing regulations and bureaucracy. Moreover, liberalization of network industries and solving the Roma problem need to continue as government priorities.[36]

Third, the key to Slovakia's future is the development of the knowledge economy. Education, science, research and information systems will become increasingly competitive and this increasing competition can be detrimental to Slovakia's prosperity if investments in education and science do not become a priority immediately. Placing a high priority on education and science requires not only priority access to public resources, whether from local, regional, national or European budgets, but also a priority from the point of view of continuously improving the system for delivering and using these resources and their outputs. While it is difficult to judge how well Slovakia is meeting these conditions, it is quite evident that many additional improvements are possible and urgently need to be implemented.

Will Fico change the socio-economic model?

Fico repeatedly declares that building a strong social state is his top priority and that this objective differentiates him from the previous government, which constitutes the current opposition. The same objective is in his government's programme declaration, which states that 'the government of the Slovak Republic will broadly support the real direction of the Slovak Republic towards fulfilment of social state characteristics'.

Are these objectives real? Can we assume that they will be fulfilled? The most important economic characteristics of a strong social state are high levels of redistribution and taxation. Changes that have been realized so far did not increase the level of redistribution; indeed, they did just the opposite. The decrease of the exempt income level for higher-income groups slightly increased their overall income tax burden, but the decreased VAT rate for pharmaceuticals and sanitary goods had an opposite and even stronger effect. Fico's tax revisions resulted in a decrease, not an increase, in the tax burden.[37]

The EU convergence programme, which is on a standardized methodology, is elaborated by all EU member countries, contains a country's basic objectives for economic development for the next four years, and is a useful way to evaluate the current government. Fico's government voted on its first convergence programme in December 2006, almost six months after it took over. Despite Fico's extensive rhetoric about strong social state building, this programme failed to propose any significant changes in the Slovak economic model. Moreover, measured by the most important and complex indicator, which is the level of redistribution and taxation, Fico's convergence programme predicts a further decrease in redistribution and taxation.

In 2006, the proportion of public expenditures financed by VAT was 37.9 per cent, but the convergence programme adopted by Fico's government in December 2006 assumed that in 2010 this figure will reach 33.6 per cent, implying a large decrease in redistribution.[38] This trend is further exacerbated by the fact that the only change in the tax system announced so far is the potential enlargement of the number of goods and services listed as eligible for the lower VAT rate. These facts prove that the thesis of strong social government is more a political marketing tool than a real objective. One of the reasons is that the government does not want to implement any unpopular measures, and increasing taxes would definitely be such a measure. Moreover, the government lacks the expertise and administrative capacity to undertake any deep system changes.

The conclusion is that, with a high probability, the current Slovak model will not be quickly changed but, rather, gradually eroded due to growing statism, corruption and distortion of certain reforms. Long-term competitiveness will also be reduced as the government fails to find effective solutions to current and emerging problems in the business environment and lags in its support for, and development of, the knowledge economy.

Conclusion

The story of Slovak reforms provides clear evidence that there exist efficient tools for overcoming economic problems and backwardness, for revitalizing and stabilizing a distorted economy and setting it on the path of high and healthy growth. Usually, it is the necessary policies that reflect well-known priorities, principles and tools. The better known they are, the more difficult it is to implement them in reality. Therefore, it is essential to summarize them. Based on our Slovak experience, I consider these to be the most important:

- Increase economic freedom, decrease redistribution, decrease taxes
- Economic and political integration in international bodies, especially membership in EU, NATO, OECD
- Macroeconomic stabilization, fiscal consolidation
- Strict budget restraint for both public institutions and the business sector
- Revitalization, restructuring and privatization of banks
- Privatization of utilities, entry of strategic investors into these companies
- Price deregulation and the creation of independent regulators
- Solving the problem of an ageing population through pension reform
- Flexible markets, especially the labour market
- A simple, neutral, effective and fair tax system
- Improvement of the business environment
- A social system that does not de-motivate and that helps those who really need it
- Decentralization on the principle of subsidiarity.

These are the most important priorities and tools that demonstrated a strong positive result in the Slovak case. Undoubtedly, there exist policies that we were not able to use, but that are important. Specifically, better law enforcement, more effective public administration and quality education, science, research and development, and the use of information technology need to be priorities for future Slovak governments. The example of Slovakia can serve as an inspiration for other countries, whether West European, Balkan or East European. This text will, hopefully, also contribute to this task.

Notes

1 A term coined by Madeleine Albright, at that time the United States Secretary of State.
2 A term coined by Zakaria (1997).
3 This term is explained by Zakaria (1997).

4 It is more than symbolic that in 1994–98 there was only one privatization through sale to a foreign investor despite the privatization of more than 400 companies (Mikloš 1999).

5 Regulated prices reached a level that covered justified expenditures and provided adequate profits only in January 2004, during the last stage of deregulation.

6 The entry of a large number of young people into the work force was a major source of the increase in unemployment.

7 One reform not implemented was the introduction of partial tuition payments for university studies.

8 In text that follows, the first two areas will be described in more detail because the author, as Minister of Finance of the Slovak Republic in 2002–06, was directly responsible for them. In the other aspects of the economic reform, as Deputy Prime Minister he had a coordinating role, and thus they will be described more briefly.

9 In the second half of 2006, the economy grew at 9.7 per cent and forecasts predicted another increase in economic growth to more than 10 per cent in 2007. In reality GDP growth reached 10.4% in real terms.

10 The best evidence of this is that the differences between contemporaneous and ex post, ESA 95-based, estimates of the deficits are, during 2002, huge.

11 After the Fico government took over, the repeated softening of budget restrictions is evident in a majority of these areas, and particularly in healthcare, as the result of the elimination of reforms.

12 Programme declaration of the Slovak government, 2002.

13 It will be seen that, after the flat tax was implemented, the progressive character of income tax was preserved.

14 There existed 37 personal and corporate income tax rates in the original tax system..

15 Increased from 38,360 SKK in 2003 to 80,832 SKK in 2004.

16 Prominent politicians of that time included German Chancellor G. Schroder, French Minister of Finance N. Sarkozy, Swedish Prime Minister Persson. However, while those politicians did not comment specifically on the Slovak tax system, they talked in general about new member countries and, in the context of such discussions, there were many allusions, direct and indirect, to the changes in the Slovak tax system.

17 A good example of tax competition efficiency is Austria, Slovakia's neighbour. Discussions about the need to decrease income tax from the original 35 per cent rate took years and nobody assumed that the decrease would go lower than 29 per cent. Literally, within a few weeks of the adoption of the tax reform that decreased the tax rate from 25 per cent to 19 per cent in Slovakia, the Austrian tax rate was decreased to 25 per cent in Austria. That led to increased pressure for a tax decrease in Germany.

18 In 2004–05, when the author of this text made the same arguments to his colleagues at the meetings of the Council of Ministers of Finance, he did not receive any counter-argument from his colleagues. Indeed, some proposed to take the Slovak base as the common base for this tax. But, in response to author's question as to whether they could imagine eliminating almost all exceptions, special regimes and deductible items in all 24 EU member states, the answer from all the ministers was negative.

19 Programme declaration of the government, 2002.
20 This implicit liability is defined as the gap between the actual accumulated funds and those funds that current savers would be entitled to in the event of total suspension of the continuous pillar.
21 More information on Slovak healthcare reform can be found at the Health Policy Institute site at www.hpi.sk
22 More on these reforms, tools and results in Beblavý (2007).
23 More on the public administration reform and fiscal decentralization at www.mesa10.sk
24 See Sapir (2005).
25 Current indicators that already mirror direct and indirect effects of reforms are similar or even better than in the Baltic countries.
26 After continuous decreases in the foreign trade deficit, in January 2007 the current account was in surplus despite the Slovak crown's steady appreciation. In reaction to this, a decision about the revision of the central parity from 38.455 to 35.4424 SKK/EUR. Except for Ireland in 1998, this is the first occurrence of such a parity appreciation in the ERMII system.
27 In reality, after the phase of government formation dominated by Smer, the pre-election promises of reform elimination have not been fulfilled, with the exception of healthcare reform, where the reform steps and measures are distorted but there is an absence of any alternative vision and strategy.
28 Both decreases of real income were closely connected to the inevitable increase of regulated prices that, despite increased expenditures, were not increased at all during Meciar's era in 1994–98.
29 It was a significant increase; for example, gas prices for households increased on average by 35 per cent.
30 The political opposition of that time predicted a diametrically opposed development of grocery prices after joining EU. Opposition leader Fico frightened the public, claiming that after joining EU we would have Slovak salaries and European prices.
31 In all these data, we consider inflation for individual income groups. For a more specific analysis of the first year of tax reform see 'The First Step of the Tax Reform or 19 Per Cent in Use' IFP MF, 205, Economic analysis 8, www.finance.gov.sk
32 We could probably talk about relative poverty because otherwise we would have to say that in Ireland, with 20 per cent, or in Great Britain, with 19 per cent, poverty is higher than in Bulgaria (15 per cent) or in Slovakia (13 per cent). An even better illustration of this incorrect interpretation of this indicator is the fact that, based on this indicator, the risk of poverty is lower in South Korea than in North Korea.
33 Since it would negatively impact more than 1.5 million people, who joined the second pillar.
34 Smer closely cooperated with labour unions before elections and promised them, among other things, a change in the Labour Code.
35 Fico on 9 March 2007, at the EU summit in Brussels, softened his previous attitude toward such harmonization, thus breaking ranks with the Baltic countries, Great Britain and Ireland in their resistance to harmonization.

36   Slovakia has a high proportion of Roma citizens (6–8 per cent), many of whom are not well integrated into society and who form the core of the long-term unemployed.
37   The decrease in deductible income for high-income groups increases revenues by 1.1 billion SKK, while the decreased VAT rate for pharmaceuticals will decrease annual tax revenues by 2.8 billion SKK (forecast of the Ministry of Finance).
38   Convergence Programme of the Slovak Republic, December 2006: 53.

References

Beblavý, M. (2007) *Social Reform and Labour Market Reform.*, www.governance.sk

Government of the Slovak Republic (2002) Programme Declaration of the Government of the Slovak Republic, Bratislava.

Government of the Slovak Republic (2006) Programme Declaration of the Government of the Slovak Republic, Bratislava.

Mikloš, I. (1999) *Privatization in Slovakia* (Bratislava: IVO).

Mikloš, I. (2005) *Book of Reforms, or How Slovakia Earned International Recognition in Economic Area*. Ministry of Finance, Slovak Republic.

Ministry of Finance of the Slovak Republic (2005) 'First Year of the Tax Reform, or 19 Per Cent in Use', IFP MF, 2005, Economic Analysis 8, www.finance.gov.sk

Ministry of Finance of the Slovak Republic (2006) 'Convergence Programme of the Slovak Republic', www.finance.gov.sk

Sapir, A. (2005) 'Globalization and the European Social Models', www.bruegel.org

EEAG (2007) 'Report on the European Economy, 2007'.

Zakaria, F. (1997) 'The Rise of Illiberal Democracy', *Foreign Affairs*, 76(6), November/December.

4
The Czech Socio-Economic Model and Its Evolution from the Start of Transition to 2007

Karel Dyba

Introduction

In this chapter, we examine the evolution of the Czech socio-economic model since the start of the transition by examining, mainly, the size of the government, as measured by taxes and expenditures, and by looking into changing characteristics of the labour market.

We start with a brief background so as to remind the reader of the long industrial history of the Czech lands and the institutions of democratic capitalism that existed before the Communists took power in 1948. We recall that 40 years of a one-party regime and authoritarian central planning brought about not only huge structural distortions in the economy, but also the wholesale destruction of the institutional foundations of democratic capitalism. Next, we briefly characterize the two opposing concepts of transformation that emerged immediately after the definitive demise of the Communist regime by the end of 1989. We try to show that the so-called radical reformers who finally managed to prevail tried to move the country towards a version of free market capitalism that was closer to Anglo-Saxon traditions. Opposing them were so-called gradualists, with their rather fuzzy and incoherent concept of a market economy with strong involvement of the state in the economy through extensive redistribution and regulatory activities.

In the sections on government size and the labour market, we will compare the developments since 1989 up to 1997, which were mainly shaped by the ideas of Vaclav Klaus's group of free-market reformers, with the developments from 1998 up to 2006, when social-democratic ideas shaped economic policies and institutions. Because the general elections in 2006 brought back a right-of-centre coalition government, we briefly analyze its proposed fiscal stabilization package involving, above all, a relative reduction in social and health expenditures and some decrease in the tax burden.

We conclude by showing that the Czech socio-economic model that emerged after Vaclav Klaus was voted out of office in late 1997 moved closer to the European continental model. In particular, this happened under coalition governments led by social-democratic prime ministers. It remains to be seen whether the right-of-centre coalition government led by Civic Democratic (ODS) Prime Minister Mirek Topolanek, which took power after the 2006 general elections, will succeed in its reform attempts, aimed at a leaner government, a more flexible labour market and less regulation and, in a sense, bring to the fore again the liberal features of the Czech socio-economic model.

Background

Czechoslovakia, composed of the industrialized Czech lands, more agrarian Slovakia and rather underdeveloped Ruthenia, was born after World War I. It was a parliamentary democracy with a market economy, albeit, as was common in those times, one with some state interventionism. In terms of policies, it practised fiscal and monetary conservativism, and it was an island of relative stability in Central Europe. Between the two World Wars, Czechoslovakia ranked among the top ten producers of industrial goods in the world and possessed a sophisticated armaments and machinery industry, mostly located in the Czech lands. In fact, this was the place where the industrial revolution had its genesis in East-Central Europe. The country traded mostly with Western Europe, and a large part of its financial and industrial assets were owned by foreign capital, especially by British and French interests.

After World War II, during which Czechoslovakia had been occupied by Nazi Germany, there was a brief period of democracy during which many financial institutions and large enterprises, as in many other European countries, were nationalized. Finally, in 1948, the Communists took over. A Soviet-type one-party political system and authoritarian central planning were quickly introduced. As a consequence, the political, social and economic development of the country was derailed for about four decades, and it cost Czechs and Slovaks dearly. Whereas, immediately after World War II, Czechoslovak GDP per capita was at least as high as Austria's, and we can reasonably infer that it was most probably higher because the Czech economy had not been as damaged by the war as had Austria's, by the end of 1989, when the Velvet Revolution removed the Communists from power, Czech GDP per capita was only slightly above half of Austria's GDP per capita when both were measured at purchasing power parity (PPP).

The search for a strategy of transition at the beginning of the 1990s: two concepts of transition

The downfall of the Communist regime in November 1989 allowed Czechoslovakia, by then a federation consisting of the Czech and Slovak Republics whose 'velvet' dissolution into two independent countries only came about on 1 January 1993, to begin the return to a normal development path, a path it would have taken after World War II had it been allowed the opportunity to do so. This path, one can assume, would have meant rebuilding and improving upon the pre-war institutions of democratic capitalism that would have probably developed similarly as in neighbouring Western countries such as Austria or Germany, and most probably would have led to a rather similar development of its GDP per capita as in, say, Austria. Instead, however, the more than 40 years of Communist rule managed to destroy almost completely the institutional foundations of democratic capitalism and to replace them by an autocratic political and economic system.

In addition, there is, as we know, a vast 'soft infrastructure' of norms of behaviour, habits, and so on that underpins democratic capitalism and is extremely important for its sound functioning. All these institutions of democratic capitalist culture had evolved over decades and generations, at a not negligible cost. This all was liquidated by the Communists and replaced by institutions such as one party rule, authoritarian central planning, disrespect for markets, outlawing private enterprise and so on. Let us also remember that overwhelming nationalization involved not only politics and economics, but also other parts of social life such as sports, culture, religion and such (Tříska 2006). Luckily, by the beginning of the 1990s, after the demise of communism, Czechs were able to abandon the wrong track and to start reconstructing the foundations of democratic capitalism, though practically from scratch and confronted also with negative legacies of four decades of communism.

A catchword used by practically all newly established and relevant political forces following the November 1989 revolution was 'rejoining Europe'. Broadly speaking and concentrating only on the economic element of this slogan, which obviously had its political, social, military, cultural content as well, had, at the beginning of transition, two divergent interpretations. With some simplification, one can say that a slightly older generation of economists, who had come into prominence during the Prague Spring era in the 1960s, sought a return to their ideas of a 'third way' and of developing them in the course of the transition. One can assume that this implicitly or explicitly meant copying the Western European economic model, either in its German or Austrian mature 'social market economy' variant or the 'Swedish welfare state'. Interestingly enough, these politicians and economists, who held top positions in the government, tended to avoid words such as 'capitalism' or 'privatization' in their writings or speeches.

As a reform strategy, their strategy for transition amounted to a piecemeal approach that, perhaps for want of better word, was dubbed 'gradualism'. It called for a stronger involvement of the state in the economy at both the macro and micro levels, including industrial policies in the sense of picking winners and nurturing them before opening the economy to outside competition. Hence, the gradualists argued for a less aggressive and more 'social' approach; for less restrictive macroeconomic policies including deficit financing; for more protection of domestic industries and subsidies for export promotion; for a smaller devaluation of the crown and hence an overvalued and managed exchange rate; for slower liberalization of prices and gradual opening of the markets; for the restructuring of state-owned enterprises (SOEs) by ministries before privatization and, if they were to be privatized, then preferably into the hands of employees, and so on. Some proponents of this strategy looked for inspiration to Japan and the South-East Asian tigers' industrial policies, conveniently forgetting such details as differences in history, in the stage of development, the cultural context and other substantial structural differences between the Czech lands in the 1990s and the Asian tigers of 20 to 30 years ago.[1]

Ranged against this fuzzy approach toward transition was an aggressive, comprehensive and consistent transformation course proposed by then Federal Minister of Finance, Vaclav Klaus, and the reformers who supported him. They did not want any 'third way', a concept reminiscent of a reform attempt in the 1960s, which, in their minds, was simply a kind of muddling through, lacking a clear transformation goal. Instead their vision was a 'market economy without any adjectives' based on private property, driven by private initiative and opened to the outside world. As Klaus (1991) put it: 'Adjectives like "social" or "environmentally conscious" are nothing other than attempts to restrain, limit, block, weaken, dissolve, or make fuzzy the clear meaning of a market economy and introduce into it non-market elements. I feel I should now advocate the use of adjectives, but adjectives with a totally different meaning. We need an unconstrained, unrestricted, full-fledged, unspoiled market economy, and we need it now.'

Radical reformers thus had in their minds a return to a type of free-market democratic capitalism. Yet, their strategy was by no means a so-called shock therapy approach. It was quite clear to the Klaus group that regime-changing measures have to be applied as a whole, in a package (see Dyba and Charap 1991; Klaus 2006). However, only some measures such as liberalization of most prices, introducing internal convertibility of the crown together with devaluation of the currency, and so on, could and had to be introduced, in a sense, over-night, but in the context of prudent macroeconomic policies. It was also quite clear to them that the system-changing wholesale privatization they envisaged would require some time to accomplish – say, several years or so, including creating the necessary legal framework – and that it would take further time before a newly-established free-market economy would work relatively smoothly. It was quite obvious that the liquidation of communist-era regulations could be, and must be, somewhat rapid, yet these laws and regulations could hardly be immediately replaced by well-functioning property rights, markets, laws, rules, behaviours and other basic institutions of mature capitalism. Radical reformers were aware that they could learn to a degree from their own rather distant capitalist past, as well as from the successes and failures of various reform attempts in developed as well as less-developed Western countries. They were also aware, however, that the institutional, legal and other foundations of a new socio-economic system could not simply be imported. They expected that to reach a similar final stage of the Czech model of democratic capitalism would take some time, that it would be a lengthier process of 'learning by doing' in which, as is usual in parliamentary democracies, the outcomes can only to some extent be shaped from above.[2]

Finally, after heated political battles in the executive as well as in parliament, the Klausean blueprint for transformation prevailed, although with certain compromises that the political situation required. The group of reformers allied with Klaus, although not holding many responsible positions from which to influence developments, succeeded in imposing a macroeconomic framework that made it possible to liberalize prices and open markets, as well as to liberalize foreign trade. Also, they were able to push through wholesale privatization, the implementation of which was a crucial and final measure of system change. On the other hand, by the beginning of the 1990s they had much less influence on developments in the social and health sectors, on environmental regulations and, partly, also on labour market and business regulations such as commercial law, licensing of businesses and trades, land and environment use and so on. These sectors and regulations, which fortunately were not critical in the early phase of reform implementation, simply had to wait for a major overhaul.

Realization of Klaus's vision

1990: the warm-up lap

It is to be noted that reformers inherited an economy which, unlike Poland or Hungary, was practically completely nationalized, suffered from deeper structural distortions such as excessive industrialization, with an especially high share of heavy industries, and a declining rate of growth.[3] On the other hand, there was less repressed inflation and little foreign debt to Western countries and less general disorganization, certainly in contrast with, for example, Poland. This relatively stable, though deteriorating, economic situation gave the reformers some breathing space, which they used in 1990 to push through important preparatory reform steps while they were competing with their opponents in the executive, parliament, academia and so on in order to have their radical economic reform scenario accepted.

Within a short period of time a number of legal, institutional and liberalizing acts and measures were introduced that effectively created the legal and institutional basis of a capitalist market economy. Most important among them were constitutional changes legalizing privately-owned firms, limiting state property only to some natural resources, and allowing expropriation only for public purposes and with remuneration. Next, legal norms allowing private businesses as well as joint stock companies were approved.[4] Needless to say, a new legal framework and other institutions could only be in a rudimentary form as is usual, and perhaps even preferable, in times of major economic and social changes. Yet, it was certainly good enough to allow orderly implementation of all major reform steps.

One of those major steps was a major overhaul of fiscal policy, begun already in 1990. From a macroeconomic point of view, the aim was to achieve a slight budget surplus in order to reduce aggregate demand in the economy, as well as to signal that fiscal policy would be oriented towards maintaining stability in the near future in order to forestall any possible destabilization after the expected full liberalization of prices and foreign trade. At the same time, there were substantial structural changes in the budget as a reflection of the first systemic changes towards an open market economy in which the redistributive role of the state would be limited. Hence, the share of government expenditures in GDP, which at the beginning of transformation was nearly 60 per cent, was decreased to about 52 per cent by substantial reductions in various expenditures; for example, by reducing defence expenditures, which had reached 7 per cent of GDP by the end of the 1980s (Kocarnik 2006), by reducing subventions to enterprises, and so on. These reductions in state expenditures were accompanied by decreasing corporate income taxes; for example, for non-financial enterprises from 75 per cent to 55 per cent.[5]

A balanced budget policy, together with a restrictive monetary policy, was considered a necessary background for liberalization of prices and foreign trade, which was to happen as of 1 January 1991. Yet, as alongside the structural changes in budget, other important reform steps had already taken place in 1990, still organized 'from above' by the Ministry of Finance under Klaus. Among the most important measures was a form of rationalization of the price structure, which involved increases in a number of retail prices and decreases in some wholesale prices so as to eliminate thousands of individual turnover taxes, some of them negative. This was accompanied by a temporary subsidy to households to soften, in part, the effects of this measure. However, as it was only a partial and temporary compensation, it was in line with a longer-term general vision to reduce state involvement in the economy, to curtail redistribution significantly and to increase economic freedom. This type of complex view of any reform measure so as not to lose wide public support for the coming transformation policies was typical of Klaus's group of reformers. Note also that their attempts to maintain a wide pro-reform political consensus led them to accept compromises in reforms, however much they would have wished to implement more of their liberal vision.

The balanced budget policy contributed to the curtailment of an inflationary jump in prices after the full liberalization of prices as of 1 January 1991. As a result, the Czech price jump was by far the lowest among post-communist economies. This helped to diminish the loss of the real value of the population's savings, which was a key goal of reformers. On the other hand, it left enterprises and the state with rather large debts to be repaid in the future, obviously contributing to eventual problems in the Czech banking sector in the mid-1990s. Also, relatively low inflation helped to ease possible tensions in the newly established social safety net so that there were practically no occurrences of outright social

deprivation and poverty, as occurred in some other transition economies. This situation remained a type of 'constant' throughout the transition years, even to date, as the recent data on the percentage of
people living under poverty line show.

Also in 1990, reformers took steps towards the opening of the economy
to global markets. First steps included auctions for foreign currencies,
which, given legal changes allowing about 300 industrial companies to
engage freely in international trade, started to influence the behaviour
of many other state-owned enterprises as well. It was such early steps
that helped to break the state's monopoly over foreign trade, through
which the communist state had isolated the domestic economy from
outside events, and that was an essential feature of authoritative central
planning. Needless to say, many new commercial agreements were
signed with Western countries, including the association agreement
with the EU, in order to improve access of Czech goods to foreign markets
as a necessary support for the transition process. Also part of the opening
up, already taking place in 1990, was Czechoslovakia's renewal of its
membership in the IMF, as well as membership in the World Bank.
These steps enhanced the credibility of reforms and were an element of
support for the peg of the crown. The resolute and rapid opening up of
the country was considered to be an extremely important reform step
because it brought strong import and export competition into the still
mostly non-privatized economy, and served an important anti-inflation
and restructuring role and created institution-changing pressures
throughout the economy.

Further, two-tier banking was also implemented during 1990. The
Constitution made the Czechoslovak National Bank a very independent
institution, with its Governor and Board members nominated only by
the President of the country. The Constitution also established external
as well as internal stability of the crown as the main targets of monetary
policy. This type of arrangement, which totally freed the Central Bank
from any political influence, was to a large extent a reaction to the
extreme suppression of independent monetary policy to physical central
planning in the previous communist economic system. With the benefit
of hindsight, the pendulum seemed to move to the other extreme, making Central Bankers responsible solely for price stability and not taking
into account any growth targets as monetary policy goals. This kind of
extreme swing also happened in some other arrangements or institutions. By way of example, I would mention new laws and institutions
aimed at the protection of the environment, which also was more
than neglected during 40 years of communism. Hence, over-regulation

of land use and environment protection was written into laws with resulting costly negative impacts on economic activity in the following years.

Similarly, the judiciary, in contrast to its status under communism, was made institutionally fully independent from the executive, and judges were, and still are, nominated for life without any probationary period. This arrangement, perhaps understandable after the totalitarian experience under communism, was, and is, because it still prevails at the time of writing, more of questionable merit for a country in times of revolutionary systemic and structural changes. As later experience showed, this policy contributed to the inefficiency of the judicial system and imposed unnecessary economic and social costs on society at large. As Olson's (1982) work predicted, subsequent attempts to correct excesses in the reform of the legal and institutional framework, committed perhaps with the best of intentions at the early stages of transition, have been rather difficult because vested interests have established themselves in the new system.

Developments after the commencement of sharp reform from 1 January 1991

Decreasing the size of government

From the time when Klaus took over the premiership in the Czech coalition cabinet after the general elections in 1992 until 1998, his government's credo was to balance the budget while decreasing the redistributional activities of the state. The success of this policy is evident from Figure 4.1.[6]

The structure of public finances, however, underwent further considerable changes. On the revenue side, there was significant tax reform as from 1 January 1993 that introduced a Western European-style value added tax system, new corporate taxes and a progressive personal income tax structure. As to the expenditure side, Klaus, together with some of his ministers, worked hard to overcome various pressures within his coalition government as well as in parliament to make excessive increases in various social expenditures, including pensions and health expenditures, over and above the level the overall growth of the economy could sustain. Keeping this 'smaller government stance' over time became rather more complex because one of the junior partners in the cabinet, the Christian Democrats, more and more openly advocated for a 'social market economy', inspired mainly by their German and Austrian colleagues. For example, when one of Klaus's Civic Democratic

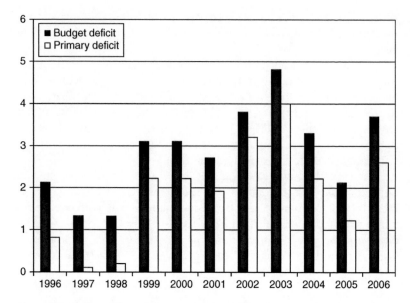

Figure 4.1   Budget deficit and primary deficit of the Czech Republic (as a percentage of GDP)
Source: International Monetary Fund, *International Financial Statistics*, 2007

ministers put forward a proposal to increase the retirement age in order to ease financial tensions in the pay-as-you go pension system that were being felt due to the ageing of the population, the Christian Democratic colleagues argued for a smaller and slower increase in the retirement age and eventually, for purely political reasons, got their way. Moreover, the Klaus cabinet faced stiff opposition from Social Democrats in parliament: in fact, their last budget, for 1998, was only approved with the help of one or two Social Democratic 'dissidents'. Nevertheless, entitlement expenditures on social and health expenditures, mostly as prescribed by law, were kept under control, albeit with increasing difficulty.[7]

Finally, after an economic slowdown and a currency mini-crisis in May 1997, both, to a large extent, produced by monetary policy mistakes,[8] Klaus was forced to resign and prematurely end his second term toward the end of 1997. CNB Governor Josef Tosovsky was appointed by then President Vaclav Havel to lead an interim government until early general elections in 1998. These were won by the Social Democrats, and their leader, Milos Zeman, formed a new left-of-centre coalition government.

His was a minority cabinet, kept in power by a type of 'soft grand coalition' formed when Klaus, on behalf of ODS, signed a political stability agreement with Zeman that included an important section on fiscal policy aimed at keeping the budget deficit under a certain limit. In addition, the agreement contained a rather important political chapter that elaborated and pledged joint support for a proposal to change the electoral law to allow parties that won the election to build a stronger and more effective government. Unfortunately, this change, which would have brought the Czech political system closer to an Anglo-Saxon majority voting system, was never realized because it was challenged by President Vaclav Havel and brought before the Constitutional Court, which excised from the draft law precisely those provisions aimed at increasing the majority party's rights in an otherwise proportional voting system.

Pro-welfare state tendencies under the left-of-centre socialist-led cabinets in the 1998–2006 period

While the agreement to limit the budget deficit perhaps helped to keep the deficit spending inclinations of the Zeman cabinet under control, Zeman's government formulated a quasi-Keynesian argument for keeping public finance balanced over the business cycle that produced a series of central government, and general government, deficits (see Figure 4.1). These deficits, as can also be seen from Figure 4.2, remained a more or less permanent characteristic of the economic policy of the coalition cabinets led by the Social Democrats after Zeman retired from active politics in 2002, when the Social Democrats again won the general election.[9]

The result was a reversal of the trend toward a 'smaller state', as practiced by Klaus's cabinet, and a turn towards inexorable growth in the taxing and spending power of the state and of its redistributive and regulatory role in the economy. This is evident from the increases in the so-called tax quota II, which consists of all direct and indirect taxes as well as payroll taxes paid by employers and obligatory charges paid by employees to cover health and other social contributions (see Figure 4.2). It is also clear from the increase in government expenditures as a share of GDP between 1999 and 2006 (Figure 4.3).[10] The increasing share of total consolidated government expenditures in GDP under cabinets led by Social Democratic premiers reached about 44 per cent in the middle of the first decade in the twenty-first century as against 40.9 per cent in 1998, the last budget that was prepared by the Klaus government

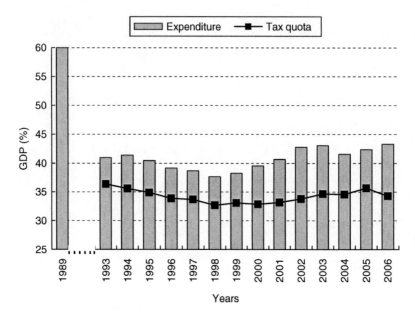

Figure 4.2   General government expenditures and tax quota II (including social and health insurance), as a percentage of GDP

Note: Tax quota II means direct and indirect taxes as well as payroll taxes paid by employers and obligatory charges paid by employees to cover health and other social contributions.

Source: Data for 1996–2006, Ministry of Finance, Czech Republic, http://www.mfcr.cz/cps/rde/xchg/mfcr/hs.xsl/makro_pre_30030.html, and earlier versions of macroeconomic prediction. Data 1993–95 provided by Petr Mach, www.cepin.cz, fully comparable with MinFin data. Estimate for 1989 not fully comparable with other data – see Note 4

before its demise. Driving this growth in expenditures was an increasing share of expenditures mandated by law in total government expenditures. These mandates were related mainly to social and healthcare claims.

In comparative terms, the Czech share of government expenditures to GDP was, by the end of the left-of-centre cabinets in 2006, the second highest among the ten recent newcomers to the EU, lower only than Hungary, and close to German and Dutch levels. Correspondingly, as shown by OECD data and thus also including insurance paid by the state for its employees, pensioners and children, the tax quota II has been growing over the past ten years or so and is the third highest among the newcomers. Figure 4.3 provides a longer-term comparison of the Czech tax quota with the OECD average.

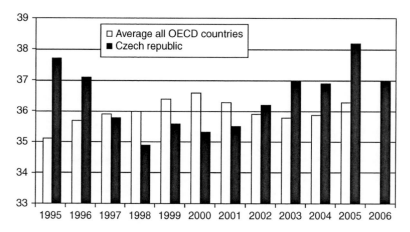

Figure 4.3 Tax quota (taxes/GDP as a percentage)
Source: See data to Figure 4.2 and Figure 4.4

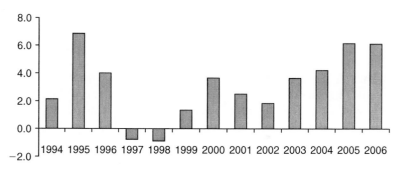

Figure 4.4 Real GDP growth in the Czech Republic (%)
Source: Czech Statistical Office (2007) *Statistical Yearbook (2006)* (Prague)

By empirical analysis, though not by any well-established theory, we know that higher levels of economic development are usually associated with higher social benefits. Therefore, the high government expenditure-to-GDP ratio achieved by the Czech Republic in the middle of this decade is clearly inappropriate because its level of development, as measured by purchasing power parity (PPP) GDP per capita, is still significantly below that of both Germany and Holland. Because this expansion of the public sector in the Czech Republic is accompanied by seemingly permanent deficits despite high recent economic growth (see Figure 4.4), and despite rising tax revenues, the Czech Republic seems to have suffered from a premature inclination toward the West European welfare state. Indeed, this welfare state, as we know, is itself in a sort of crisis in a number of more developed EU 'social market econo-mies', and thus it is even less appropriate for a country such as the Czech Republic, which is still in a catching-up phase.

It should be noted that after the general election in 2002, when Vladi-mir Spidla took over, after having tried to continue the pro-welfare Social Democratic fiscal policy, claiming that 'there are enough resources', he was forced to change his course and attempt a consolidation of public finances. A medium-term 2003–06 budgeting outline together with a type of reform of public finances were elaborated. This retrenchment included some curtailment of government expenditures, including social expenditures, as well as their restructuring in favour of spending on edu-cation, R&D and infrastructure. Also, there were changes in terms of rev-enue, such as steps towards a relative increase in indirect taxes and decrease in direct taxes, the net effect of which would have been to increase government revenues. These changes included increases in con-sumption taxes (for example, on gasoline), as well as in VAT, and these were to be compensated to some extent by a decrease in corporate and also individual taxes. Corporate taxes were reduced from 28 per cent in 2004 to 24 per cent in 2006, and the top marginal personal income tax rate was reduced. Also, there was a promise to use any additional revenues only for the purpose of decreasing deficits and not to spend them. The outcome should have been a decreasing budget deficit trending towards a sustainable level significantly under 3 per cent of GDP in the medium term, as required by the Maastricht criteria, achieved to a greater extent by reductions in government expenditures and to a lesser extent by increases in revenues related to tax restructuring.

As public budgeting had already became too fragmented under Zeman's government, Spidla's government also tried to increase its transparency by terminating the existence of some of extra-budgetary funds; so, for example, the liquidation of the National Property Fund commenced. Note also that the consolidation of public finances was related to the Czech Republic's admission to the EU in May 2004 and thus implicitly had the blessing of the EU Commission.

While some steps envisaged by Spidla's consolidation programme were undertaken, more important efforts towards controlling budget expen-ditures, especially to stem the increasing share of mandated expenditures in total expenditures, to keep within legally binding medium-term expen-diture targets and to put an end to the pro-cyclical tendencies of fiscal policy, were repeatedly cast aside. Finally, the Social Democrat-led cabinet, with the support of, mainly, the Communist Party, introduced indexation of various social payments, and, before the 2006 elections, pushed through new social programmes resulting in a large increase of the deficit-to-GDP ratio in 2007 and, thereafter, well above the original medium-term targets.

Note also that, in terms of transparency and simplification of the tax laws, the Social Democratic coalition cabinets have not achieved much. In fact, the tax law enacted in 1992 has become much more complex. By 2006, it had undergone 90 revisions, bloating it to 66,000 words, and recognized about 450 various kinds of taxable incomes and 363 tax exemptions. Its increasing complexity and lack of transparency thus led to increasing 'tax optimalization' and tax avoidance with additional negative consequences for public finances.

In contrast to Klaus's vision, the Social Democratic governments sought a larger government by increasing various social expenditures disproportionately and by increasing regulatory functions that required more government expenditures. They thus tilted the Czech social economic model of democratic capitalism towards a 'social market economy' in the style of Germany and away from the type of 'less-state and more pro-market' model found in Anglo-Saxon economies.

General elections, 2006: will the right-of-centre coalition cabinet change the nation's course?

The general elections in 2006 ushered in a right-of-centre coalition government led by Civic Democratic Party (ODS) premier Mirek Topolanek. In its campaign, ODS promised a very strong dose of reform, including fiscal reform, pension reform, health reform and similar measures reminiscent of the comprehensive and thorough reforms implemented under the second Dzurinda government in Slovakia. The reform's centrepiece was the introduction of a 15 per cent flat tax rate, valid for corporations, personal income and also VAT, while abolishing a number of tax exemptions and thus simplifying the tax and fiscal system enormously. Also, radical changes in the structure of social expenditures were proposed by ODS, including a complete review of the pension and health system, so as to bring persistent budget deficits under control in the medium term as well as to cope with the cost of aging in the longer term. Needless to say that a number of deregulatory measures was envisaged in order to make the business environment more transparent and to decrease the regulatory burden for firms significantly.

Main features of the fiscal stabilization package

However, because the results of the election were rather inconclusive, it took several months before a coalition government with the Greens and Christian Democrats as junior partners was formed and passed a vote of confidence in the Lower House. Therefore, this package of fiscal, social and healthcare reforms represents a compromise proposal only aimed at stabilizing public finances. Its aim is to reduce the deficit-to-GDP ratio permanently below 3 per cent in the medium term by curtailing certain social and health expenditures and also by changing the tax system. It is consequently to be seen as a first phase of reform measures and, later on, possibly more radical steps similar to the Slovak reforms should follow.

Key aspects include the following: corporate taxes will gradually decrease from the current 24 per cent to 19 per cent by 2010. There is a 15 per cent income tax on personal income as of 2008. However, it will be based on the so-called 'super-gross wage', which includes social and health insurance paid by employers, and, therefore, the effective income tax rate will be slightly over 20 per cent. Eliminating certain tax exemptions will widen the tax base. The result of changes in taxes on personal incomes, in view of a rather high income threshold, is to decrease the income tax burden for everybody, though relatively more so for higher-income earners and families with children. There is a new and rather moderate environmental tax on certain energy sources, whose passage the Greens made a condition for participating in the coalition government. As a main way of raising revenues, however, the lower VAT rate was increased from 5 per cent to 9 per cent while the basic VAT rate will remain at 19 per cent.

Some social spending is being cut or curtailed, mainly by eliminating the automatic indexation of various social transfers introduced during the pre-election frenzy in 2006. Pensions will be exempted.

Outline of the proposed pension and health reforms

The cabinet also wants to undertake a major pension reform. One of the first measures will be to raise the retirement age to 65 and prolong the period of insurance payment to 35 years in order to qualify for a pension from the pay-as-you-go pillar. Moreover, the government will seek multipartisan support for a major reform based on the recommendations of a commission composed of experts and politicians nominated by all the parties represented in parliament. This commission had already prepared several reform variants before the elections in 2006. These variants included some form of capitalization pillar, reduced weight for the pay-as-you go pillar, and so on, and were similar to what had already been introduced in a number of newcomers to the EU before their entry in 2005. Note, however, that various forms of voluntary pension savings plans provided by pension funds and other financial institutions, and benefiting from tax advantages, have already existed for some years.

Finally, proposals for cost saving measures in healthcare reform have also been put forward, including implementation of fees for certain health services, such as visits to the doctor, prescriptions, lodging and food in hospitals. As in Slovakia, these payments are of a somewhat symbolic value, and there will also be an annual cap put on them. Nevertheless, they should help to decrease the extremely bloated demand for some of these services by reducing unnecessary visits to doctors and the waste of prescription drugs, as well as helping to remove certain corrupt practices, as was the case in Slovakia when they introduced such fees. More importantly, legal changes allowing for genuine competition among health insurance companies, which would be buying health services from their providers and offering them under market conditions to clients, are being prepared and should be implemented in 2008 or 2009. Note that the reformed health system retains its solidarity principle based on obligatory health insurance payments and continues to cover all citizens, yet works more efficiently and motivates people to care more about their health. Also, a number of regional hospitals were privatized or rented by regional governors, 12 out of 13 of whom are ODS members, with the expectation of cost reductions and quality improvements. Up to now, experience confirms that this is possible.

These measures have already resulted in improvements in public finance and helped to increase the transparency of the government's role in the economy. They should also help sustain the currently strong growth of the Czech economy in an increasingly volatile international environment.

It should be noted that the cabinet, after it had received a vote of confidence in parliament in early 2007, managed to get this stabilization package enacted with the aid of its coalition partners despite its lack of a working majority. Nevertheless, this stabilization package represents only a first step in the right direction. The next phase of reform, involving deeper structural changes in the tax, health and social service systems, may prove less appealing to coalition partners and thus more difficult to move through parliament.

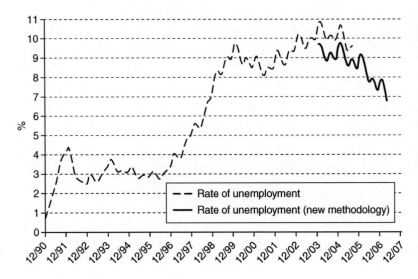

Figure 4.5   Rate of unemployment
Source: Based on data provided by Ministry of Labour and Social Affairs of the Czech Republic,
http://www.mpsv.sz

Labour market reforms under transition

Looking at the development of the labour market as reflected by unemployment statistics over the last 17 years, we can clearly recognize three periods in Figure 4.5.

First, we can see rather stable and low unemployment rate in the early years of transition, say from 1991 until 1997. Next, after 1997, the unemployment rate started to grow significantly from between 3 per cent to 4 per cent, reaching a new level of over 9 per cent in 1999. A significant part of its increase was related to a natural cyclical slowdown that was made more pronounced by monetary policy mistakes in the second half of the 1990s. The unemployment rate stayed at that higher level even when the economy picked up from 2000 onwards, obviously a type of Western European hysteresis effect, and started to decline only when growth of GDP reached over 4 per cent in 2004. Finally, significantly improved growth performance of over 6 per cent in 2005 until 2007 led to a further decrease of the unemployment rate, which, however, levelled off at between 6 per cent to 7 per cent, still relatively high in view of the booming economy.

The labour market in the Klaus era

In comparison with most transition economies, there was no significant unemployment in the Czech Republic at the beginning of transition, say, until 1997 or so. There are evidently several reasons why this was so. First, one should stress the dynamics released in the newly liberalized market economy by privatization and competition. This resulted in a rather fast restructuring in a number of firms, including large enterprises, and to the rapid emergence of new firms in industry and, above all, in services. These absorbed many workers released by industry and agriculture. Second, real labour costs were low at the beginning of transition, which made labour cheaper and therefore increased the level of labour demanded by firms. Also, women's exceptionally high participation rate, a legacy of the socialist centrally planned economy, 'normalized' itself and, similarly, some pensioners who were a part of the labour force in communist times left the labour force for good. Finally, some people made use of the newly arrived freedom of movement and left to work abroad.

As to specific labour market institutions and policies adopted already in early 1990 as a part of newly implemented social safety net, they, as mentioned earlier, were not under the direct control of Klaus's group of reformers. Newly established labour offices modelled along German lines were located in a number of districts and placed in charge of a passive employment programme. At the beginning, this programme contained very generous benefits; for example, for most laid-off workers the replacement ratio was 65 per cent in the first six months and there was no cap on the level of benefits. For those who were laid off for organizational reasons or took care of small children, the benefit could have reached 90 per cent of their previous earnings. However, because of inherent disincentives to work and high budgetary costs, there were already reductions in benefits in 1990 and, as of January 1992, the entitlement period was generalized to 6 months and replacement ratios reduced to 60 per cent in the first three months and 50 per cent thereafter. Under the heading of active employment policies, labour offices also administered the creation of new jobs by subsidizing employers as well as through the provision of short-term public works jobs, jobs for new graduates and retraining.

What the real contribution of labour market policies to the creation of a relatively well functioning labour market in the first half of the 1990s was remains unclear. Much more important in this respect seemed to be the rather low real labour costs combined with de facto labour market flexibility, which made hiring and firing people relatively easy and not too costly. One has to stress at this point that one of the most important institutional factors contributing to labour market flexibility was the relative weakness of labour unions. Labour unions were somewhat compromised by their full subservience to the Communist Party during its almost 40 years of rule, when membership in trade unions was practically obligatory. Therefore, immediately after the demise of communism many people stopped being members of unions and the authority of trade unions, tainted by their past, suffered another blow because of significantly decreasing membership. There was thus practically no strong rank and file support for the introduction of such measures as legally mandated sector-wide collective wage bargaining as in Germany, which some Czech trade union leaders favoured. Wage agreements thus remained at the factory level, which is always more rational. Also, Klaus and his ministers were able to resist pressures to introduce wage indexation and the removal official closing days; hours for opening of shops were legislated, and there existed in practice a large degree of freedom regarding the form of labour contracts, and so on.

The labour market under Socialist-led cabinets

The decrease in the growth rate after 1997 and the partly self-inflicted and unnecessarily deep recession in 1998–99 increased the unemployment rate to over 9 per cent, where it remained from 2000 until 2003, although the economy resumed its growth. As mentioned above, only since 2004, when the growth rate of GDP surpassed 6 per cent, have we witnessed a significant decline in the rate of unemployment to around 6 per cent when measured as an annual average, still a rather high level in times of annual GDP growth rates exceeding 6 per cent. In absolute numbers, this means that, in mid-2007, close to 380,000 persons remained officially unemployed despite increasing vacancies. Together with an increasing number of official and unofficial foreign workers, this situation seems to suggest that social transfers are too high, which keeps a number of Czech workers out of the workforce.

As to the structure of unemployment, we have seen persistent growth in the share of longer-term unemployed in total unemployment, in particular among people with a low level of education. Over the past dozen years, the share of the long-term unemployed, meaning those unemployed for over one year, increased from about 24 per cent of the unemployed in 1995 to about 54 per cent in 2006, most probably one of the highest ratios of this kind in the EU-25 countries. The share of those who were unemployed for more than 6 months rose from about 40 per cent to about 70 per cent in the same period. Overall unemployment, as well as long-term unemployment, is especially high among labourers with low skills and only a basic education, so that, in the group of people with basic education, unemployment was about 70 per cent in 2007. There are also significant and lasting differences in the regional structure of unemployment despite the existence of various active and passive labour market policies, as well as FDI incentives favouring structurally weak regions.

This means that the relatively high unemployment and its structure, in combination with the relatively high growth rates that the Czech Republic has experienced in the past few years, suggests the existence of structural similarities to some developed EU countries in labour market rigidities.[11]

Over time, under coalition cabinets led by Social Democrats, measures were implemented that, if they did not negatively influence the functioning of the labour market, certainly did not improve it. First, increases in the minimum wage relative to the average wage[12] and increases in various social benefits relative to wages for low-skilled work lead to a situation where it does not pay firms to employ low-skilled people, and, at the same time, low-skilled people lack incentives to seek jobs actively and to work in the official economy. Next, because of weak controls and soft rules, people can supplement their unemployment benefits and/or social allowances through income from unregistered work. Moreover, the tax wedge has remained rather high, since mandated social and health insurance payments by employers were 35 per cent of gross wages. When social and health insurance payments made by employees out of their gross wages are included, the rate reaches 47.5 per cent. This sharply reduces the demand for labour in general and especially for low skilled work.[13] At the macro level, these high labour taxes are reflected in the rather high share of payroll taxes in government revenues, which, as we have seen is close to the top among the EU-25, third highest in 2005, and topped only by Germany and France.

Just before the 2006 general elections, a coalition cabinet led by Social Democratic Prime Minister Paroubek, with the help of Communist legislators, pushed through parliament a hastily written new labour code prepared in close collaboration with the trade unions.[14] This is not to say that there was no need for a new labour code because the existing one had been passed deep in communist times, and, although much amended, it remained in spirit a relic of those times. Yet, the new legislation did not represent any significant improvement over the existing one in terms of its contribution to labour market flexibility because it regulated many details of labour contracts. Especially at the level of the firm, it gives too much power to the major trade union at the expense of unorganized workers or any other minor trade union organization when negotiating a collective contract. Also, it introduces higher-level collective contracts with a kind of nebulous relation to firm-level collective contracts.[15] Moreover, it goes well beyond setting basic standards for labour contracts, leaving it to the parties to negotiate details such as full- or part-time jobs, time-limited labour contracts, flexible hours of work, conditions of dismissal and lay-off compensation, and so on. On the contrary, it regulates many of these 'details'. This is a move in the wrong direction because increased flexibility of the labour market, which would make hiring and firing workers less costly and easier, is needed to offset the fast growth of real wages that has taken place in the Czech Republic in the past few years and that is expected to continue in the future as well, moving real wages closer and closer to the levels in advanced EU countries.

There have recently been negotiations between employers' representatives and trade union representatives sponsored by various Chambers of Commerce. A number of technical amendments to the new labour code was agreed on; for example, on overtime for managers, employee approvals of changes to work time accounts and transfer of employees that would reduce strains between employers and employees. This has been sent to the Ministry of Labour in the hope that these technical changes will garner bipartisan support and will be passed quickly rather than waiting for a major overhaul of the labour code that the new ODS Labour Minister has already announced and that will be strongly opposed by Social Democrats and Communists once it reaches Parliament.

Relating social system reforms to labour market reforms under Topolanek's cabinet

Topolanek's new coalition government also wants to improve the functioning of the labour market by measures other than labour code changes. It intends to combine social system adjustments and labour market reforms in such a way as to tie payments of social transfers to the behaviour of unemployed people, so that those who actively seek work are rewarded and those who remain passive and misuse the system are penalized. Thus, there should be participation benefits for those who take part in retraining courses, in public works, occasional short-time jobs and so on. Retraining programmes, education and public works – that is, active employment policies – should also receive more resources at the cost of government support for foreign direct investments, which, as the recent evidence from the automobile industry shows,[16] helps to attract foreign workers using Czech taxpayers' money.[17]

Also, the system of unemployment support, currently 50 per cent in the first three months, 40 per cent for another three months, and only a subsistence allowance after that, should be changed so that it penalizes misuse; for example, by increasing the level of support in the first two months and severely decreasing it after that so that those who remain unemployed after one year will receive only a subsistence allowance or food and other coupons for necessities only. Restrictions on working pensioners, which were partly eased by Social Democratic cabinets, should further be eliminated so as to help labour market flexibility.

Most of these measures aiming at improvements in labour market flexibility require changes in the respective laws. As in case of public finance reforms, it will not be easy for the current government to get them passed.[18]

Conclusions

We have examined the evolution of the size of government and the characteristics of the labour market in the Czech Republic after the fall of communism so as to shed some light on the Czech socio-economic model through the transition years and after. Under Vaclav Klaus's administrations, the size of government was decreased and more responsibility was shifted to individuals. Also, his cabinet succeeded in keeping the labour market quite flexible, partly helped by a positive legacy of communist times in terms of weak labour unions.

Though Vaclav Klaus's group of resolute reformers were able to establish the sound basics of free market democratic capitalism relatively early in the 1990s, they continued to be confronted by proponents of 'social market' ideology, increasingly also within Klaus's coalition governments of 1992–97. Hence, when Klaus was forced to resign, his legacy was a Czech variant of democratic capitalism with prevalently Anglo-Saxon free market features, but also containing elements of pro-welfare and regulatory inclinations of the European continental socio-economic model. Left-of-centre cabinets led by Social Democratic premiers from 1998–2006 moved the Czech socio-economic structure slightly backwards to a more continental model by increasing spending and the regulatory powers of the state, especially in the area of mandatory social expenditures. The result was persistent government deficits that proved to have a structural nature when the economy reached rather dynamic growth in 2004–07. This is a legacy to be solved by the right-of centre government headed by the Civic Democratic Party (ODS) government that came to power in 2006. To do so will require implementation of significant social, health, pension and labour market reforms that, in the final analysis, as with the trends in Slovakia or the Baltic States, would mean changes in the Czech variant of democratic capitalism aimed towards a leaner government, a more flexible labour market and less regulation and, in a sense, that would uphold the liberal features of the Czech socio-economic structure again.

Addendum

As shown above, Czech economic performance as measured by GDP growth has been averaging over 5 per cent from 2003 until 2007. This is much better performance than the EU-12 average, which one would expect because of obvious reasons related to catching up, but significantly worse than the growth performance of Slovakia and the Baltic States, which have reached close to 9 per cent growth on average in the same or an even longer period. Moreover, Czech growth, as we have shown, has been accompanied by a persistent structural deficit in public finance reaching more than 3 per cent of GDP, whereas Slovakia and the Baltic Republics, especially, have either much smaller deficits or even surpluses, which one would expect in fast-growing and healthy economies. Interestingly enough, these economies have also made significant reforms in recent years in the case of Slovakia or in the more distant past in the case of the Baltic States. The hallmark of these reforms was a low flat tax rate and its positive effects on motivation and growth. Thus, one can agree with the view of Mart Laart,[19] former Prime Minister of Estonia, that transition economies, including the Czech Republic, could improve their long-term growth performance at least 1 per cent per year by replacing their progressive tax systems by a flat rate. Obviously, this would have to occur with all the other associated changes in the fiscal, social and health sectors, as well as in the labour market, while, at the same time, other things equal, achieving a sustainable balance in their public finances. Hopefully, Czechs will succeed in accepting such a policy before any kind of crisis or economic turbulence forces it on them at a time when the necessary reforms will be much more costly than they would be in the relatively good times in which they are currently living.

Notes

1 For a useful discussion of the role of industrial policies in the spectacular performance of the Asian tigers and their irrelevance for Central Eastern European transition countries, see Sachs (1993).

2 For more on that, see various lectures by Vaclav Klaus (1994), in particular his address to the Mont Pelerin Society General Meeting, 26 September 1994, in Cannes, France.

3 It may well be that there was no growth at all, if we take hidden inflation under authoritarian socialism into account.

4 In Poland or Hungary, these norms either survived communism or were already approved by communist governments. The Hungarians even passed a privatization law at the end of communism.

5 These numbers apply to federal Czechoslovakia. Also they are not directly comparable to the numbers given in Table 4.1 as the methodologies of computation differ. However, as to trends, they tell the same story.

6 Note that the budget for 1998 was the last one prepared by Klaus's cabinet.

7 There was always a price for staying within these limits, such as a slowdown or stop of further privatization of the remaining state stakes in major commercial banks. Note also that the Czech National Bank under Tosovsky, evidently supported by the IMF and/or the World Bank, was in favour of keeping the state as a strong shareholder in the three major Czech commercial banks, which by the mid-1990s controlled more than 80 per cent of the credit market, so as to enhance their stability.

8 By mid-1996, the CNB had tightened its monetary policy, worried by signs of overheating of the economy such as the increasing current account deficit and allegedly high inflation; annual inflation as measured by the CPI was only around 9 per cent. However, the Bank did not take into account the fragility of the microeconomic and institutional framework of an economy and society still in course of transformation and pushed an already slowing economy into recession. For more on that, see Dyba (1999).

9 First, there was a cabinet lead by Vladimir Spidla, who was replaced by Stanislav Gross when Spidla was forced to resign by a 'mutiny' against him in his own party. Finally, still in the same term (2002–06), Jiri Paroubek replaced Gross when the latter was forced to resign because of some family financial irregularities.

10 Under Zeeman various strains in the budget, already visible in the last year or so of Klaus's coalition cabinets, intensified and were allowed to leak into open deficits. Among these strains was the proliferation of various state funds that started to take on an independent life without regard to macroeconomic developments. Also, there were expenditures to rescue commercial banks, a policy favoured by various pressure groups, as well as a weakening of control over expenditures by municipal and newly created regional governments.

11 Perhaps surprisingly, the Austrian situation is significantly better compared with that of Germany. Unlike Germany, Austria was to some extent influenced towards or 'forced into' labour market reforms by the newcomers to the EU. Austria has recently implemented significant reform measures in fiscal policy, including a decrease in corporate taxes, as well as in the labour market aimed at making it more flexible; see Butner *et al.* (2007).

12   Currently this ratio is above 40 per cent, but it used to be about half of that in the mid-1990s.
13   According to J.-P. Cotis, Chief Economist of OECD, as quoted by the Czech press (see http://ihned.cz/3-20427470-Cotis-000000_d-36), non-wage labour costs in the Czech republic are extremely high. For example, for a person earning two thirds of the average wage, the income tax plus social security and health insurance payments comprise 41 per cent of the wage whereas the OECD average for a person with the same two thirds of the average wage it is only 34 per cent.
14   Note that the current as well as past Chairmen of the Federation of Trade Unions are Social Democrats, the current Chairman is a Senator, and the past Chairman is a member of the European Parliament.
15   There is a pending case with the Constitutional Court as a group of MPs claims that the new labour code violates the basic rights of citizens.
16   This reflects the findings of the study of effects of a new Toyota and Peugeot car factory in Kolin commissioned by the Ministry of Industry and Trade. See the interview of Martin Říman, Minister of Industry and Trade, in Novotný (2007).
17   Interestingly enough, OECD statistics shows that active labour market programmes, as a percentage of GDP in the Czech Republic, are nearly as low as in the US, which is around 0.20 per cent. Slovakia spends twice as much, which is close to the British situation. Denmark, practicing 'flexicurity', currently spends about 1.7 per cent, a rather expensive policy hardly transferable to other countries in the short term. See Chapter 2 on Denmark in this volume.
18   Note, however, that the high tax wedge that makes labour so expensive to companies is not to be changed in the first phase of the Topolanek cabinet's stabilization reforms.
19   See his interview 'Flat Rate Tax Reforms for Transition and Developing Countries' by W. Schelkle, in *Development and Transition*, December 2006, 5: 2–3.

References

Butner, T., Egger, P., Werding, M. *et al.* (2006) 'Tu felix Austria: Wachstum und Beschaeftigungspolitik in Oesterreich und Deutschland in Vergleich', *Ifo Forschungsbericht*, 31 (Munich: ifo Institute fuer Wirtschaftsforschung).

Czech Statistical Office (2007) *Statistical Yearbook (2006)* (Prague: Czech Statistical Office).

Dyba, K. (1999) 'Macroeconomic Policy and Growth during Transition', *Eastern European Economies*, July/August 1999.

Dyba, K. and Charap, J. (1991) 'Transition to a Market Economy: The Case of Czechoslovakia', *European Economic Review*, 35.

IMF (2007) *International Financial Statistics* (Washington, DC: IMF).

Klaus, V. (1991) 'Dismantling Socialism: A Preliminary Report', 1991 John Bonython Lecture delivered by Václav Klaus at the Centre for Independent Studies in Australia and New Zealand; http://cis.org.au/EVENTS/JBL/JBLhome.html

Klaus, V. (1994) *Rebirth of a Country. Five Years After* (Prague: Ringier ČR, a.s.).

Klaus, V. (2006) 'Patnáct let od zahájení ekonomické transformace', in *Patnáct let od obnovení kapitalismu v naší zemi*, Sborník textů č.47/2006, CEP-Centrum pro ekonomiku a politiku, duben 2006, Prague, www.cepin.cz

Kočárník, I. (2006) 'Těžký střet o reformu', in *Patnáct let od obnovení kapitalismu v naší zemi*, Sborník textů č.47/2006, CEP-Centrum pro ekonomiku a politiku, duben 2006, Prague, www.cepin.cz

Novotný, S. (2007) 'Nadšený z toho nejsem... Rozhovor s Ministrem průmyslu a obchodu M. Římanem', *Ekonom*, č. 25/2007.

Olson, M. (1982) *The Rise and Decline of Nations: Economic Growth, Stagflation and Social Rigidities* (New Haven, CT: Yale University Press).

Sachs, J. (1993) *Poland's Jump to the Market Economy* (Cambridge, MA/London: MIT Press).

Schelkle, W. (2006) 'Flat Rate Tax Reforms for Transition and Developing Countries', Waltraud Schelkle interviews Mart Laar, *Development and Transition*, 5, December.

Tříska, D. (2006) 'Privatizace při zakládání kapitalizmu v ČR', in *Patnáct let od obnovení kapitalismu v naší zemi*, Sborník textů č.47/2006, CEP-Centrum pro ekonomiku a politiku, duben 2006, Prague, www.cepin.cz

5
Institutional Transplants in the Transformation of Poland's Economy and Polity

Jacek Rostowski

Introduction

Why different economies grow at different rates is one of the most important questions in economics. Barro's (1991) classical paper on economic growth across the world introduced dummies for sub-Saharan Africa and Latin America, and found that their coefficients were significant, but he did not explain why this was the case. Many empirical studies show that so-called total factor productivity accounts for most of the observed cross-country variations in income levels, yet, although it may well be more important than the accumulation of capital, population growth and even educational improvement, productivity is 'the unexplained part of economic growth' (Easterly and Levine 2002).

One of the reasons for the presence of this residual in cross-country comparisons could be that the neoclassical framework ignores institutions, 'the humanly devised constraints that structure political, economic and social interaction'. These include both 'informal constraints (sanctions, taboos, customs, traditions, and codes of conduct), and formal rules (constitutions, laws, property rights)' (North 1991). Institutions are usually stable over time, and they have a lasting effect that might explain the long-run persistence of discrepancies in economic performance. Two ways in which the impact of institutions on growth can be introduced into standard models of economic growth are presented in the Appendix.

The collapse of communism faced Poland and other former Soviet bloc countries with the need for a massive 'institutional refit', as the institutions that existed under communism were naturally largely unsuitable for the needs of a market economy. It is the purpose of this chapter to describe where these institutions were derived from either in the form of transplants from other countries, revivals of pre-communist domestic institutions or local institutional innovations, and to propose some tentative views as to why the particular developments we observe took place, and to what extent they corresponded to needs at the time. In the case of transplants, one of the interesting questions is why they were copied from a particular country rather than from others.

Previous research on the economic importance of institutions and institutional transplants

Hayek (1960) argued that common law is superior to the civil law in its economic effects, not so much because of substantively different legal rules, but because of their differing assumptions about the rights of the individual and the state, which go back to the philosophical writings of Locke and Hume on the one hand and Rousseau on the other. According to Posner, the efficiency of common law is due to the ability of judges to adapt old rules and create new ones suitable for new and difficult to predict circumstances.

La Porta *et al.* (1997) found that 'countries with poorer investor protections, measured by both character of legal rules and the quality of law enforcement, have smaller and narrower capital markets'. Countries belonging to the French civil law school, a subset of all civil law countries, have the weakest investor protection and the least developed financial systems. Common law countries tend to have the opposite characteristics. La Porta *et al.* (2004) find that, thanks to greater judicial independence, common law countries have more economic freedom – that is, protection of property and contract rights – than do others. They also point to the findings of King and Levine (1993) and subsequent authors, indicating that financial development promotes economic growth.

Furthermore, Levine *et al.* (2000) found that, when they use legal school as an instrument for financial sector development, this instrumented financial development has a large and significant impact on economic growth over the 1960–95 period. Finally, Rostowski and Stasescu (2006) found that, although legal school does not have a significant impact on growth, former British colonies grow significantly faster than former French colonies in the post-independence period. Thus, there is both theoretical and empirical work suggesting that, when institutions are transplanted, it matters from which country or countries they are transplanted.

Historical background

In 1989, Poland and other former Soviet bloc states faced several key tasks. The two most pressing were, first, to restore macroeconomic stability and, second, to privatize state assets, which constituted the vast bulk of the productive capital of the economy. A third, less immediately obvious task, was to create the laws and accompanying institutions of enforcement that would sustain a macro-economically stable market economy that would generate sufficiently high levels of economic growth to allow the country to make up for the lost years of communism, and catch up with Western Europe.[1]

The three tasks were closely intertwined. Inflationary pressure stemmed primarily from the existence of absolute full employment under communism. Under absolute full employment both 'vertical' and 'upward sloping' models of the Phillips curve lead to explosively spiralling prices (Rostowski 1998a). This pressure had been restrained through administrative price controls, which, over the years had led to the massive misallocation of resources at the micro-economic level and to generalized shortages, often called 'suppressed inflation'. At the same time, wage pressure from the fully employed workers was restrained by the banning of trade unions and the suppression of strikes by secret police action. When strikes were allowed, as during the so-called Solidarity period of 1980–01, while prices continued to be set centrally, shortages spiralled out of control.

Markets cannot work without free prices, but free prices combined with absolute full employment can only lead to hyperinflation. Yet, under conditions of hyperinflation it is also the case that prices cannot efficiently perform their function as signals of relative scarcity. Agents cannot be sure to what extent a given price change reflects the general movement in prices and to what extent it reflects changes in demand for or supply of the good in question. Thus, absolute full employment had to be abolished for the market to begin to function in Poland.

It was unclear to what extent managers of un-privatized state enterprises would be willing to sack employees, bringing us back to the question of privatization. Yet, many methods of privatization were themselves unlikely to be possible unless the value of privatized enterprises could be realistically assessed. This, in turn, required market clearing; that is, free, yet stable prices, requiring the mastering of high inflation.

Moreover, state ownership of enterprises was not the only potential problem faced in attempting to end absolute full employment. For enterprises to sack workers, it was likely that they needed to be subject to bankruptcy if they failed to meet their financial obligations. Yet, most post-communist states had no bankruptcy law, and those that did had legislation that left much to be desired, bringing us back to the need for new legal rules and their effective enforcement. Indeed, even if an efficient bankruptcy law existed, what good would it do if there were no mechanism to ensure that enterprises were forced to pay for the inputs they bought with money, rather than relying on trade credit willingly granted to them by their friends from other state enterprises (Rostowski 1998b).

The foregoing description might seem to suggest that it was a miracle that any former communist economy managed to transform itself successfully into a stable market economy. And that is without mentioning the problems of massive foreign debt, immature new political and business elites, or corrupt old ones, or the need for a simultaneous political transition to democracy in countries that had suffered from 40 or 70 years of totalitarianism, and often had previously had little experience of either democracy or the rule of law. Yet, despite these quite abominable initial conditions most of the countries have succeeded in their transitions, both economic and political, from communism.

In each country in which the transition succeeded, there was some chink in the vicious circle of impossibility described above that seemed to require that, in order for any problem to be solved, all had to be solved simultaneously. In the case of Poland, the chink was the existence of a formal legal structure for the independence and corporate governance of state enterprises that was based on elected workers' councils and on the existence, even under communism, of quite a large private sector both in agriculture and outside of it. In Hungary, it was the willingness of the political elite to acquiesce to the selling of almost the whole of the industrial sector to foreign investors. In Russia, it was the political elite's acquiescence in massive nomenklatura privatization, in which the persistence of hyperinflation and arrested transformation actually played a crucial part (Hellman 1998).

The presence of chinks in the cycle of impossibility in so many countries suggests that something was driving political and economic systems towards sustainable, if not necessarily optimal, solutions. In certain cases, such as Russia, this sustainability has not included proper democracy as well as a functioning market economy.

Policies versus institutions in the transition from communism: some problems and definitions

Glaeser *et al.* (2004) are critical of explanations of growth based on differences in institutions; first, because of the subjective nature of most of the institutional indicators used in the literature, and second, because of the strong influence of human capital stock on the very different ways in which quite similar institutions actually operate.[2] They therefore argue that it is policies that respect property rights and encourage education that determine growth. However, Rostowski and Stasescu (2006) argue that it is hard to distinguish clearly between economic policies and institutions. For example, are the rights to price stability and to trade freely policies or institutions? Is an efficient system of universal schooling a policy or an institution?

Rostowski and Stasescu therefore suggest that institutions should be distinguished from policies through their far greater persistence or, even better, through the expectation of their future persistence.[3] Thus, a short period of stable prices or of a fixed exchange rate should be thought of as a policy, but if they are expected to last for the foreseeable future they become institutions. However, this criterion is far less useful during the transition from communism to capitalism, when, at least initially, almost everything was very 'young' and short-lived, and people had few strong expectations as to the long-term persistence of any particular arrangement. Under these circumstances, it might be more useful to use the following commonsensical distinctions: institutions are those rules that allow a very small degree of discretion in their application; bureaucracies are organizations that apply rules and formulate policies. In doing so, they might have more or less discretion. Policies are decisions made by bureaucracies in those cases in which they have a high degree of discretion. Thus, a council of ministers, a bureaucracy, might embark on a policy of economic reform that involves passing a large number of laws, some of which permit of very little discretion in their application and should therefore be considered institutions, while others allow for considerable discretion, and, if pursued with some minimal degree of consistency, should therefore themselves be considered lower-level policies. Some fundamental systemic rules that might allow for the exercise of wide discretion by well-defined actors are also often called institutions. Examples here would be constitutional review of acts of parliament by supreme or constitutional courts, or review of the decisions of the state bureaucracy by ordinary or administrative courts. Another is the principle of private property, by which owners are allowed to dispose of their property largely as they wish. We will call these institutions systemic rules. All of the above come in at least two variants: economic and political. Thus, we have both political and economic systemic rules, political and economic institutions, political and economic policies, and political and economic bureaucracies.

Finally, it needs to be remembered that many institutional outcomes, in the widest sense of the term, turn out not as they were intended, and that in free societies and market economies, a vast number of institutional outcomes are not primarily determined by the state or political processes, but rather by the interplay of private-sector actors. Thus, for example, British banking law allows for the existence of German-style universal banks, which both serve retail customers and have close ties to industry, while until recently US banking law did not. Yet, the structure of the British banking system is far closer to that of the US than to that of Germany.

Institutional transformation and transplantation in Poland in the early transition

The years 1989–93 were a period in which speed was crucial. The economy was in deep crisis before the dismantling of communism. Indeed, it was this crisis that induced the Communists to surrender power. The dissolution of many communist institutions as a result of the loss of power by the Polish United Workers Party, as well as the dissolution of the Council for Mutual Economic Assistance, which had regulated trade between communist countries, only added to the problems. Reformers and politicians therefore acted opportunistically, often following the line of least resistance so as to make pre-existing institutions fit for purpose under the new circumstances.

Political institutions

These were initially heterogeneous, with elements borrowed from a number of countries. The powers of the presidency were modelled on those of the French Fifth Republic: foreign affairs, defence and internal affairs were reserved to President Jaruzelski, who also appointed the relevant ministers. In this way, Jaruzelski could be the guarantor of Poland's loyalty to the Soviet Union, in much the same way that De Gaulle could guarantee that Communists would never take France out of the Western Alliance unless they won the presidency. A similar institutional set-up was later established in South Africa, when free elections to parliament were preceded by the transfer of the Foreign, Defence and Interior

Ministries to the control of President De Klerk, providing a guarantee of white security for a further period.

The similarity to France was increased when Lech Wałesa, who was elected by direct universal suffrage, succeeded Jaruzelski, who had been elected by parliament. The voting system for parliamentary elections was also based on the Fifth Republic model of two-round voting, with only the top two candidates going through from the first round to the second. This system makes sense when, as in France, the political stage is highly polarized into two camps, both of which consist of several competing parties. The first round then effectively acts as a primary for the selection of the left- or right-wing candidate for the second round. In Poland, however, although the political stage was highly polarized between Solidarity and the Communist Party, the two camps were not at this time internally fragmented into independent parties.

The June 1989 elections were only partly free. Two fifths of all seats in the lower chamber of Parliament, the Sejm, were to be freely contested. The remaining seats were to be contested only among the parties of the ruling coalition, the Communist Party, the Peasants' Party and the so-called Democratic Party, as well as Communist-friendly independents. Again, this system recalls other cases of de-colonization. For instance, in British colonies, when elections were introduced they often provided for so-called reserved seats. These either involved only voters of a particular ethnic group electing their representative, or alternatively all voters could vote, but only a member of the group for whom the seat was reserved could stand for election to it. The purpose was often to guarantee members of geographically widely dispersed ethnic minorities parliamentary representation that they otherwise would not obtain in a first-past-the-post system, but sometimes it was also to weight representation in favour of such minorities and away from the majority, which might be in conflict with Britain.

Economic institutions

Among the hundreds of acts and regulations introduced or revived in the late 1980s and early 1990s, four stand out as particularly important. The first was the re-activation of the provisions of the pre-War Commercial Code regarding private companies, which fortunately had been merely suspended, and not repealed, when communism was imposed on the country in the late 1940s. This code was itself a transplant, having been largely copied in 1934 from the German Commercial Code of 1901. As important was the re-activation of fundamental property rights to own private property and to form partnerships.[4] These were contained in the Civil Code, which had originally been transplanted from France to the Grand Duchy of Warsaw in Napoleonic times.

The second was the system of workers' councils and of workers' council election of state enterprise directors. This had been introduced during the early 1980s, at the height of repression of the Solidarity movement, in spite of the fact that workers' councils were a key demand of Solidarity. Of course, during communist rule the freedom of workers to elect their representatives to the councils and of the councils to act were limited by the activity of Communist Party branches in the state enterprises. Nevertheless, it sufficed to remove the Communist Party branches from the enterprises for the councils to start functioning independently. While the interests of workers, which the councils represented, were not entirely congruent with those of the enterprise, as they tended to over-stress the short-term interests of current workers against the interests of capital and potential or future workers, they were nevertheless able to provide some degree of corporate governance and to ensure that managers were not able to steal enterprise assets on a massive scale. Workers' councils had first been introduced in Poland after World War II, then suppressed under Stalinism, re-introduced in 1956, then suppressed again, and re-introduced once more in 1982. They were a truly domestic institution, although they also existed in other countries, such as Yugoslavia.

Third, there came a whole host of liberalizing measures: to free prices, wages, commercial property rents, sales and purchase of almost all goods and services, to engage freely in international trade, to exchange currency freely, and to use whatever currency one wished in domestic trade. None of these vital measures can be said to have had any particular national origin, although they were clearly inspired by a belief in free markets, which has recently been particularly strong in Anglo-Saxon countries.

Yet, what was probably the most important element of the legal aspect of the transformation of the Polish economy did not need to be changed at all. This was the fourth institution that made the systemic transformation possible in Poland. It was the existence of a clear legislative hierarchy and of a clear judicial hierarchy in the country's legal doctrine. In accordance with Western legal tradition, Acts of Parliament had to be in accord with the Constitution, decisions of the Council of Ministers or regulations issued by the Council could only be issued on the basis of Acts of Parliament that expressly envisaged them, and decisions of Ministers or regulations issued by them could only by issued on the basis of Acts of Parliament or decisions of the Council of Ministers, and so on.

The moment a superior legal act was changed, for example removing the legal basis for price control in the country as a whole, all subordinate regulations that depended on it for their legal force automatically ceased to be binding.

This was quite different from the situation in the USSR, where the complete subordination of the whole of the state apparatus to the Communist Party (CP) for 70 years, meant that regulations were even formally issued by a state agency on the basis of a decision by the relevant CP branch without reference to a coherent nationwide legal hierarchy. As a result, when the power of the CP collapsed, regulations issued by local governments and ministries had often to be repealed or reformed one by one, as their authority did not depend on a higher act, and therefore did not automatically cease with the repeal or change of that act. Reformers therefore had to hunt down thousands of pieces of legislation giving power over the economy to bureaucrats and change them one at a time, a massive undertaking that made a swift jump to the market economy far harder in the former USSR.[5]

In Poland also, there were of course many problems, some of them resulting from a failure by the courts to understand key concepts of the market economy in the usual way. Thus, it took some time until all courts were willing to allow newly established limited companies to spend the money they had collected as capital freely. This was because of the practice in the 1980s, when private companies were first allowed, of treating capital in them as a kind of deposit that guaranteed that a firm would fulfil its obligations to suppliers and the tax authorities. Naturally, some of the institutions transplanted from the West were worse than the ones they replaced, even in the context of a market economy. Thus, ironically, it was the reformers who abolished the enterprise wage bill tax, which was effectively a flat employment income tax, and replaced it with a progressive income tax. This was done in the name of educating taxpayers to understand that state services were provided out of their taxes. Subsequently reformers have attempted, unsuccessfully, on several occasions to replace the progressive income tax with a flat rate in order to compete with countries such as Estonia.

The period of consolidation

From roughly 1992, Poland began to establish its more permanent institutional structure. This focused mainly on the drafting and ratification of the new constitution, which came into force in 1997, and on the passing of a series of new laws or amendments to old laws that gave institutional expression and detail to the principles embodied in the constitution. The main source of inspiration for these new institutions was Germany, and the second most important was the European Union, both in that the new laws needed to be future EU membership compatible and as a direct source of institutional transplants.

Political institutions

Inspired by German ordo-liberalism, the political structure became more similar to that of Germany and less French.[6] Thus, the power of both the President and Parliament were reduced, while that of the Prime Minister was increased. This happened, above all, as a result of three main changes introduced under the new constitution:

1 The prime minister could now be removed only through a constructive vote of no confidence by which his/her successor was simultaneously elected to the post. This contrasted with the situation under the previous 'Small Constitution' of 1992 by which the prime minister was required to resign if he lost a confidence vote, and it was only once this had happened that a new prime minister was elected;
2 The prime minister could appoint and remove ministers at will. Under the provisions that held until the enactment of the 'Small Constitution', ministers were directly approved by the Sejm and could only be removed if the Sejm approved their dismissal;
3 The right of the president to be consulted on the appointment of ministers to the three power ministries, Defence, Foreign Affairs and the Interior, was abolished.[7]

The result of these changes was observable at once. Whereas, in the years following the partially free elections of 1989, Poland had experienced eight prime ministers in as many years, under the 1997 constitution there were only three in the first eight years of its operation. Two further very important German-type transplants were strengthened as a result of the following measures:

1 Decisions of the Constitutional Court, a separate supreme court, charged with pronouncing on acts of parliament and decisions of the highest levels of the executive branch, which could previously be overturned by a two thirds majority of the Sejm, were now made irreversible;[8]

2 Judges of the Court were to be appointed in such a way as to have overlapping nine-year, non-renewable tenures, so as to increase their political independence;
3 The independence of the central bank (National Bank of Poland (NBP)) was constitutionally guaranteed;
4 The composition of its interest rate setting Monetary Policy Council (MPC) was designed so as to encourage its independence.

Nevertheless, many French-type elements remained in the new Constitution, such as the direct two-round elections of the President by voters, and the potentially wide use of referendums in legislation.

Economic institution

In two key areas the independence of institutions was strengthened, so as to increase the rules-based nature of decision-making and to help ensure macro economic stability. The first was the independence and governance of the central bank, while the second was rules regarding the drafting of the budget, and the permitted level public sector debt. As mentioned earlier, the independence of the NBP was written into the 1997 Constitution. Even more important, so was the composition and selection of the interest rate setting MPC. The MPC consists of the governor, who is nominated by the president and approved by the Sejm, and nine members appointed for six-year terms that overlap that of the governor by three years. Three of the MPC members are appointed by the president, three are elected by the Sejm, and three by the Senate.

These provisions made the NBP legally and politically one of the most independent central banks in the world, comparable to the European Central Bank. Not only was its independence guaranteed by the constitution (by comparison, the independence of the Bank of England is based on an administrative decision of the chancellor of the Exchequer), but all of its main officers, the governor, deputy governors and members of the MPC, are appointed for fixed terms. Possibly, even more important, the members of the MPC are chosen by the state's three directly elected legislative bodies, the Sejm, the senate and the president, while the governor is not only nominated by the president but also approved by the Sejm. The democratic legitimacy of such office holders is therefore similar to that of those elected in other countries for fixed terms by parliaments to protect various kinds of citizens' rights. Examples of such offices include the state presidents of Germany and Italy, ombudsmen and chairmen of national accounting chambers in a number of countries, including Poland, and also the president of the European Commission. Analogous to these, the office holders of the NBP are charged by the 1997 constitution with maintaining the value of the national currency. Thus, when a conflict arises between the central bank and the government over monetary policy, it is not clear which side has the greater claim to democratic and constitutional legitimacy.[9] Indeed, conflicts with governments in 2003 and 2006 were decisively won by the NBP.

On the fiscal side, the 1997 constitution made it impossible for parliament to increase the budget deficit above that originally contained in the draft proposed by the government, and limited public sector debt to three fifths of annual GDP. The first provision was, again, in line with German practice, which goes even further, with the German basic law forbidding deficits in excess of net public sector investment. Taken together with the Polish provision, which allows the government to implement the draft budget even if it is rejected by parliament, this provided a huge strengthening of the government's ability to impose budget discipline in the face of a recalcitrant parliament. Indeed, taken together, these powers come close to those of French governments, which can pass laws, including on the budget, by decree, as long as they have the confidence of parliament. Such powers can be important for the maintenance of budget discipline. In the Polish case, this is because proportional representation has led to a fragmented Sejm in which both the opposition and junior partners in the governing coalition often attempt to gain popularity at the expense of the main governing party through fiscal incontinence.[10]

The second important fiscal provision of the 1997 constitution was the limitation of public sector debt to three fifths of annual GDP. This was taken directly from the criteria contained in the Maastricht Treaty for the adoption of the euro by EU member states. Taken together with the provisions of the Law on Public Finance of 1998, which provided for corrective measures to be taken when public debt exceeded the 50 per cent and 55 per cent of GDP thresholds, this legal straitjacket successfully imposed a degree of fiscal discipline on the Miller and Belka governments of 2001–05, which would rather have spent their way out of the 2001–04 growth slowdown.

Future challenges

One of the key problems associated with economic decision-making is that in a democracy it is inevitable that politicians are only elected for a temporary period, otherwise there would be little scope for their accountability through citizens' ability to refuse them re-election. Nevertheless, this results in the danger that politicians will act opportunistically if they can find a source of revenue that can fund current consumption but only has to be repaid at a date subsequent to their eventual departure from office. In this way, benefits to voters can be front-loaded, while costs are deferred for successors to deal with. This mechanism can be thought of as a form of asset stripping of various kinds of implicit citizens' rights, of whose existence voters might not be aware. A classical example is loose monetary policy, which initially increases aggregate demand, real output, real income and employment, all of which are reversed once inflationary expectations catch up with reality. Such a policy exploits the stability of citizens' price expectations, which is a social asset that is no longer available to subsequent governments once it has been used up. Establishing an independent central bank is a way of inhibiting such social asset stripping behaviour. Another example of a political Ponzi scheme of this kind is excessive government borrowing, something that the Polish constitution prevents through public debt limits.

Nevertheless, when inhibited by institutional prohibitions of this kind, it is in the nature of temporarily elected officials to seek out new opportunities for mortgaging the future. A recent example in Poland has been the approval of high pensions for miners, which, although approved in 2005, will have its largest impact on the public finances only after 2010. For this reason Bratkowski and Rostowski (2005) have proposed the establishment of a National Actuarial Board (*Państwowa Izba Aktuarialna*) that would assess the long term impact of proposed spending legislation and pronounce on whether it would require offsetting revenues to be provided for simultaneously by legislation.[11]

Bratkowski and Rostowski have also suggested comprehensive reforms to the political structure so as to strengthen budget discipline across the board. These include:

1 Shifting to a more bi-polar political system through a reduction in the size of multi-member constituencies for elections to the Sejm;
2 Further strengthening the position of the government vis-à-vis the Sejm in the budget-making process. Thus, for example, the Sejm would only be allowed to reduce government revenue forecasts, but not its spending forecasts, which it could, however, increase. Also, it could only amend the provisions of the budget by voting measures that increase revenues or reduce expenditures as compared with the government submitted draft;
3 Strengthening the position of the minister of Finance vis-à-vis the spending ministries by allowing the government to reject the draft

budget in its entirety, rather than amending it before it was sent to Parliament for approval.[12]

Conclusions

We shall try to answer three questions. First, to what extent was the relatively high level of success of the transformation of the Polish economy due to the adoption of the right policies and, rather, to what extent was it the result of good systemic rules, institutions and bureaucracies as defined earlier? Second, to the extent to which the success of the transformation in Poland was not the result of good policies, to what extent were the good systemic rules, institutions and bureaucracies that made it possible new, and to what extent did they already exist before the beginning of the transformation? Third, to the extent to which systemic rules, institutions and bureaucracies were new, to what extent were they home-grown rather than transplanted? And, if transplanted, can we say anything interesting about why they were transplanted from one country rather than another?

Our description of the key institutional elements in the success of the early period of the transformation of the Polish economy suggests the following answers to our questions. First, the early transformation succeeded in Poland thanks to daring policies that were adopted within a framework of either pre-existing or revived systemic rules and institutions. For example, had the systemic rule of legislative hierarchy not existed, the legal instruments used to implement the new policies of free price setting, free international trade, internal convertibility of the zloty, small budget deficits financed by borrowing rather than money creation and so on, could not have been introduced successfully, and it is possible that, as a result, the policies themselves could not have been implemented as rapidly as they were.

Second, some completely new or revived systemic rules were introduced and proved vital. They included: the legal equality of private and social ownership; a wide degree of economic freedom for individuals and companies; political freedom and democracy; the rule of law rather than the leading role of the party. However, the policies, institutions and systemic rules that were central to the transformation were implemented almost exclusively using pre-existing bureaucracies: parliament, the presidency, the Council of Ministers, the ministries, the National Bank of Poland and so on. In the early transition, very few new public sector bureaucracies were created. One of the very few that was, was the Ministry of Ownership Transformation (that is, privatization), and the extent of its success has been seriously challenged.

Third, in the early transition, new systemic rules and institutions were, on the whole, either home-grown (such as the system of workers control of state enterprises) or, when transplanted, of such universal application for their origin not to be easily identifiable (such as the legal equality of all forms of property, or the freedom of owners and producers to set prices). However, as we have seen, the picture is far more complicated in the field of political institutions, with many more apparently being transplanted from abroad, in the early period mainly from France and Germany.

In the second period of the Polish transformation, post-1992, institution building appears to have played a more important role in the country's economic success. Indeed, one of the striking aspects of the story is the way in which, after having achieved a real breakthrough via economic liberalization and stabilization in the context of pre-existing or easily adapted institutions in the early transformation, the Polish political elites were able to adapt to the opportunity provided by a more stable economic and, indeed, political environment post-1992, and turn their attention to institution building, both political and economic.

Monetary and fiscal institutions and bureaucracies were strengthened under the 1997 constitution and accompanying legislation. This institutional strengthening helped to reduce inflation to a very low level, to reduce the fiscal deficit significantly and to limit the growth of public sector debt/GDP, which has set the framework for the resumption of rapid economic growth in the period after 2003. The institutional strengthening also made Poland's accession to the EU easier, although weaker institutions have not kept Hungary out of the Union. On the political side, there was also a strengthening of the mechanism for constitutional review by the Constitutional Court, which provides a framework for guaranteeing all the other political and property rights of citizens, and of the position of the prime minister vis-à-vis parliament and the presidency. As we have seen, the new strengthened institutions were largely based on German ordo-liberal models.

Given the present state of research, it is impossible to say to what extent the success of the second phase of the Polish transformation was due to new institutions or new bureaucracies, rather than new policies.[13] It certainly appears to be the case that Polish governments have felt constrained by the limitations on their freedom of action imposed by the independent state institutions such as the NBP and the Constitutional Court that were strengthened by the 1997 Constitution, and that these constraints have, on the whole, had a positive effect as far as the quality of economic decision-making and economic performance are concerned.[14]

Appendix

Modelling the effects of institutions and geography on economic growth

Diminishing returns to reproducible factors

We start with a Cobb–Douglas type production function with both human and physical capital:

$$Y(t) = K(t)^{\alpha}[A(t)L(t)]^{1-\alpha} \qquad (5.1A)$$

where the symbols have the conventional meanings; that is, $Y =$ output, $K =$ capital, $L =$ labour. We assume that $\alpha < 1$, which gives diminishing returns to capital and labour and constant returns to scale. With constant or increasing returns to capital we have endogenous growth, which we address below. The evolution of the economy is determined by:

$$\partial k / \partial t = sy(t) - (n + g + \delta)k(t) \qquad (5.2A)$$

where n is the proportional growth rate of the labour force, g is the proportional growth rate of the efficiency of labour, δ is the depreciation rate at which capital wears out, s is the economy's saving-investment rate, and k is the economy's capital-output ratio.

The steady state of the economy is defined by:

$$k^* = [s/(n + g + \delta)]^{1/(1-\alpha)} \qquad (5.3A)$$

Substituting equation 5.3A into equation 5.1A and taking logs gives the log of steady state income per capita:

$$\ln[Y(t)/L(t)]^* = \ln A(0) + gt - [\alpha/(1-\alpha)]\ln(n + g + \delta) + [\alpha/(1-\alpha)]\ln s \qquad (5.4A)$$

Better institutions can affect the rate of economic growth in two ways. The first is through better incentives for agents in a given country to adopt new technologies, which gives a higher rate of technical change, g, and thus a higher long-run growth rate for the economy. This will be the case whether technical innovations are domestically produced, as in advanced countries, or imported from countries at the world technological frontier, as occurs in poorer countries.

However, there a problem with this model: the adoption of new technologies must be assumed to be costless, otherwise it is a form of capital expenditure, and yet, at the same time, it is not automatic, occurring everywhere as soon as an improvement is devised at the world technological frontier, because then it would be uniform across countries. Bad institutions work in this framework to inhibit the adoption of innovations to such an extent that no amount of capital expenditure will overcome this handicap, whereas good ones allow the innovations to be adopted without the need for any special expense.

A second channel allows an improvement in institutions to affect growth. Such an improvement might increase the rate of return on capital, which increases the steady state level of per capita capital for any given saving rate given by equation 5.3A. This increases the steady state level of per capita income. To the extent that the actual level of income is now below the steady state, or further below it, this increases the rate of growth of output per capita, which is given by:

$$\gamma = \lambda\{\ln[Y(t)/L(t)]^* - \ln[Y(t)/L(t)]\} \tag{5.5A}$$

Another way of thinking about this is that the increase in the marginal product of capital increases the growth rate of output/head for given increases in capital/head at the given saving rate assumed in the Solow model. Furthermore, if we go outside the Solow framework and make the savings rate endogenous and positively dependent on the rate of return on capital, we will have an even faster increase in k and, therefore, in y.

However, in the Solow model, countries that have had good institutions for a long time will not grow faster than those with worse institutions due to such effects via the productivity of capital. This is because faster growth via this channel can only occur as a result of a greater gap between actual and steady state income, something that is unlikely to be the case after particular institutions have existed for a long period. The same is true for the positive or negative effects of geography, which operate in this model through the impact of $A(0)$, representing endowments, on the steady state.

Constant or increasing returns

If we use a function with constant returns to broad capital, both physical and human, we can write:

$$Y = AK \tag{5.6A}$$

Then we get the growth rate:

$$\gamma = sA - (n + g + \delta) \tag{5.7A}$$

Even if $g = 0$, γ will be constant as long as savings, population growth and depreciation rates are constant and positive as long as $sA > n + \delta$.

What is more, different countries will have different long-term growth rates depending on the values of these parameters, and there will be no tendency for income levels to converge. In this case, any factors that affect the rate of savings and investment, be they institutions or geography (for example, via transport costs in the latter case as illustrated by Gallup *et al.* (1998)), will affect the long-run growth rate of an economy.

The problem with the *AK* function is that it does not allow for any, even conditional, convergence of income levels. However, a mixed *AK* and Cobb–Douglas function will give us both differences in long-term growth rates, which depend on the savings rate, and therefore might depend on institutions or geography, and shorter-term convergence in income levels:

$$Y = AK + BK^{\alpha} L^{(1-\alpha)} \tag{5.8A}$$

where $A > 0$, $B > 0$ and $0 < \alpha < 1$. In per capita terms, the function is:

$$Y = Ak + Bk^{\alpha} \tag{5.9A}$$

The average productivity of capital is given by:

$$y/k = A + Bk^{-(1-\alpha)} \tag{5.10A}$$

which decreases in *k* but approaches *A*, rather than zero, as *k* tends to infinity, so that given:

$$\gamma = sy/k - (n + \delta) \tag{5.11A}$$

$$\gamma = sA + sBk^{-(1-\alpha)} - (n + \delta) \tag{5.12A}$$

a higher savings rate gives a higher growth of GDP/capita at a given population growth rate and rate of depreciation, but that higher rate is itself smaller the higher is *k*.

Notes

1 Before World War II many East European countries were no poorer than those in Western Europe. Thus, the Czech lands (Bohemia and Moravia) were as rich as France, richer than Germany and far richer than Austria, while Poland was richer than Spain and about as rich as Italy. Estonia was far richer than Finland.
2 Glaeser and Saks (2006) argue that levels of corruption, which importantly determine how formal institutions actually operate, differ across US states as a function of their level of education.

3 I am grateful to Andrzej Bratkowski for this latter suggestion.

4 None of these rights had been formally abolished. Neither was the ability of physical persons and private and social legal persons to enter into binding contracts formally withdrawn either. The only problem was the absolute need of socialized legal persons to follow the instructions of their bureaucratic superiors in ministries or HQs of federations of cooperatives, and the very limited access of private persons to assets.

5 Even the USSR had a clear hierarchy of criminal and civil courts. But, in some ways, it was even worse off in this sphere than in that of legislation, as formally it had no commercial courts at all! This was the logical consequence of all production and exchange being in the hands of the state for 70 years. It made little sense for different state agencies to be able to sue each other. The state arbitration system (*Gosarbitrazh*) was only able to decide in cases of disputes between state entities (the assumption being that in a dispute between a private person and a state entity, the state entity must automatically be right, unless individuals within the state organization had acted in an illegal – and therefore criminal – manner). In 1991 the *Gosarbitrazh* system was transformed into arbitrage courts available to all legal persons, not merely state-owned ones. However, they are not available to physical persons. Over time, these arbitrage courts developed into the commercial court system of the post-Soviet states.

6 Although it is worth noting that German ordo-liberalism was itself strongly influenced by American constitutional ideas of citizens' rights, the division of powers and constitutional checks and balances.

7 The super-majority required to override the presidential veto was reduced from two thirds to three fifths.

8 The legality of lower level bureaucratic decisions was, and continues to be, controlled by so-called administrative courts, which constitute a parallel judicial hierarchy that is topped by the third supreme court, the *Naczelny Sąd Administracyjny*.

9 For the forcefully expressed presentation of the contrary view, though one that is not strongly grounded in Polish constitutional realities, see Mishkin (2002).

10 This is especially the case in the last years of a parliamentary term, when the 5 per cent threshold of votes obtained for entry into the new parliament often becomes a looming threat, particularly for smaller parties.

11 I have recently learned that Deputy Prime Minister Jerzy Hausner has made a similar proposal.

12 A different approach to strengthening budget discipline in Poland is suggested by Hallerberg and von Hagen 2006). Their main proposal is that a multi-year budgetary pact between the political parties forming a multi-party coalition government become a part of standard political practice.

13 Most of the key new systemic rules that needed to be changed for the economy to move from socialism to capitalism had already been introduced in the first phase of the transformation.

14 Nevertheless, it is almost impossible at this stage to judge the relative impact of transplanted as opposed to home-grown institutions on economic performance during this period.

References

Barro, R. (1991) 'Economic Growth in a Cross Section of Countries, *Quarterly Journal of Economics*, 106(2).

Bratkowski, A. and Rostowski, J. (2005) 'Jakie zmiany instytucjonalne są potrzebne, aby wzmocnić dyscyplinę budżetową w Polsce?', *Ius et Lex*, 3, 1/2005: 401–15.

Easterly, W. and Levine, R. (2002) 'It's Not Factor Accumulation: Stylized Facts And Growth Models', Central Bank of Chile Working Papers, 164, June.

Gallup J.L., Sachs, J.D. and Mellinger, A.D. (1998) 'Geography and Economic Development', NBER Working Paper W6849, December.

Glaeser, E., La Porta, R., Lopez de Silanes, F. and Shleifer, A. (2004) 'Do Institutions Cause Growth?', *Journal of Economic Growth*, 9: 271–303.

Glaeser, E.R. and Saks, R.F. (2006) 'Corruption in America', *Journal of Public Economics*, 90: 1053–72.

Hallerberg, M. and Von Hagen, J. (2006) 'Budget Processes in Poland: Promoting Fiscal and Economic Stability', *'Sprawne Państwo'* Program Ernst&Young, Warsaw, Ernst&Young. http://webapp01.ey.com.pl/EYP/WEB/ey.com_download.nsf/resources/Budget_processes_in_Poland.pdf/$FILE/Budget_processes_in_ Poland.pdf

Hayek, F. (1960) *The Constitution of Liberty* (London: Routledge & Kegan Paul).

Hellman, J. (1998) 'Winners Take All: The Politics of Partial Reform in Post-Communist Transition', *World Politics*, 50(2): 203–34.

King, R.G. and Levine, R. (1993) 'Finance and Growth: Schumpeter Might Be Right', *Quarterly Journal of Economics*, 108: 717–37.

La Porta, R., Lopez-de-Silanes, F., Pop-Eleches, C. and Shleifer, A. (2004) 'Judicial Checks and Balances', *Journal of Political Economy*, 112(2).

La Porta, R., Lopez-de-Silanes, F., Shleifer, A. and Vishny, R. (1997) 'Legal Determinants of External Finance', *Journal of Finance*, 52(2).

Levine, R., Loayza, N. and Beck, T. (2000) 'Financial Intermediation and Growth: Causality and Causes', *Journal of Monetary Economics*, 66: 31–77.

Mishkin, F. (2002) 'Structural Issues for Successful Inflation Targeting in Transition Economies', Paper presented at the Conference on Monetary Policy in the Environment of Structural Changes, at the National Bank of Poland, Falenty, Poland, 24–25 October.

North, D.C. (1991) 'Institutions', *Journal of Economic Perspectives*, 5(1).

Rostowski, J. (1998a) 'The Inter-Enterprise Debt Explosion in the Former Soviet Union: Causes, Consequences and Cures', in Rostowski, J. (1998) *Macroeconomic Instability in Post-communist Countries* (Oxford: Clarendon Press).

Rostowski, J. (1998b) 'Market Socialism Is Not Enough: Inflation v. Unemployment in Reformed Communist Economies', in Rostowski, J. (1998) *Macroeconomic Instability in Post-Communist Countries* (Oxford: Clarendon Press).

Rostowski, J. and Stasescu, B. (2006) 'The Wig and the Pith Helmet, The Impact of "Legal School" versus Colonial Institutions on Economic Performance', (2nd version), *CASE Studies and Analyses*, 300, Warsaw, available at www.case.com.pl

6
The European Union and the New Member States' Dilemmas: The Case of Poland

Wojciech Bieńkowski

Introduction

When we analyze statistical data concerning Poland's economic growth at present, things seems satisfactory. The economy is booming, GDP growth rates in 2006–07 are around 6–7 per cent annually, inflation is low and the budget deficit is within Maastricht Treaty limits. Unemployment has been reduced dramatically thus, here and there, causing some labour shortage problems. Our exports are expanding at more than satisfactory rates. What is more, productivity growth for most of the transformation period has easily allowed steady wage increases as well currency appreciation. What is most encouraging, however, is an investment growth rate at above 20 per cent and foreign direct investment (FDI) inflows exceeding US$15 billion in 2006, and over US$6.4 billion in the first five months of 2007 and reaching over US$110 billion since the start of the transformation.

But these positive results create a danger for Poland's longer-term prospects. History has taught us that good times are not good for structural reforms in an economy, even when society needs them badly. Economic reforms are, as always, in the hands of politicians and they are known for risk avoidance rather than for dramatic, or even gradual, changes when those could bring some negative reactions from voters in the short run. This is exactly the case of Poland at present. A booming economy, as well as internal political struggles within the ruling coalition and in Poland's parliament, mean that the administration is reluctant to push the overdue reforms. The problems, constraints and choices politicians and economic experts in Poland have to face at present are many, and they will not be easily resolved. Some are of internal origin, related to systemic transformation and the economic and technological underdevelopment inherited from the communist past. Others are external, related to various international standards Poland has had to meet, such the laws and rules related to our EU membership.

But sitting above all these constraints and considerations, there is a more visible and urgent ideological and structural problem Poland has been facing that relates to the question of choosing the correct socio-economic model to make our economy competitive in the long term. The choice Estonia or Slovakia faced and solved some years ago, or the choice Ireland made in 1986–87 has yet to be made in Poland. This is exactly the topic of this chapter but we will approach it in steps, leaving some space for the necessary background information first.

Legacy of the previous system and the transaction cost

Systemic transformation in Poland: its nature, process of implementation and legacy

Internally, a country in transition from communism to a market economy is always difficult to manage because several layers of systemic transformation problems multiply economic difficulties that exist in any 'normal' country anyway. What is more, both categories of problem – that is, political economy and economic policy, as such – have to be solved at the same time. Often, they interact negatively. Despite 18 mostly successful years of transformation in Poland, there are still many old system-related problems to deal with.

Its nature

The systemic transformation in Poland, which began in 1989, is depicted in Figure 6.1. The critical thing in the process as depicted is rooted in the foundation of the system, or the lower layer of it, which is an ideological level comprising the basic set of values on which any system is based.

Prior to 1989, state ideology or communist party ideology, which people were forced to follow, dominated. Citizens in were unimportant in setting priorities and treated mostly as a tool with which to implement the political objectives. As a result, there was a party or dictator in the political layer of the system whose role was to lead the nation and use the nation to achieve the goals. Consequently, the economic part of the system was given full command over all resources. The best way to command the economy was to have it 100 per cent state-owned. There was virtually no room for individual or private initiative and, consequently, no room for private property, money or market forces.

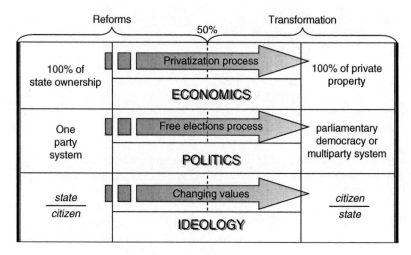

Figure 6.1   Model of system transformation
Source: Bieńkowski (2002)

Poland was fortunate to have a pretty smart communist party elite in the 1980s (which was the time of the obvious decay of the communist system in this part of Europe) and they had found a way out of the systemic trap by making a deal with Solidarity and the Church. The elite decided, in the spring of 1989, to embark on a systemic transformation process by signing the famous 'Round Table Agreement' or 'Magdalenka Agreement', named after the Warsaw suburb where the negotiations were completed.

What was critical at the time was the fact that both sides agreed to the complete change of the entire system, but only gradually. Namely, what the party elite agreed to was that the new system for Poland would be aiming to be a multi-party political one, and that private property in the economy would regain the same legal status as government ownership, which had dominated the economy for over 40 years. Moreover, the system change would be permanent, not temporary, as happened during the NEP (New Economic Period) period in the Soviet Union or during certain other short periods when the communist economy was in a grave state and the party injected some private initiative into it in order to avoid total disaster. What was very important during the Magdalenka talks was the agreement on a timetable for the coming change to which the parties had agreed. Soon after the conclusions of

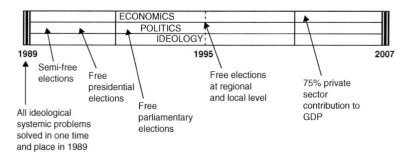

Figure 6.2 Model of system transformation: Polish economic course since 1989
Source: Bieńkowski (2002)

the talks, in the summer of 1989, Poland had semi-free elections and later, by December of that year, the new Deputy Prime Minister and Minister of Finance, Leszek Balcerowicz, had prepared a plan to stabilize Poland's economy and to make it 70 per cent private and open to international trade within a 10-year period. So as not to repeat a well-known story, we depict the transformation process in Figure 6.2.

Implementation

Figure 6.2 shows that, at the ideological layer, Poland's political elite has reached a consensus right away in the spring of 1989 and, by all accounts, they agreed on everything with respect to ideology, the political system and privatization of the economy. The making of this decision is worth stressing because, for example, in Russia, Ukraine or even China for that matter, giving private property equal status with social property or accepting a multi-party system came very late. Quite often, it came many years after the systemic transformation took off or still has not been fully accepted – or not accepted at all, as in the case of China with respect to its multi-party political system.

The political transformation in Poland took off in the summer of 1989, even though 66 per cent of parliamentary seats were reserved for the communist party members, General Jaruzelski remained as President and four critical ministerial posts (defence, interior affairs, foreign affairs and the Central Bank) remained in the hands of communist party members. But, in 1990, a free presidential election took place, which Lech Wałesa, the Solidarity Leader at that time, won: a year later we had completely free parliamentary elections. By 1994–95, or six years after formal take-off, the systemic transformation in the political sphere was formally completed.

A similar process could be seen with respect to the economy. The process of privatization took place in two ways: by privatizing state-owned corporations and by making room for new private enterprises. As the result, by the mid-1990s 50 per cent of Poland's GDP was provided by the private sector. In 2007, about 84 per cent of GDP came from the private sector, and about 78 per cent of Poland's workforce was dependent on that sector as well. Due to its international obligations and the EU membership, Polish economy is completely open to trade and international investment. What is more, the Polish zloty has become convertible and stable. In short, the process of economic transformation from command to market economy has also been completed.

Legacy of the previous system and the transaction cost

What Poland still needs to do, however, is filter out old habits derived from two centuries' of our old, bad experiences, when Poland was either occupied by stronger neighbours or demoralized by the communist system, which had created an absurd set of values for over 50 years. People with such experiences tend to have little respect for government; mostly foreign, aggressive and corrupt. They learned to have more respect for various ways of surviving in an unfriendly environment. The problem we are talking about is depicted in Table 6.1.

Salvia and Alberto (2007) have conducted similar studies. The above analyses place Poland at the bottom of the ranking tables when it comes to ethics ratio, market and transparency indicators among European Union countries.

Certainly, Poland has been fully in accord with formal Western institutions as shown by her constitution, laws and regulations, as well as by the way government agencies responsible for the implementation of laws should behave. But there are equally important informal institutions derived from historical experience, religion and so on that make people reluctant to follow these rules.

As a result, in a new or restored democracy, a slightly chaotic society and a fragile parliamentary democracy, Poland finds it difficult to form a stable political majority, and, therefore, the compatibility of formal and informal institutions suffers. That situation translates into inefficient bureaucracy, corruption, non-competitive financial institutions and inflexible markets that make transaction costs high. And when transaction costs are high, the competitiveness of the economy is weakened and the whole country suffers.

Table 6.1 Corruption and ethics in different institutions in 2006

Country	Political Parties	Parliament/ Legislature	Business/ Private Sector	Media	The Military	NGOs	Religious Bodies	Education System	Legal System/ Judiciary	Medical Services	Police	Registry and Permit Service	Utilities	Tax Revenue Authorities
Austria	3.2	2.9	3.2	3.0	2.9	2.5	2.7	2.5	2.6	2.5	2.8	2.6	2.3	2.7
Bulgaria	4.3	4.2	3.9	3.0	2.8	3.2	3.0	3.4	4.3	4.1	4.0	3.3	2.7	3.6
Czech Republic	3.6	3.4	3.3	2.8	3.2	2.6	2.4	2.9	3.6	3.4	3.8	3.4	2.5	2.6
Denmark	3.1	2.5	3.2	3.1	2.4	2.6	3.3	2.3	2.0	2.5	2.2	1.9	2.5	2.2
Finland	3.3	2.5	2.9	3.0	1.8	2.5	2.6	2.0	2.1	2.1	1.8	1.7	2.2	2.1
France	3.7	2.9	3.5	3.4	2.1	2.4	2.5	1.9	2.6	2.3	2.8	2.2	2.3	2.6
Germany	3.5	3.0	3.5	3.1	2.4	2.8	2.5	2.2	2.5	2.8	2.3	2.0	3.1	2.3
Greece	4.1	3.4	3.3	3.7	2.6	2.5	3.1	2.9	3.6	3.5	3.3	2.3	3.3	3.8
Iceland	3.7	2.9	3.8	3.3	x	2.7	2.8	2.2	2.8	2.5	2.4	2.2	2.7	2.3
Ireland	3.4	2.8	3.0	2.8	2.1	2.3	2.7	2.1	2.9	2.5	2.7	2.2	2.4	2.6
Italy	4.2	3.7	3.3	3.2	2.2	2.6	2.5	2.4	3.1	3.2	2.3	3.4	2.8	3.4
Lithuania	4.0	4.0	3.6	3.0	2.3	2.6	2.0	2.9	3.9	3.9	3.7	2.9	2.1	2.4
Luxemburg	3.7	3.2	3.5	3.4	2.7	2.7	3.1	2.6	3.0	2.7	3.0	2.6	2.5	2.8
Netherlands	3.0	2.7	3.0	3.0	2.5	2.7	2.8	2.3	2.5	2.6	2.7	2.1	2.7	2.4
Norway	3.0	2.6	3.9	3.5	3.1	3.2	3.3	2.4	2.4	2.6	2.5	2.0	2.7	2.2
Poland	4.2	3.9	3.9	3.4	3.1	3.3	3.2	3.1	3.8	4.0	3.8	3.7	2.7	3.2
Portugal	4.1	3.6	3.6	3.0	2.6	2.8	2.8	2.9	3.4	3.2	3.2	2.6	2.8	3.6
Romania	3.9	3.9	3.6	2.8	2.4	2.6	2.2	3.0	3.8	3.7	3.7	2.9	2.4	2.6
Spain	3.9	3.1	3.6	3.4	2.5	2.7	2.8	2.3	3.0	2.2	2.8	2.9	3.1	3.0
Sweden	3.2	2.5	3.1	3.2	2.4	2.3	3.1	2.1	2.4	2.4	2.5	2.2	2.4	1.9
Switzerland	2.8	2.5	3.0	2.9	2.2	2.3	2.4	1.9	2.2	2.2	2.2	2.2	1.9	2.4
United Kingdom	3.5	3.1	3.2	3.4	2.4	2.7	2.8	2.3	2.9	2.3	2.7	2.0	2.6	2.7
EU	3.7	3.2	3.4	3.2	2.4	2.7	2.6	2.3	2.9	2.7	2.7	2.5	2.7	2.8

Notes: 1 = not all corrupt, 5 = extremely corrupt, x – no data available. Figures are weighted. Shaded scores are the highest for that particular country.
Source: Transparency International Global Corruption Barometer (2007): 22

Some factors that determine transaction costs include:

- Time to get a license to start a business
- Access to credits and quality of financial institutions
- Access to and mobility of working force
- Scale of corruption
- Ability to close a business quickly and cheaply.

The World Bank has been publishing the so-called 'Ease of Doing Business' index in an attempt to assess transaction costs in the member countries. Poland has been placed at about 75 out of 175 countries (see Table 6.2).

At first glance, Poland's score does not seem too bad, given our historical background and 50 years of communism. Still, the score is definitely unsatisfactory. Poland has to lower transactions costs by getting rid of the rigidities of the present economic system caused by the communist past or various populist promises added by Solidarity-based or post-communist dominated governments during the 18 years of transformation that congested our institutions with 'pro-social' laws and regulations that either extended employees' privileges or constrained entrepreneurs. The consequences can best be illustrated by Figure 6.3, which depicts the still existing difficulties Polish entrepreneurs face every day.

Poland's institutional setting shows clearly that Poland's governments have not been business-friendly and have not created enough incentives to make people work hard. Poland's currently booming economy cannot, and should not cloud the underlying picture. Poland needs to unchain itself from its post-communist and populist institutional setting by introducing a business-friendly legal environment, by improving the functioning of government agencies, and by making its markets, including the labour market, flexible. Cutting many social programmes and limiting bureaucratic power, which contribute to corruption, is indispensable. In short, Poland's political elite, when looking for better policy solutions, should search for models that could provide and secure the desired business-friendly environment in the long run.

What to do next, when transformation is over and EU membership has been secured?

As indicated earlier, the real dilemma for Poland, and many other countries in transition, relates to a very important political or, to be more precise, ideological question: What socio-economic model should Poland follow

Table 6.2 Ease in doing business – international ranking from the year 2007

Country	Overall rank	Starting a business	Dealing with licenses	Employing workers	Protecting investors	Paying taxes	Enforcing contracts	Closing a business
Continental model								
France	35	12	26	134	60	92	19	32
Germany	21	66	21	129	83	73	29	28
Italy	82	52	104	101	83	117	141	49
Scandinavian model								
Denmark	7	14	6	15	19	15	1	20
Finland	14	18	35	111	46	75	13	6
Sweden	13	20	17	94	46	39	2	17
Anglo-Saxon model								
Ireland	10	6	20	83	5	2	24	7
United Kingdom	6	9	46	17	9	12	22	10
Anglo-Saxon model overseas								
Australia	8	2	29	9	46	35	7	12
Canada	4	1	32	13	5	22	16	5
Chile	28	32	40	58	19	37	73	107
New Zealand	2	3	18	10	1	10	15	21
Singapore	1	11	8	3	2	8	23	2
USA	3	3	22	1	5	63	6	16

(Continued)

144

Table 6.2 (Continued)

Country	Overall rank	Starting a business	Dealing with licenses	Employing workers	Protecting investors	Paying taxes	Enforcing contracts	Closing a business
New EU member states (8 post communist countries)								
Czech Republik	52	74	110	45	83	110	57	113
Estonia	17	51	13	151	33	29	20	47
Hungary	66	87	143	90	118	118	12	48
Latvia	24	25	65	123	46	52	11	62
Lithuania	16	48	23	119	60	40	4	30
Poland	**75**	**114**	**146**	**49**	**33**	**71**	**112**	**85**
Slovakia	36	63	47	72	118	113	59	31
Slovenia	61	98	63	146	46	84	84	35

Source: World Bank (2007)

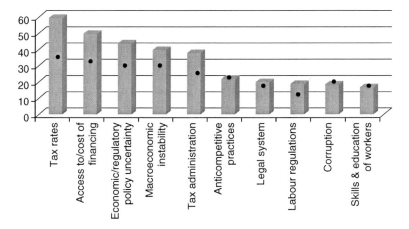

• Average for region of Eastern Europe, former Soviet
▨ Union and Central Asia

Figure 6.3 Where the shoe pinches: percentage of firms identifying as having 'major' or 'very severe' obstacles to business investment in Poland, 2005
Source: World Bank (2005)

once the chains of communist system have been broken, the systemic transformation is about to be completed and EU membership has been secured? To be more specific, the key components of this question are:

- Should Poland follow the traditional EU socio-economic model that has dominated in most European continental countries such as France, Germany or Italy, or
- Should Poland choose the Anglo-Saxon model followed by the UK since the time of Margaret Thatcher and Ireland since 1986/87 with great success, or, perhaps
- Should we opt for the Scandinavian model, because countries in this region have been doing relatively well and rank high in international competitiveness reports. Many 'reformers' in the EU, including the EU Council leaders as of March 2006, have started to think of it as the possible best reference point for further economic policy reform, or perhaps
- As some as some experts still insist, we should opt for the Japanese or industrial policy model, concentrating on selected industries that, supposedly, have better prospects of becoming globally competitive.

Figure 6.4 depicts these choices against the systemic transformation model. Nations that have secured private property dominance,

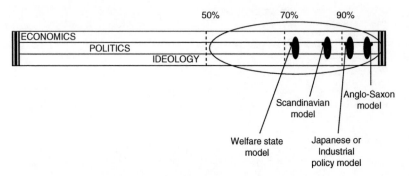

Figure 6.4   Possible scenarios (models) within market and democracy
Source: Bieńkowski (2002)

multi-party political systems and, above all, the value system espoused by John Locke and the Founding Fathers, could still have a variety of ideas as to which path of development to follow and what should be the proportions of power sharing between the state and individuals at all levels.

At this moment, at an early stage of Poland's EU membership, the choices, as depicted above, might look merely theoretical. We are happy to accept EU financial assistance programmes, and Poland's present government has plenty of internal problems to solve in order to survive. Above all, the economy is booming, which pushes the debate and the decision aside.

But, in the longer run, the Polish political and economic elites, to the extent they are willing to think long-term, face the dilemma because the EU model as espoused by Poland's closest economic partners, and main economic policy guidelines as advocated by Brussels and by most of the European continental countries, does not provide for high growth and competitiveness, a fact that even experts working for the frames of the Lisbon Strategy (LS) admit openly in their annual progress review reports (see Kok (2004), for example).

Why should we choose to opt openly within the EU for an Anglo-Saxon model?

There are at least two main reasons why Poland should opt for the Anglo-Saxon model rather than vacillate between the continental and Scandinavian options. One is our national character, as shaped by historical experience if not inherited in our genes. I strongly believe that we Poles have been plagued by individualism. We better feel when being

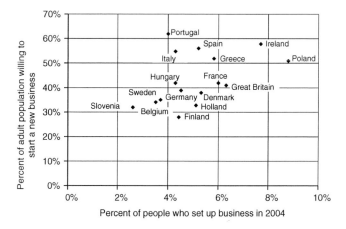

Figure 6.5 Entrepreneurial spirit in selected countries
Source: Adam Smith Research Centre (2004)

independent and being on our own rather than preferring risk avoidance, group behaviour or government dependence. Both our long history and the recent communist experience provide the same guidance for us on how to survive and be better off. Under the previous environment, one had to invent ways to circumvent the formal institutional environment. Perhaps that is why it is not surprising that, in international rankings, our attitude towards business is rated as high as far as entrepreneurial spirit is concerned (see Figure 6.5).

The second reason that makes us inclined to think about the Anglo-Saxon model positively is the evidence that countries whose economy is based on Anglo-Saxon foundations perform better than others over the longer term. The data presented in Table 6.3 illustrate clearly that the major macroeconomic indicators – such as GDP growth rates, unemployment, employment growth, the level of productivity growth – are far superior in countries using the Anglo-Saxon model than in most of the remaining countries that prefer other socio-economic models.

What is more, the Anglo-Saxon countries have relatively greater worker-forces willing to work longer hours, and this helps to achieve a higher per capita income. In addition, one should stress that the unemployed in Anglo-Saxon model countries stay unemployed for a shorter time and find new jobs within weeks rather than months. See the data in Table 6.4 to compare the situation in this respect between the countries in question.

Table 6.3 Major economic indicators of selected OECD and EU countries in 1997–2006

Country	Average real GDP growth rate 1997–2005	Real GDP growth rate 2006	Labour productivity per person employed* 1997–2005	Labour productivity per person employed* 2006	Unemployment rate 1997–2005	Unemployment rate 2006
Continental model						
France	2.3	2.0	121.1	120.7	9.8	9.5
Germany	1.3	2.8	102.8	101.9	8.5	8.4
Italy	1.4	1.9	116.6	105.5	9.5	6.8
Scandinavian model						
Denmark	2.0	3.1	103.1	104.4	4.9	3.9
Finland	3.6	5.5	109.1	107.4	9.8	7.7
Sweden	3.0	4.2	104.6	106.1	6.6	7.1
Anglo-Saxon model						
Ireland	7.4	6.0	124.6	128.3	5.5	4.4
United Kingdom	2.9	2.8	105.9	106.3	5.4	5.3
Anglo-Saxon model overseas						
USA	3.2	3.3	132.9	134	5.0	4.6

New EU member states (8 post communists countries)

Czech Republik	2.4	6.1	60.5	67.9	7.9[a]	7.1
Estonia	7.6	10.5	45.8	60.6	10.4	5.9
Hungary	4.5	3.9	64.8	72.1	6.8	7.5
Latvia	7.1	11.9	39.5	50.9	12.1[a]	6.8
Lithuania	6.4	7.5	44.5	56.5	13.2[a]	5.6
Poland	**4.0**	**6.1**	**53.8**	**59.2**	**16.1**	**13.8**
Slovakia	3.7	8.3	56.6	67.8	17.2[a]	13.4
Slovenia	3.9	5.2	71.8	80.4	6.7	6.0

Notes: *GDP in Purchasing Power Standards per person employed relative to EU-25 = 100; [a]average of 1998–2005.
Source: Own calculations based on Eurostat (2007)

Table 6.4 Wages, labour costs and long-term unemployment levels in selected OECD and EU countries, 1997–2006

Country	Minimum wage/Euro per month/* 2003	Minimum wage/Euro per month/* 2006	Hourly labour cost/in Euro/ 1997–2004	Hourly labour cost/in Euro/ 2005	Long-term unemployment rate/total as % of total active population/ 1997–2005	Long-term unemployment rate/total as % of total active population/ 2006
Continental model						
France	1154.0	1218.0	25.38	29.29	3.8	4.0
Germany	x	x	24.52	26.43	4.4	4.7
Italy	x	x	19.52	x	5.6	3.4
Scandinavian model						
Denmark	x	x	27.39	x	1.1	0.8
Finland	x	x	22.71	26.39	2.9	1.9
Sweden	x	x	26.91[a]	x	1.6	1.1
Anglo-Saxon model						
Ireland	1073.0	1293.0	x	x	2.3	1.4
United Kingdom	1106.0	1269.0	22.43	24.47	1.4	1.2
Anglo-Saxon model overseas						
USA	877.0	753.2	x	x	0.5	0.5

New EU member states (8 post communists countries)

Czech Republic	199.0	261.3	4.35	6.63	3.7[b]	3.9
Estonia	138.0	191.7	3.14	4.67	5.0[b]	2.8
Hungary	212.0	247.0	4.07	6.14	3.2	3.4
Latvia	116.0	129.2	2.12	2.77	6.2[b]	2.5
Lithuania	125.0	159.3	2.55	3.56	6.7[b]	2.5
Poland	**201.0**	**233.5**	**4.56**	**5.55**	**8.3**	**7.8**
Slovakia	133.0	183.2	3.33	4.80	10.4[b]	10.2
Slovenia	451.0	511.9	9.32	10.76	– 3.5	2.9

Notes: *Gross amounts (before the deduction of income tax and social security contributions); [a] average of 1997–2003; [b] average of 1998–2005; x - no data available.

Source: Own calculations based on Eurostat (2007)

This all stems from more flexible labour markets in countries following the Anglo-Saxon model and less government interference in wage level regulations, a smaller role for trade unions and lower social assistance transfers when people stay unemployed generally. This is confirmed by the data collected and analyzed by Aiginger (2005), as well as by Aiginger and Gruber (2005) and many others who have discriminated data performance of various economic models.

Other reasons or possible causes of the big differences in economic performance relate to other features of economic policy, such as tax policy, character and scale of the social programmes, the role of trade unions, the educational system, or even direct or indirect but decisive government involvement in running business, at least in part of the economy. Tax level differences and tax wedge differences are shown in Tables 6.5 and 6.6.

Table 6.5   Total tax receipts as a percentage of GDP in selected OECD and EU countries, 1996 and 2004

Country	Total tax receipts as % of GDP in 1996	Total tax receipts as % of GDP in 2004
Continental model		
France	44.1	43.4
Germany	36.5	34.7
Italy	41.8	41.1
Scandinavian model		
Denmark	49.2	48.8
Finland	46.9	44.2
Sweden	50.0	50.4
Anglo-Saxon model		
Ireland	32.4	30.1
United Kingdom	34.6	36.0
Anglo-Saxon model overseas		
Australia	29.4	31.2
Canada	35.9	33.5
New Zealand	34.8	35.6
USA	28.3	25.5
New EU member states (3 post communists countries)		
Czech Republik	36.5	38.4
Hungary	40.4	38.1
Poland	36.8	**34.4**
EU-15 average	40.2	39.7
EU/USA	1.4	1.6
OECD average	35.7	35.9

Source: OECD (2007)

Table 6.6 Comparison on total tax wedge (as a percentage of labour costs)[1]

Country	Total tax wedge 2005	Annual change 2005/04 (in percentage points)			
		Tax wedge	Income tax	Employee SSC	Employer SSC
Continental model					
France	50.05	0.21	0.12	−0.02	0.11
Germany	51.77	−1.50	−1.50	0.00	0.00
Italy	45.40	0.00	0.00	0.00	0.00
Scandinavian model					
Denmark	41.35	0.09	0.16	−0.04	−0.02
Finland	44.60	0.10	−0.09	0.19	0.00
Sweden	47.93	−0.45	−0.31	0.00	−0.14
Anglo-Saxon model					
Ireland	25.72	−0.44	−0.47	0.04	0.00
United Kingdom	33.52	0.15	0.08	0.03	0.04
Anglo-Saxon model overseas					
USA	29.11	−0.02	−0.01	−0.01	−0.01
New EU member states (3 post communist countries)					
Czech Republic	43.79	0.26	0.26	0.00	0.00
Hungary	50.54	−1.24	−1.11	0.02	−0.15
Poland	43.56	0.23	0.06	0.17	0.00
EU-15 average	42.07	−0.07	−0.09	0.00	0.02
OECD average	37.28	−0.14	−0.02	0.04	−0.16

Source: OECD (2006)

As we can see, the faster economic growth in countries using the Anglo-Saxon model over the last ten years or so and their superiority in productivity trends (see Table 6.3) must somehow be correlated with more flexible markets and lower taxes. Higher taxes inhibit entrepreneurship; employers are discouraged from hiring if taxes are high and if the employer contribution to social programmes is high. The best illustration is the tax wedge problem with which many countries have been struggling. Table 6.7 provides the relevant information.

Again, most countries with a lower tax wedge use the Anglo-Saxon model and, as indicated earlier, they grew more rapidly over the last 10–15 years, exhibiting equal or better productivity rates, creating more jobs and reaching lower levels of unemployment, not to mention its better structure. Given the present dangerous demographic trends, these data are very telling. The same could be said about Anglo-Saxon countries' superiority with respect to innovation or tertiary education. But we are not going to multiply these proofs of the Anglo-Saxon model's superiority with respect to economic performance and ability to secure relatively better prospects for aging populations. The main aim of this chapter is to indicate clearly that Poland, and certain other countries of Eastern and Central Europe who joined the EU, cannot be satisfied with their relatively good growth rates at the moment, and should not be satisfied with the opportunities created by their EU membership. Especially since many, if not most, of the EU countries, and the EU itself, advocate the Lisbon Strategy or the Scandinavian model, which does not guarantee good long-term prospects. Poland should look for different, far-reaching solutions that can be found predominantly in the Anglo-Saxon model. This is a conclusion that we should have arrived at when analyzing the data provided by international experience.

Conclusion

No doubt Poland has performed well over the last 18 years of transformation, both in relation to other post-communist countries and in comparison with the EU average. At the outset of systemic transformation in 1989, Poland's GDP per capita in terms of purchasing power parity amounted to 38 per cent of the EU average. In 2006, Poland's GDP per capita in PPP terms stood at 46.3 per cent of it. EU membership helps to help to accelerate the catching up process. This year (that is, in 2007), we are going to have over 6.5 per cent GDP growth. But the easy utilization of the growth and productivity factors stemming from the systemic transformation and EU membership might not suffice to secure permanent long-term growth and structural adjustment. Poland should restructure its economic policy and also encourage the EU to consider the intelligent implementation of the Anglo-Saxon model, or selected elements of it. Both the character of the Polish people as well as statistical evidence seem to suggest strongly that choosing the Anglo-Saxon model would benefit Poland's ambition to catch up with the Western world and to prosper.

References

Adam Smith Research Centre (2004) Raport Otwarcia 2005/2006, Adam Smith Research Centre, Warsaw.

Aiginger, K. and Guger, A. (2005) 'The European Social Model: From an Alleged Barrier to a Competitive Advantage', *Journal of Progressive Politics*, 4.3, Autumn, 40–7.

Aiginger, K. (2005) *Towards a New European Model of the Reformed Welfare State: An Alternative to the United States Model, Economic Survey of Europe*, 1, 2005 (New York/ Geneva: United Nations).

Bieńkowski, W. (2005) *Instytucje jako czynnik konkurencyjności krajów postkomunistycznych. Kilka uwag ogólnych dotyczących Europy Środkowo-wschodniej* (Warsaw: Kolegium Gospodarki Światowej Szkoła Główna Handlowa).

Bieńkowski, W. (2002) 'Completion of Systemic Transformation as the Condition for Further Economic Cooperation of the Post-Communist Countries', *Eastern European Economics*, M.E. Sharpe, Inc., USA, 2.

Bieńkowski, W., Brada, J.C. and Radło, M.J. (2006) *Reaganomics Goes Global. What Can the EU, Russia and Other Transition Countries Learn from the USA?* (Basingstoke and New York: Palgrave Macmillan).

Dialog Pismo Dialogu Społecznego (2007) Centrum Partnerstwa Społecznego 'Dialog', 2/2007 (15) (Warsaw: Czerwiec).

EBRD (2006) *EBRD Transition Report 2006* (London: EBRD).

Hockuba, Z. (ed.) (2007) *Gospodarka Polski Prognozy i Opinie*, Instytut Nauk Ekonomicznych Polskiej Akademii Nauk, Warsaw, May.

Eurostat (2007)

Kok, W. (2004) *Facing the Challenge: The Lisbon Strategy for Growth and Employment*, Report from the High Level Group, November, Office for Official Publications of the European Communities.

New Europe. Report on Transformation (2006) XVI Economic Forum, Krynica, Poland, 6–9 September.

OECD (2006) *Taxing Wages 2004–2005* (Paris: OECD).

OECD (2007) Source: OECD Statistical Databases, Online OECD Databases: http://www.sourceoecd.org/.

Phelps, E.S. (2006) 'The Justice of Inclusive Free Enterprise: Aristotle, Hayek, Tocqueville and Rawls', Lecture at the Honoris Causa Ceremony, Institut d'Etudes Politiques de Paris, Paris, 22 June 2006.

Poland 2005 Survey (2005) World Bank Enterprise Surveys, Washington D.C. 2007.

Poland. Competitiveness Report 2007. The role of FDY (2007) World Economy Research Institute, Warsaw School of Economics, Warsaw.

Policy and Research Department Transparency International (2007) *Report on the Transparency International Global Corruption Barometer 2007*, 6 December, Berlin.

Salvia, G.C. and Alberro, H. (2007) *Democracy, Markets and Transparency 2007*, Centro Para la Apertura y el Desarrollo de America Latina, November.

Schenk, K.-E. (2003) *Economic Institutions and Complexity, Structures, Interactions and Emergent Properties* (Cheltenham, UK/Northampton, MA: Edward Elgar).

Weresa M. (2007) *Poland. Competitiveness Report 2007. The role of FDI* (2007) World Economy Research Institute, Warsaw School of Economics, Warsaw.

World Bank (2005) *Poland 2005 Survey*, World Bank Enterprise Surveys, Washington. http://www.enterprisesurveys.org/documents/EnterpriseSurveys/Reports/Poland-2005.pdf

World Bank (2007) *Doing Business 2007. How to Reform* (Washington, DC: World Bank and International Finance Corporation).

Part II

Economic Growth and Security in Comparative Perspective

7
New Challenges for the European Model and How to Cope with It

Karl Aiginger[1]

Introduction

Disappointing growth in Europe since the beginnings of the 1990s and persistently high unemployment raised the question as to whether it was the specific features of the European social model that stopped Europe catching up with the US. This chapter defines the characteristics of the European socio-economic model and the differences between sub-models in different European countries (following Aiginger and Guger, 2006a; 2006b). It then identifies which policy changes and strategies made these countries more successful over the past 10–15 years, after several crises in the 1970s and 1980s, and even the first years of the 1990s. Specifically, we look for indicators on adaptability that might explain why these economies were so successful during the period of accelerated globalization.

The chapter is structured as follows: the next section defines the European socio-economic model and its variants. Then we compare the performance of the model types in the long and in the short run. We go on to delineate the strategy of the successful European countries, carving out five elements of change in economic policy since the nineties. Next, we analyze the ability of the Scandinavian countries to adapt to changes and possible reform blocs in the continental countries. The closing section to the chapter summarizes our argument.

The European model: its variants and performance

The European countries share some common characteristics. We define the European socio-economic model pragmatically in terms of

159

responsibility, regulation and redistribution (see also Aiginger and Guger 2006a; 2006b):

Responsibility   A rather broad responsibility of society exists for the welfare of individuals, sheltering them against poverty, and providing support in case of illness, disability, unemployment and old age; society actively promotes and often provides education and health. It supports families either through transfers or by the provision of care and housing facilities.

Regulation   Labour relations are institutionalized; they are based on social dialogue, labour laws and collective agreements. Business relations are somewhat regulated and are partly shaped by social partners on the branch and firm levels. Administrative and economic regulation for product markets exists. Business start-ups depend on permits and partly on qualification of owners or managers.

Redistribution   Transfers, financial support and social services are open to all groups; differences in incomes are limited by redistributive financial transfers, income taxation and taxes on property and bequests.

Thus, the European model is more than just a social model in the narrow sense. Indeed, it also influences production, employment and productivity and, thus, growth and competitiveness and all other objectives of economic policy. Furthermore, the European model influences social relationships, cultural institutions and behaviour, learning, and the creation and diffusion of knowledge. Finally, and this is specifically relevant to this chapter, it defines the ability to cope with external shocks and changes such as globalization. We therefore prefer to speak about a European socio-economic model rather than merely a social model.

As important as the common elements, are the differences across countries. It is standard practice to distinguish between the Scandinavian model, and the Continental model (also known as the 'corporatist model' and sometimes as the 'Rhineland model'), and the Anglo-Saxon (or 'liberal') model applicable to countries with less market interference, low transfers, but targeted assistance to poor people. We furthermore ascribe the name 'Mediterranean model' to the southern European countries, in which a still low level of expenditures is combined with existing family networks. A fifth model, as yet not elaborated, might emerge in the future, consisting of the new member countries. In these countries, some social institutions have been founded but only after transition; they are short of the financial means for a comprehensive welfare system and they are determined to catch up with the old member countries and have been very successful in this respect over the past ten years. We will therefore call this fifth model the 'catching-up model'. Outside Europe, the US model has lower levels of social expenditures and low regulation, thus sharing characteristics with the liberal model in Europe. We therefore group Canada, Australia and New Zealand into the Anglo-Saxon 'overseas model'. Japan, as well as the other industrialized Asian economies, remains outside this discussion.

The Scandinavian model is the most comprehensive, with a high degree of emphasis on redistribution; social benefits are financed by taxes. This model relies on institutions working closely together with the government. Trade unions are strongly involved in the administration of unemployment insurance and training, and the model is characterized by an active labour market policy and high employment rates. The continental model emphasizes employment and wages as the basis of social transfers. Transfers are financed through the contributions of employers and employees. Social partners play an important role in industrial relations, and wage bargaining is centralized. Redistribution and the inclusion of outsiders are not high on the agenda. The Anglo-Saxon model emphasizes the responsibility of individuals for themselves, its labour market is not regulated; and its competition policy is rather ambitious. Social transfers are smaller than in the other models, more targeted and means tested. Labour relations are decentralized, and bargaining takes place primarily at the firm level. In the Mediterranean countries, social transfers are small; families still play a significant role in the provision of security and shelter. Trade unions and employer representatives are important to the somewhat centralized bargaining process for wages and work conditions. Employment rates, specifically those of women, are low.

The Scandinavian model is practised in five countries, including the three countries with the best overall performance over the past 15 years: Denmark, Finland and Sweden. These are called the top three countries in Aiginger (2005a) and the model is also employed in Norway and the Netherlands. The inclusion of the Netherlands in this group is the most contentious choice, because the Dutch model is less ambitious, redistributes less and places less emphasis on gender equality, at least until the 1990s.[2] We pool five countries in the continental model, France, Germany and Italy, which are the three big continental countries, plus Belgium and Austria, two high-growth countries with top positions in per capita GDP.[3] It is striking that the social model typology groups Germany and France together. When analyzed in terms of intervention (high in France, low in Germany), the mode of industrial policy (sectoral in France, horizontal in Germany), or the importance of nationalization and competition policy (with France favouring nationalized champions, while in Germany competition policy is similar to a holy grail), these two

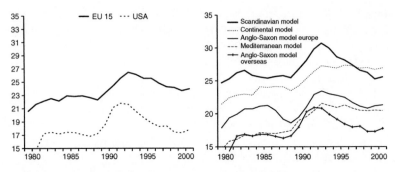

Figure 7.1   Social expenditures as a percentage of GDP
As to sub-aggregates and EU-15 weighted average over countries.
Source: OECD

countries would be ascribed to different policy approaches. However, the literature is unanimous when it comes to the inclusion of France and Germany in the same group of social model. There is a certain amount of disagreement as to whether Italy fits better into this group or into the Mediterranean group. Since we have placed Italy in the continental group, the Mediterranean model comprises Spain, Portugal and Greece. The Anglo-Saxon model is championed in Europe by the United Kingdom. As far as the low degree of regulation and the social system are concerned, Ireland exhibits a certain degree of similarity to the United Kingdom, but policy interventions have been intense, as is typical of a country in course of catching-up. High shares of inward FDI, low taxes for business, and a regional policy supporting small and medium sized firms are among the main examples of such intervention. In Europe, these strategies are now the paradigm for catching-up economies. Outside of Europe, we group Canada, the US, New Zealand and Australia together, under the heading Anglo-Saxon model overseas. Table 7.1 summarizes the performance of the different models.

Surprising similarity in the long run and even more surprising differences in the short run

Looking at economic performance, in the long run there are surprisingly small differences between the European sub-models and no difference in economic growth between the US and the EU-15. If anything, the Mediterranean countries did achieve a slightly higher growth, which is interpreted as a catching-up process, and the European Anglo-Saxon countries suffered from the policies first of 'old Labour' and then of 'the Iron Lady',

Table 7.1 Performance: short- and long-run growth of GDP

	1960/ 1990	1990/ 2005	Unemploy- ment rate		Employment rate	
	Annual growth in %		1990	2005	1990	2005
Scandinavian model	**3.3**	**2.3**	**4.7**	**5.6**	**73.3**	**74.2**
Denmark	2.7	2.2	7.2	4.6	76.4	77.2
Finland	3.9	2.0	3.2	8.4	73.9	68.6
Netherlands	3.4	2.2	5.8	5.1	64.9	73.6
Sweden	2.9	2.0	1.7	6.8	83.0	73.7
Norway	3.9	3.2	5.2	4.0	74.8	77.7
Continental model	**3.5**	**1.7**	**7.3**	**8.9**	**64.1**	**66.2**
Germany	3.2	1.7	6.2	9.5	69.6	70.0
France	3.8	1.9	8.5	9.6	61.2	63.8
Italy	3.9	1.3	8.9	7.7	57.4	62.0
Belgium	3.4	1.9	6.6	8.0	58.3	61.8
Austria	3.5	2.2	3.1	5.2	74.6	74.8
Anglo-Saxon model Europe	**2.6**	**2.7**	**7.3**	**4.6**	**70.7**	**71.9**
Irland	4.1	6.5	13.4	4.3	54.6	68.6
United Kingdom	2.5	2.4	6.9	4.6	71.8	72.1
Mediterrean model	**4.6**	**2.8**	**11.0**	**9.1**	**55.7**	**63.6**
Greece	4.5	3.0	6.4	10.4	54.7	55.0
Portugal	4.8	2.1	4.8	7.4	70.0	70.5
Spain	4.6	2.9	13.1	9.2	53.2	64.1
Anglo-Saxon model Overseas	**3.6**	**3.1**	**5.7**	**5.2**	**72.0**	**72.9**
USA	3.5	3.1	5.5	5.1	72.3	72.9
Canada	4.0	2.8	8.1	6.8	71.2	74.1
Australia	3.8	3.5	7.0	5.2	69.2	72.1
New Zealand	2.4	3.2	7.8	4.0	53.7	59.6
EU 15	**3.4**	**2.0**	**7.5**	**7.9**	**64.5**	**67.2**
Japan	6.1	1.3	2.1	4.5	74.8	77.2
Catching-up model	**.**	**2.5**	**.**	**7.5**	**.**	**61.2**
Czech Republic	.	1.3	.	7.9	.	65.4
Hungary	.	3.9	.	7.0	.	56.2
EU 15/USA	0.96	0.65	1.36	1.55	0.89	0.92

Source: Eurostat (AMECO) – as to sub-aggregates weighted average over countries – EU-15 reported.

Margaret Thatcher. The interesting divide occurred since the 1990s, whether measured from 1990 to 2005 or from 1995 to 2005. Europe's growth trails that of the US and, more surprisingly and with a greater difference, that of the continental countries, France, Germany and Italy lag the most. In contrast, the Scandinavian countries reached an average growth of 2.6 per cent and the Anglo-Saxon countries in Europe enjoyed a growth very near that of the US. The greatest surprise in our view is the recovery of the Scandinavian model. This is the most comprehensive social model, with the largest share of taxes and government in GDP. This destroys the usual foregone conclusion that Europe's growth problem has its origins in the high cost of its social system.[4]

If we extend the performance evaluation to other indicators than economic growth, the difference becomes even greater. Unemployment is much lower, the employment rate higher in the Scandinavian model, specifically if compared with the Continental model. The fiscal balance shows a surplus in the Scandinavian countries, while the continental countries and the Anglo-Saxon model in Europe, as well as in the US, run deficits.

Carving out five strategy elements

If we look at the economic policy of the successful Scandinavian countries over the past 10–15 years, their strategy rests on five pillars. The strategies tried, in general, to maintain core elements of the existing socio-economic model but also to make firms, individuals and institutions better able to cope with changes in the economic environment.

Pillar 1: managed and balanced flexibility

Many economists stress the importance of flexibility for firms. Firms that can hire and fire can adjust production to demand. Reducing regulation, and specifically labour regulation, is high on the agenda of many liberal or neo-liberal economic think tanks. But it is not this notion of flexibility that has been pushed recently in the Scandinavian countries. Flexibility of firms is supplemented, and even enabled, by security for the individual person; those who lose their job are either offered new ones or a training programme. Replacement ratios, unemployment benefit in relation to wages, are high, specifically for low-income earners. Part-time work and temporary contracts are somewhat common and connected with social benefits and individual choices. The share of male employees on flexible contracts is much greater than in continental countries. Reduction of work time is often voluntary and reversible, and adjusted to personal choices. Thus, it is flexibility for firms and persons, embedded in a

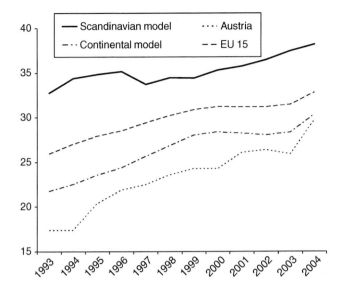

Figure 7.2 Flexible contracts: share of part-time plus fixed-term contracts

system of security, upgrading of skills, and choice and gender equality that characterizes the model. The decision about the specific work time and income depends not only on the needs of the market, but also on the preferences of individuals. Government interferes a little in the rules, and guarantees the balance between firms and employees. This new type of flexibility, different from the liberal notion of hiring and firing out of a large pool of low-qualified labour, is sometimes called flexicurity. I prefer to call it 'managed and balanced flexibility'.

Pillar 2: work pays and training is an obligation

Economies, especially those under the stress of rapid change, offer jobs with different wages, and individuals have different capabilities. Government tries to limit income differences by offering either subsidies or tax credits to those earning low wages. Under such a policy, it is always better to work than to rely on subsistence payments. Wages are held high in the short run by tax credits or subsidies, and people in this situation are trained on the job and off the job. The tax wedge is low, increasing the incentive to work for the employee and to hire for firms. Despite the higher taxes in general, tax wedges in the Scandinavian countries are now lower than in the continental economies.

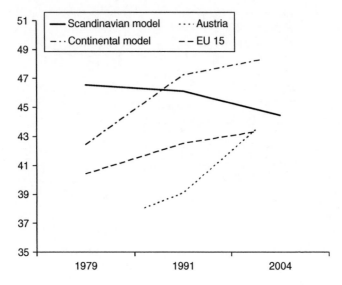

Figure 7.3   Tax wedge: difference between gross and net wages
Pillar 3: fiscal prudence plus quality of government

Business taxes are relatively low, while wealth and energy is taxed in the Nordic countries. Mobility in retraining is an obligation, encouraged not only by financial instruments, but also by the pressure of efficient labour market institutions and trust.

Pillar 3: fiscal prudence plus quality of government

The Scandinavian countries were known in the 1970s and 1980s for their permissive fiscal policy, suffering one unsuccessful fiscal consolidation after the other. Since the mid-1990s, they target the achievement of fiscal surpluses, mainly by capping expenditures. They now all have fiscal surpluses, a success reinvigorated by accelerating economic growth. Within the budget, the priority of future investment and new activities is evident. The quality of budgets is important, in the sense of boosting growth stimulating expenditures. Public sector management has been installed, schools are efficient and quality is monitored.

Pillar 4: investment for the future

The Scandinavian countries increased their investment into research, education, lifelong learning and modern technologies such as ICT and biotechnology. The difference in the rate of future investment in GDP, which

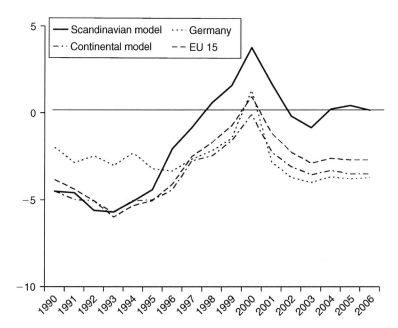

Figure 7.4 Budget surplus/deficit
Pillar 4: investment for the future

had been about two percentage points at the beginning of the 1990s, widened despite the severe crises in 1993. Now, these investments into the future are higher relative to GDP than in the US. Sweden, Finland and Denmark are leading in most rankings for innovation or education systems, as well as for the information society. These expenditures are also targeted in the Lisbon Strategy, but without much success in other countries.

Pillar 5: consistent long-run strategy

The Scandinavian countries follow a systematic four-part approach economic policy-making. The trade unions, employers' organizations, economic experts and government share the strategy for change. The strategy is continued even if the political party in power changes. Long-run strategies are followed; they are not only discussed but also implemented not on one level of government only but on all levels, and also in schools and organizations. The societies are inclusive, specifically supporting the poor, including immigrants. Income differences are limited. People trust society and the government, and changes are interpreted as new opportunities, not as imminent danger.[5]

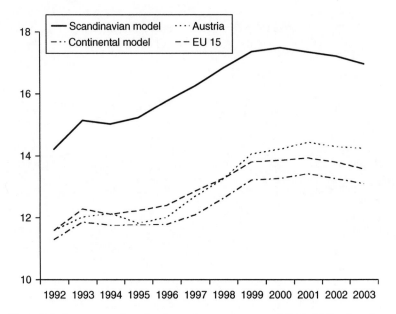

Figure 7.5   Investment into the future (as a percentage of GDP: R&D, education, ICT expenditures)
Pillar 5: consistent long-run strategy

The ability to change and the role of institutions

Why have the continental economies been unable to cope with change despite having a lower tax burden and lower wages, at least for the low-skilled sector? There is no definite answer, but I will venture five hypotheses.

The continental countries underestimated the need for change. This might have been the case for the large countries (Germany, France and Italy), since export ratios are rather low in large countries and the countries are home to sizeable, successful firms producing for the world markets. These countries had experienced no big crisis in the 1990s, and they all enjoyed modest growth. The countries were further distracted by certain experiments and shocks, such as radical privatization and the reduction in working hours in France, unification of very different economies under the pressure of a single currency in Germany, or regional conflicts and political turmoil in Italy. The big continental economies furthermore had the 'middle of the road' problem: since taxes were not excessively high, social expenditures not excessive, and research and

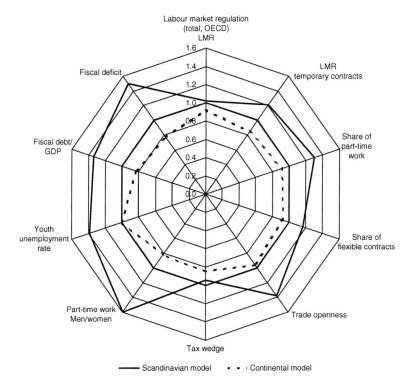

Figure 7.6 Adaptivity profiles: Scandinavia versus Continental Europe
Notes: Data refer to 2003, 2004 or 2005; values outside the unit circle delineate less regulation, more flexible contracts, lower tax wedge and lower unemployment, lower deficits and debts (relative to the average of EU-15).

education expenditures not really low, the countries thought they could go on without policy change and without careful monitoring of the quality and efficiency of institutions. Deregulation was low on the agenda despite the fact that the labour markets in all countries and product markets in France and Italy were rather strictly regulated. Investment in the future did not increase; neither did expenditure on research or on education. The Scandinavian countries realized that they could finance their, marginally trimmed, welfare model only if they excelled in future investment and generated higher economic growth.

The continental countries did not pay attention to the problem that their institutions were less comprehensive, specifically favouring insiders. The Scandinavian countries have more inclusive institutions and maintained this approach in the 1990s: they always had a high union density

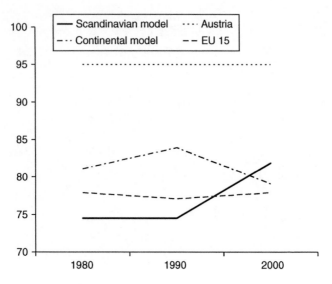

Figure 7.7   Collective bargaining coverage

and succeeded in keeping it high despite booming flexible contracts (part-time plus fixed-term) as well as increasing the coverage of collective agreements. This inclusiveness allowed the reduction of regulation specifically for irregular contracts, since people felt sheltered by minimum wages, social assistance with high replacement ratios specifically for the lowest-wage sector, and trust.

The economic role of government and experts is greater in Scandinavian countries, complementary to the influence of social partners. Trade union density is one of the best-documented indicators of the importance of institutions in general, and of social partners in particular. It declined from 50 per cent in 1980 to 39 per cent in 2000 in the EU-15. This average figure hides the fact that it is plunging from 36 per cent to 25 per cent in the continental countries, while being the highest and decreasing only from 59 per cent (1980) to 54 per cent (2000) in the Scandinavian countries. Also, the figure was higher in 2000 in the Scandinavian countries than in 1970. On the level of individual countries, there is a modest positive correlation between trade union density and economic performance (Aiginger 2007). This cooperation between government and social partners is often called tripartite decision-making, in contrast to two-partite if only employers and employees cooperate. We prefer to call the system four-partite decision-making because the experts are a fourth constituent group. Consistent, consensual

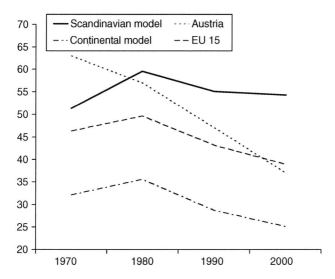

Figure 7.8 Trade union density

decision-making, with two groups focusing on special interests and two agents on more general interests, allows a quick response to changes in the economic environment. Two-partite systems sometimes favour special interests and rents, be it rents of oligopolistic firms or of existing employees in large sheltered firms. We use the term 'sometimes' since there are examples in which social partners are pursuing the general economic interest on their own, such as integration into the EU or fostering technological change in the printing industry in Austria, and others in which they serve more special interests.

The development of institutions was, in general, not smooth in most countries. There had been some pacts and partnerships brokered with and without government, such as the Waasenar Agreement and the Haarlem Agreement in the Netherlands and the National Mediation Commission (Rehnberg Commission) in Sweden. Less successful examples in the same vein might have been the Alliances for Jobs for Germany, Italy and Spain. Complementary institutions were created, such as the Socio-Economic Council in the Netherlands, and the National Economic and Social Forum in Ireland. Existing institutions such as TEKES in Finland were complemented with institutions focusing on smaller firms or regional activities. There were periods of conflict, such as the demise of intersectoral wage negotiation, the opting out of employer's organization, breakdown of bilateral negotiations and so on. Alternative trade unions were founded to cover new employment contracts, and conflicts between big firms and SMEs in employers' organizations came up. This all means that external shocks led to conflicts in existing institutions, and the economies and the social system had to adapt.

How could it be the case that strong, inclusive institutions could be good for performance? The role of institutions in a world of globalization and technological change has to change from defending the self-interest of insiders to providing solutions for outsiders and those disadvantaged by rapid change, thus leading to growth, employment and competitiveness. Or, to state it in more economic language: institutions change from preserving rents to creating positive externalities. Modern institutions encourage new abilities and qualifications, and are shaping and balancing flexibility rules. Strong, inclusive institutions will be better able to internalize positive externalities and to manage flexible contracts than weak decentralized institutions, which can only protect the small and decreasing members.

Summary

Are there lessons to be drawn from this analysis for European countries in general and the new members of the European Union? The European model is no barrier to competitiveness, if it is reformed in the direction of fostering change and growth, and improving incentives and qualifications. This is demonstrated by the Scandinavian countries, which now combine – after several crises, devaluations, and unsuccessful fiscal consolidations – rapid growth, full employment and fiscal prudence with a comprehensive welfare system and a high priority for ecological concerns and fairness.

The successful countries had to undergo substantial changes to be able to adapt their specific version of the European socio-economic model to the challenges of globalization. The reform strategy rested on five pillars: managed and balanced flexibility, making work pay and training as an obligation, fiscal consolidation plus quality of government, fostering investment into the future, and following a consistent long-run strategy embedded in trust and strong institutions.

As far as institutions were concerned, the Scandinavian countries always had more inclusive institutions and fewer insider–outsider problems. They managed to maintain and exploit this property: the coverage of collective agreements is increasing, trade union membership is stable, both in contrast with continental economies. The inclusiveness of institutions and the trust in society enabled these countries to deregulate contracts and to make use of part-time work and fixed-term contracts without increasing poverty and exclusion. Four-partite decision-making seems to be more open for radical change, than two-partite policy-making, since at least two partners – government and experts – will represent general interests. And the strong position of firm representatives and trade unions enables the countries to cope with the burden of change and with the reintegration of losers. The burden of change is acceptable if it is derived from a positive vision and if the burden is distributed in a fair way. Complex reforms – such as increasing flexibility and security at the same time – are feasible in trusting societies. Strong and inclusive institutions will mitigate the pressure from specific interests, thus preventing Olson's petrification hypothesis. In the ideal situation, they will help to foster externalities such as innovation, education and lifelong learning, thus making the economies more competitive.

Drawing conclusions from countries with a market-oriented welfare state is dangerous because the new EU member countries had experienced a planned economy with a very different role of government only 15 years ago. It is even more difficult if we acknowledge the differences between the socio-economic models within 'old' Europe.

But there are some hints about what may be important for the catching-up model:

- Institutions should be inclusive, preventing a dichotomy between outsiders and insiders
- No specific positions in existing firms or industries should be guaranteed, but mobility, upgrading skills and finding new jobs should be encouraged
- Part-time jobs, learning on the job, transition jobs between education and permanent job, sabbaticals and part time exits should be encouraged. Part-time work, entry and exit should be a choice and the jobs should be connected with social benefits
- Microeconomic changes and willingness to adapt to new challenges need a high and stable macroeconomic growth rate
- The role of economic policy does not decrease in periods of integration and globalization, only instruments change. Enforcing activities with a high external effect, such as innovation, education, lifelong learning and technological excellence, become first priorities
- The burden of change is not equally distributed by market forces, those less well-trained, with lower skills and the newcomers have to be assisted if they lose jobs
- A comprehensive welfare state is no barrier to change, but it needs to be complemented by a trusting society, high mobility, a challenging environment and excellence in innovation and education.

Appendix

Table 7.A1 Adaptivity indicators: Scandinavia versus Continental Europe

		Scandinavian model			Continental model			Scandinavian model – Continental model
		1990	2005	2005–1990	1990	2005	2005–1990	2005
Labour market regulation All contracts; 1990/2003	(−)	2.81	2.32	−0.49	3.11	2.58	−0.53	−0.26
Labour market regulation Regular contracts; 1990/2003	(−)	2.65	2.59	−0.07	2.30	2.38	0.08	−0.21
Labour market regulation Temporary contracts; 1990/2003	(−)	3.01	1.67	−1.34	3.92	2.40	−1.52	−0.73
Share of part–time work 1993/2004	(+)	21.77	26.20	4.44	12.50	18.32	5.81	7.89
Share of fix–term contracts 1993/2004	(+)	10.99	11.97	0.98	9.23	12.08	2.85	−0.11
Share of flexible contracts 1993/2004	(+)	32.75	38.18	5.42	21.73	30.39	8.66	7.78

FDI/GDP 1995/2004	(+)	3.17	0.89	−2.28	1.33	0.95	−0.38	−0.06
Trade openness 1990/2004	(+)	59.80	62.08	2.28	42.84	43.21	0.38	18.86
Tax wedge 1991/2004	(−)	45.35	43.25	−2.10	47.24	48.56	1.32	−5.31
Share of part-time work Men in relation to women 1993/2004	(+)	0.27	0.36	0.09	0.15	0.19	0.04	0.18
Long-term unemployment 1992/2004	(−)	1.26	1.35	0.09	3.49	4.42	0.94	−3.08
Youth unemployment 1993/2004	(−)	17.17	11.99	−5.18	16.05	16.53	0.48	−4.54
Fiscal debt in % of GDP; 1991/2004	(−)	58.44	48.22	−10.22	57.94	77.71	19.77	−29.49
Fiscal deficit/surplus in % of GDP; 1990/2005	(+)	−4.51	0.44	4.96	−4.49	−3.51	0.99	3.95

Notes: Higher values in this table indicate greater flexibility – some indicators had therefore to be invented, for example, since the original indicator on labour market regulation had increased if flexibility was lower; + = not inverted; − = inverted if the indicator is to be used as an adaptivity indicator (as in Figure 7.6).

Notes

1 The author thanks Alois Guger, Gunther Tichy and Ewald Walterskirchen for critical comments and acknowledges the research assistance of Dagmar Guttmann and Karolina Trebicka.
2 Some authors classify the Netherlands as member of the continental model group.
3 It is interesting that at least four of the six founding members of the EU belong to this group. The Netherlands is on the borderline between the Continental and the Scandinavian models, and Luxembourg is between the Continental and the Anglo-Saxon models.
4 The second surprise is that the two extreme models proved better than the intermediate Continental model. However, it is not clear whether the recovery of the Anglo-Saxon countries is permanent, or is a rebound from poor growth in the preceding decades.
5 It is interesting that some of these changes (summarised in Appendix 7.A1) are implemented in the Scandinavian model as well as in the liberal model, albeit at a different level. Wage supplements exist in both models, the same holds for stick-and-carrot strategies, and policies to balance the budget by limiting expenditures. But the greater surprise is that the Scandinavian economies are able to make their socio-economic system adapt to change despite high taxes and government regulation.

References

Aiginger, K. (2005a) *Towards a New European Model of the Reformed Welfare State: An Alternative to the United States Model, Economic Survey of Europe*, 1, 2005 (New York/ Geneva: United Nations).

Aiginger, K. (2005b) 'Labour Market Reforms and Economic Growth – The European Experience in the Nineties', *Journal of Economic Studies*, 32(6): 540–73.

Aiginger, K. (2007) 'Performance Differences in Europe: Tentative Hypotheses on the Role of Institutions', *WIFO Working Paper No 302/2007*, WIFO, Vienna. http://www.wifo.ac.at/wwa/servlet/wwa.upload.DownloadServlet/bdoc/WP_ 2007_302$.PDF

Aiginger, K. and Guger, A. (2005) 'The European Social Model: From an Alleged Barrier to a Competitive Advantage', *Journal of Progressive Politics*, 4.3, Autumn, 40–47.

Aiginger, K. and Guger, A. (2006a) 'The European Socioeconomic Model: Differences to the US and Changes Over Time', in Giddens, A., Diamond, P. and Liddle, R. (eds) (2006) *Global Europe; Social Europe* (Cambridge; Malden: Polity Press).

Aiginger, K. and Guger, A. (2006b) 'The Ability to Adapt: Why It Differs between the Scandinavian and Continental Models', *Intereconomics, Review of European Economic Policy*, 41(1), January/February: 14–23.

Alesina, A., Perotti, R. and Tavares, J. (1998) 'The Political Economy of Fiscal Adjustments', Brookings Papers on Economic Activity, 197–266.

Blanchard, O. (2004) 'The Economic Future of Europe', *Journal of Economic Perspectives*, 18(4), Fall, 3–26.

Boeri, T. (2002) 'Does Europe Need a Harmonized Social Policy?', Paper prepared for the Conference on Competition of Regions and Integration in EMU, 30th Volkswirtschaftliche Tagung der ÖNB, 13–14 June 2002.

Esping-Andersen, G. (1990) *Three Worlds of Welfare Capitalism* (Cambridge: Polity).

Esping-Andersen, G., Gallie, D., Hemerijck, A. and Myles, J. (2002) *Why We Need a New Welfare State* (Oxford: Oxford University Press).

EU-Kommissionsdokument, 'The European Social Model', Manuskript, 14 July 2005.

Fitoussi, J.-P. and Kostoris Padoa Schioppa, F.K. (eds) (2005) *Report on the State of the European Union, vol.1* (Basingstoke: Palgrave Macmillan).

Guger, A. (2006) 'Die Effektivität wohlfahrtsstaatlicher Distributionspolitiken – Trends im internationalen Vergleich', in M. Held, G. Kubon-Gilke and R. Sturn (Hg.), *Normative und institutionelle Grundfragen der Ökonomik. Jahrbuch 5: Soziale Sicherung in Marktgesellschaften* (Marburg: Metropolis).

Guger, A., Marterbauer, M. and Walterskirchen, E. (2004) 'Growth Policy in the Spirit of Steindl and Kalecki', WIFO Working Papers, 240/2004.

Pisani-Ferri, J. (2005) 'Only Teamwork Can Put the Eurozone on a Steady Course', *Financial Times*, 31 August.

Sapir, A., Aghion, Ph., Bertola, G., Hellwig, M., Pisani-Ferry, J., Rosati, D., Vinals, J. and Wallace, H. (2004) *An Agenda for a Growing Europe: Sapir Report* (Oxford: Oxford University Press).

Tichy, G. (2005) 'Die 'Neue Unsicherheit' als Ursache der europäischen Wachstumsschwäche', *Perspektiven der Wirtschaftspolitik*, 6(3): 385–407.

8
Beyond Models and Regulations: Eastward Expansion versus Retrenchment in the 'New' EU?

Walter D. Connor

Introduction

The European Union's New Year 2007 admission of Romania and Bulgaria, and the several months' run-up to it, had, atmospherically and administratively, a different feel from the earlier 2004 expansion that had included eight ex-communist states. It took place in an EU whose bureaucratic confidence was badly shaken by the failure of critical 'old Europe' states to ratify the Constitution. The two Balkan countries, in a sense, represented unfinished or deferred business from 2004: not admitted at that time, as Brussels drew an implicit distinction between East Central Europe and the Balkans, which were given a 'delay' that amounted to a promise of admission in 2007, 'unless ...'. The discipline imposed on their further clean-up prior to entry was not all that onerous. In 2005 and 2006, warnings about corruption and flawed justice systems, surprisingly more focused on Bulgarian backsliding than Romanian, were issued, but these remained only warnings. There was no real opposition mobilized to their entry, but, at the end, there was no real enthusiasm in Brussels either. The principle 'better (to have them, whatever the problems) in, than out' that had guided the EU in the 2004 expansion as well, although with less agonizing, was applied again.

The general view was that, first, the two had had more to do to come up to the EU level than most of the other eight post-communist states had, from the perspective of the late 1990s and 2000. Second, that they had improved markedly after 2000, though not so as to overtake any of the class of 2004. Third, they were nonetheless admitted in January 2007 without having improved their performance or readiness to the point of reaching the average level of the eight 2004 entrants. The bar was lowered for Romania and Bulgaria in a way it had not been for eight other states in 2004 – but acknowledging the whys and wherefores was a complicated and, from certain angles, a very sensitive matter. In a bizarre but suggestive side development, it emerged at the same time that the creators of the comic film *Borat: Cultural Learnings of America for Make Benefit Glorious Nation of Kazakhstan*, depicting the adventures of a disaster-prone anti-hero from post-Soviet Asian rural depths, had found the poverty, mud and backwardness needed to characterize Borat's milieu for non-expert audiences in the residents and scenes of a village in new European Union member Romania.

The current chapter highlights some aspects of the 2007 accessions, cultural-historical as well as economic-organizational, in the context of the 2004 expansions and their implications for some future lines of EU development. It is, perhaps, a bit of an 'outlier' in the present book (and not only because its author, whose background is in political science, sociology and international relations, is outnumbered by the economists who make up the majority of the contributors), and some words on its rationale are probably in order.

This book on the whole grapples with a set of interrelated issues:

1 The 'fitness' of the models and practices of the 'old' EU market economies – the pre-2004–15, historically immensely successful in providing high living standards and security in a 'civilized' market – to
   respond to new challenges, to achieve growth rates beyond the
   modest ones of the present time, to be innovative, to show greater
   'competitiveness' in the age of globalization;
2 The prospects of, and policy issues facing, the post-communist states
   of the 'new' Europe, recently admitted to the EU the eight entering,
   along with Cyprus and Malta, in 2004, as well as Bulgaria and Romania, recently arrived. After 40-plus years in the wilderness, they
   entered upon the rigours of transition to democracy and the market
   and, after about a decade-and-a-half, found themselves in that very
   successful club whose beginning goes back 50 years to the 1957
   Treaty of Rome.

The post-communist states have joined the EU at a time when many old verities are being questioned as well as defended, when formulae and models seemingly successful in meeting the challenges of the past are found wanting for the future. A major axis of contention is growth versus security, and related formulations of the question of how much modification of the social market, the European-style welfare state and its appurtenances is feasible, permissible and politically sustainable in the pursuit of the increased measures of economic growth without which living standards and security are imperilled. There are different positions among old EU members, a major divide being reflected in the notion of Anglo-Saxon versus continental European models.

Certainly, phrasing the divide that way is by itself misleading. It understates, first, the differences between the much higher degree of state involvement in the Anglo than in the American economy, and American is implied in the formulation, especially by those who use it as criticism. Second, continental Europe is not a single model; major differences in the conduct of the welfare state's business between Nordic countries and those further south are clearly evident.

But it is choices between these two broad orientations that post-communist states have been facing, and making, for some time, and continue to make today.

The stories of the eight entrants of 2004 are diverse, but there is an historical and cultural unity among them that makes them different from Balkan Romania and Bulgaria. Accession of these two countries brings 30 million new souls into the EU, people distinguished as well by historical economic-development deficiencies and recent performance levels that have made them poorer, in both general and rather specific ways, than their fellow-sufferers of 40-plus years of the revolution from above and abroad that Soviet power imposed after 1945. The objectives of this chapter are to discuss the nature and sources of those differences, cultural/historical as much as economic; to spotlight some of the major differences in contemporary *economic* levels and performance, not only between the new Balkan members and the 'old' 15- and less old 25-member EU, but between the new members of the 2004 and 2007 vintages and those post-communist states east and south outside the EU and, however desirous of entry, for the most part unlikely to be invited but fated to be the EU's neighbours nonetheless; and finally to offer some thoughts on how the recent accession might affect the ongoing European discussion about competitiveness and readiness to respond to the challenges the twenty-first century poses.

Culture and history: boundaries and linkages

The EU-15 that reached out in 2004 to finally welcome ten new members, eight of them ex-communist states, was culturally largely homogeneous. With one exception, to be specified below, the member countries were 'Western,' marked by attributes that amount to membership in

Western civilization, as it has been generally understood. Their core religious heritage was Western Christianity in its Catholic or Protestant variants, their territories the lands over which the battles of the Reformation and Counter-Reformation were fought. It is a heritage quite distinct from that of the lands and peoples of the Europe to the east and south, lands of Eastern Orthodox Christianity and the cultures rooted in it, lands where Christianity confronted Islam, and Christian peoples were fated to fall under Moslem rule.[1]

A point worth making here is that objections to using religious heritage as a marker of civilizational difference on the basis of the ongoing secularization of Europe are largely beside the point. The West–East Christian divide is part of the reality that religion was the most critical base of civilizational/cultural differences; they flowed in one manner or another from it, and they are not easily dissolved or outgrown. That large numbers of people in the old and new EU, as well as many in the states not yet members, neither believe in their theological doctrines, nor engage, except episodically, in the observances and rituals of their traditions, is, to a large degree, still beside the point. People might no longer go to church, but it is different churches they no longer attend, and those differences still find reflection in the present.

In a general sense, we are dealing with a West that is defined, as in the traditional history books, by a recognizable Middle Ages, Renaissance, Reformation and Counter-Reformation as well as Enlightenment. The eight Central or East Central European and Baltic states admitted in 2004 represent, in a sense, the eastern and northern boundaries of lands formed by these constitutive features of Western development. They are, as EU and NATO members, recovered parts of the West. To the south and east, the historical experiences were different, and these Western developments were absent, or came only in an exceedingly attenuated form. With the accession of Romania and Bulgaria in January 2007, however, the EU added two members from the other Europe, and perforce contemplated the membership of yet more states out there beyond the West, most desirous of entering under the EU umbrella though not yet welcomed. The West – including the eight new EU members of 2004 – uses the Latin alphabet. East and south, various versions of the Greek or Cyrillic are used, Romania being an exception.

The boundary line that divides these two worlds, a bit vague, of course, in places, is more or less the boundary between the old western and eastern Roman empires, Latin Rome and Greek Byzantium, a line drawn over 1500 years ago. Different cartographers might place it differently in certain border areas and also move it about depending on whether they wish to describe historical or contemporary ethno-national demography. But generally, the line, and its historical reality, is not in question.[2]

In the north, the line separates Protestant Estonia and Latvia, and Catholic Lithuania from Orthodox Russia and Belarus, further south Catholic Poland, the ethnic Poland of the Curzon line, and the nearly ethnically homogeneous post-1944 state, not the larger Poland of 1921–39, from the Orthodox and Eastern-rite Uniate Belarussian and Ukrainian world. Further south yet, it traces the borderline of the old Austro-Hungarian Empire and the decaying Orthodox Christian frontiers of the Ottoman Empire. With the collapse of these two empires in World War I, the line ran through successor states Romania and Yugoslavia. In the former, it divided the ethnic Romanian Orthodox east and south, roughly Moldavia and Wallachia, from the Saxon and Magyar Transylvania. In the latter's 1944–91 version, the Socialist Federal Republic of Yugoslavia, the line separates Western Slovenia and Croatia from the Orthodox and Moslem lands of Bosnia-Herzegovina, Montenegro, Macedonia and Serbia. It transects the last of these, running between the northern autonomous province of Vojvodina, in the pre-1918 world part of Austria–Hungary, and Serbia proper. Over time, demographic changes have affected both of these latter divisions. By the time Yugoslavia came to its bloody end, Vojvodina's autonomy within Serbia had been abolished, but to no great public outcry. By that time, it had been quite Serbian-ized, and no longer had the large Magyar population that had earlier justified its being separately designated. Very different, obviously, was the case of Serbia's southern autonomous region, the 90 per cent ethnic-Albanian Kosovo, where Milosevic's attacks on autonomy led to consequences still palpable, and unresolved, in the diplomacy of 2007, in a further demonstration of the relevance of cultural and ethnic borders.

The delayed EU entrants of 2007, and the thus far excluded European lands further out, are, again, part of the East in the framework just laid out. Linked mechanically with the states of East Central Europe from the late 1940s to 1989 in the Soviet bloc in the Warsaw Pact and in CMEA/Comecon, organizations that took no account of these differences, they have now entered a Western club. They are more alien to the world of Brussels, London, and Paris and such than were the Poles, Czechs, Hungarians and so on who entered the EU three years earlier, and they are perceived as such.

But they are not unique. They join a member of the pre-2004 EU-15, Greece, as something other in that Western club. Greece was the only member of the EU-15 not of the Western heritage as outlined above.[3]

With Spain and Portugal, it shared a history of relative economic backwardness compared with those who signed the Treaty of Rome in 1957, and a political heritage of authoritarianism and instability. But Greece, of late an undeniable success story, whose hosting of the 2004 Olympics was, before the fact, a matter of worried national pride, carries, still, a distinct set of burdens, not irrelevant to the prospects for Romania and Bulgaria. It shares with them, and with Serbia, Montenegro, Bosnia-Herzegovina, Macedonia and so on the experience of centuries-long Ottoman and Moslem domination. This was, it is useful to remember, the fate from the thirteenth century onwards of all the Orthodox peoples save the Russians. Greece's location within this historical and geographic frame has made it, from time to time, a rather 'unhappy camper' on the grounds of the EU and NATO of which it is a member.

Aside from Greece's sensitive location in the EU's wrangling over Turkey's candidacy for membership, and its linkages to new EU member Cyprus's more recent and higher profile involvement with the same, Greek discomfort in the enterprises of EU and of NATO, the Western club to which it and Turkey have belonged for over five decades, was most evident in the Kosovo crisis of 1999. While NATO, once it mobilized to confront the disorder in its ex-Yugoslav backyard, was resolved in effect to intervene against Christian Orthodox Serbs on behalf of overwhelmingly Moslem Kosovar Albanians, Orthodox Greece was anything but happy. Serge Schmemann of the *New York Times* focused in on the core of the problem at the time: it was 'pain at the military attacks against a heroic and glorious Christian people, such as the Serbs' that the synod of the Greek Orthodox Church had vented, reminding those who needed reminding that Greece 'had always felt itself a junior member of the Western club, included for geographical, not cultural, reasons'.[4]

Indeed, Greece joined NATO along with Turkey early, in 1952. It joined the EU late, in 1981, has made a good job of its membership, but remains one of the economic back-markers among the states of the 15-member pre-2004 EU. It is the only Balkan state that did not go communist after World War II, but it nearly did. It is now much closer to stable democracy in the respectable EU mode, but it was not ever thus. Even in relatively recent times, some cracks have been visible at the core of the Greek state that go back to issues first broached in the European powers' brokering of its emergence from Ottoman domination in the first half of the nineteenth century. These are not, even with the monarchy gone, completely resolved. Even since the collapse of the colonels' regime, 1967–73, elements of fundamental division on the legitimacy of the Greek state have broken through in terrorist incidents with components of anti-Americanism not totally attributable to US backing for that 1967–73 junta. Much of this, again, surfaced in its own way during Kosovo 1999. As Robert Kaplan put it at the time, the other NATO members engaged demanded 'that Greece behave like they do because it is middle class and a member of NATO', but Greece could not, 'because it is in the Balkans and ... fated to live next door to the Serbs long after any NATO groups leave'.[5]

The Orthodox countries are different; observing this is not a matter of specifying a constituting other in order to specify what the West really is. It is not a matter of ignoring social differentiation within Orthodox societies. Nor is it a matter of ignoring the dynamic for the static, of assuming that present gaps in culture, and in economic development, practice and performance, as we will see below, are fated to persist unaltered. But they are real enough now, however gingerly referred to, and will continue to distinguish the states concerned for some time.

In a *Financial Times* opinion page, arguing against Turkish EU membership, Frits Bolkestein, a former European Commission member, noted that its history, while 'marvellous', was:

> not a European history. Europe is marked by the great developments of its past: Christianity, Renaissance, Enlightenment, democracy, industrialisation. Turkey does not fit in that mould.[6]

But, except for Christianity in its Eastern version, the same reservations in a sense have applied to Greece as well, and to Bulgaria and Romania, and other states, EU candidates or not, on the eastern side of the line discussed earlier. This is a matter of a very tangled history, including the impact of centuries of Ottoman Turkish rule of the Balkans, and the imprint of their civilization on the Christian Serbs, Romanians, Bulgarians and so on, as well as the Greeks. To some degree, the Christian Balkan east is different because of this impact of an Ottoman imperial state, the predecessor to the Turkey of today, against whose admission to the EU many counsel, because of its differences.

Bringing home the lost: the 2004 expansion

The 2004 EU expansion was quite different, both in the processes among the 15 and the eight post-communist would-be entrants. Shortly after the end of communism, Poland, Hungary and the then Czechoslovakia constituted themselves the Visegrad group, and signalled their desire to enter both NATO and the EU. They did this in a manner that explicitly reminded and informed Western capitals that this was 'like calling out to like', that the 'kidnapped West' made part of the Soviet external empire in 1944–89, wanted in, wanted acceptance, and was entitled to join these Western clubs.

This was an important enterprise, wherein the national interests of the three, soon to be four, states were at stake. The same was true of the separate but similar case that the compact Baltic States and ex-Soviet republics Estonia, Latvia and Lithuania were making at the same time. These countries did not argue for the inclusion of states further east. They were asserting, in a sense, an East–Central European, or Central European, identity, distinct from an Eastern European, South-Eastern Europe, or Balkan, identity. No one, of course, in a politically correct age, was to use phraseology such as the words attributed to Metternich – 'Asia begins at the *Landgasse*' – about Vienna's eastern gate being the terminus of Western civilization, nor Bismarck's refusal to weigh the Balkans equal to the 'bones of one Pomeranian grenadier'. But such formulations, patterns and stereotypes were familiar to the players, and if they carried the feel of an age now distant, they nonetheless pointed to cultural and historical linkages on which the aspirant countries were betting.

Their readiness to enter these Western clubs, the EU especially, was questioned by many. That their security needs were best met, in the post-Cold War world of a decade ago, by NATO membership was also, to some experienced observers, anything but evident.[7] But NATO membership was a prize, a reassurance for those whose geography and history lessons had been learned in a stern school, and it was again the 'kidnapped West' that made the successful argument for special treatment. Poland, Hungary and the Czech Republic were admitted in 1999. Schmemann appreciated the significance:

> The recent expansion of NATO to include Poland, Hungary and the Czech Republic – all Catholic or Protestant countries – while excluding the Orthodox states of Bulgaria and Romania affirmed a sense that the West was promoting its own into its exclusive club. The Poles, for example, have always insisted that their Catholicism is their true membership card in the West, even if they are ethnic cousins of the Russians.[8]

But NATO is a military alliance. *Realpolitik* in girding against anticipated Soviet aggression was, in the past, as important for its purposes as cultural or historical affinity, or domestic adherence to a full Western package of democratic and civil society rules. NATO already included both

Orthodox Greece and Moslem Turkey, both admitted in 1952. They thenceforward constituted what became known as NATO's troubled southern flank, more because of the mutual enmity of these allies than major Soviet activity in the area. Thus, post-Cold War NATO did not remain culturally picky all that long, and the rest of the post-communist would-be entrants, including Romania and Bulgaria, along with the three Baltics, Slovakia and Slovenia, none of them capable of adding much to arsenals or boots-on-the-ground, got formal invitations in 2003 and entered in 2004.

The EU has been, appropriately enough, something of a different story, with its barriers and criteria relating to economic development, rules and practices of the economic and political game, state–society–individual relations rather more specific and demanding. Indeed, at the century's end, it looked likely that a first-wave EU expansion would include only the Visegrad core Poland, Hungary and the Czech Republic. Slovakia, its post-velvet divorce performance blotted by Meciar's authoritarianism, the three Baltic countries and Slovenia compromised as much as advantaged by their miniature geography and demography, Romania and Bulgaria with problems of political corruption languishing out beyond the troubled ex-Yugoslav space, all appeared to be facing probationary periods.

But things worked out differently. In the grossest sense, faced with either a small expansion with inclusion based on Western histories and cultures and clean post-communist records, or a larger one that would include states that did not really yet meet the criteria, on the principle that inclusion itself would drive domestic developments in the right direction and reduce risks of regional disorder, the EU opted for the 2004 expansion.

By their performance and policy choices both before and since admission, as hinted earlier on, the eight have spread across the boundary between Anglo-Saxon and European economic directions. The aspirations and choices have made for hard neo-liberal options in some cases, for attempts to maintain welfare-state type provisions beyond their financing capacities in others,[9] and raised many questions of what to 'do' with the added economic resources EU membership, as well as their own exertions, have provided.

2007: the reluctant expansion

We return to the point at which this chapter began. The deferral in 2004 of Bulgaria and Romania, sweetened with a near-promise that it would, in the end, be no more than a deferral, invited further attention to these, and other non-Western states in the Balkans and beyond, states whose lag relative to the states of the 2004 and 2007 expansions we will examine later. The *Economist*'s 'Charlemagne' column in January 2006 took a long look at the situation as of that time:

> The Balkans will anyway not respond to the EU's gravitational pull in the same way as they did the central and eastern Europeans. The Balkan people are further removed than the Czechs and Poles were from EU standards of democracy and free markets. They have to set up functioning governments before they can become functioning democracies.[10]

Looking back to the occasion of the EU's reaffirmation that Bulgaria and Romania could come aboard at the year's end, the *Financial Times* quoted a 'senior EU official' on how the new additions would be different, and would mark an exhaustion of the Union's capacity for welcome. The words employed again touched on things that had happened in central Europe, but not further east in those Balkan states that had seemed over time more habituated and quiescent under Soviet despotism:

> You could sell the Czech Republic, Hungary or Poland joining ... People knew about the Prague Spring or Budapest 1956 or Solidarity. With Bulgaria and Romania it is more difficult to make the case on an emotional level, and it's going to keep getting harder.[11]

These words mean much more than they say. The Czechs, Hungarians and Poles can be 'sold' because each, in one way or another, clearly rebelled against the USSR-imposed political order, testifying to political values and aspirations the West thinks characteristic of itself. Romania and Bulgaria did not. Romanians lived under Ceausescu's especially squalid dictatorship from the mid-1960s and had been, generally, among Europe's most misgoverned peoples for centuries. Bulgaria's cultural links with Russia and lack of any democratic traditions made for quiescence under Moscow's domination. Neither society fielded dissident movements of the sort that the relatively liberal regimes in Poland and Hungary, and the more repressive one in Czechoslovakia, had. Both had been more habituated to despotism, to Soviet-style totalitarian rule.

This heritage invited various assessments when EU accession was a recently accomplished fact. The middlebrow, English-language *Warsaw Voice*, aimed at an expatriate audience, did a good job of trying to put the best cultural and historical construction on these developments, along the way introducing its audience to elements of history undeniably relevant but not necessarily familiar to it.

In the case of Romania, there is perhaps an attempt to have it 'both ways' with a country that, oddly for its location, speaks a Romance language:

> The Romanians' strong support for EU membership comes as no surprise. Until 1945 Romania remained, in broad terms, under the influence of the West in terms of culture and civilization, despite the fact that Orthodox Christian faith was the dominant religion in the country. The Church in Romania had stronger ties with the legacy of Constantinople and the Byzantine Empire however than with the tradition of the Russian Church controlled by the Moscow Patriarchate. The Habsburg Empire also left its mark on Romania, connecting this area to Europe and the European system of values. Through their language, the Romanians had strong links with francophone culture – in the 1920s and 1930s, Bucharest was referred to as the 'Paris of the East'. EU flags have been seen in Romanian cities for several years now. Romanians themselves comment on this ironically: 'Romania has been in Europe for a long time, only Brussels is unaware of it.'[12]

Here, one might say, 'broad terms' are stretched a bit – with reference to 'culture and civilization'. A look at the Romanian countryside, as opposed to the somewhat Art Deco façades of Bucharest architecture, would show the East. The West in Romania is more to be seen in the architecture and culture of the Saxons and Magyars of Transylvania.

With Bulgaria, there is a more straightforward recognition of what is happening, and what makes the country different:

> Despite its ancient Greek and Byzantine traditions, the nation, which lived under Turkish occupation for five centuries and was freed from the Turks by a Russian tsar in the nineteenth century, has lost the links to its European heritage and strongly identifies itself with Russia. For instance, Bulgarians use the Cyrillic alphabet. Former Bulgarian President Petyr Stoyanov recently commented on these Bulgarian cultural dilemmas by pointing to the declaration he made 10 years ago when he spoke of his country's aspirations to join NATO and the EU as Bulgaria's 'new civilizational choice'.
>
> 'Since the time of liberation from the Turkish occupation, Bulgaria's politics have been marked by a clash of civilizations. Russophiles

against germanophiles [sic], supporters of a pro-Western orientation against supporters of stronger ties with Russia, communists against anti-communists.' According to Stoyanov, EU membership puts an end to this era because all political forces in Bulgaria now agree that NATO and EU membership means a new future for the country.[13]

These rather wordy attempts to clarify a complicated case aside, a major element of the EU's problem with the promise it had, more or less already made in 2004, came down to the economic status and performance of Romania and Bulgaria, judged against both 15- and 25-member EU averages, and the economic specifics of the ex-communist states of the class of 2004. This was a matter of relative poverty, as we shall see, but not only that. The 15-member EU had made numerous special provisions for the 2004 expansion, imposing certain 'cost-limiting' restrictions with respect to labour mobility and the Schengen Agreement, the full application of which was to be delayed, the Common Agricultural Policy, so that rural Poland's millions would reap no subsidy bonanza, and other areas as well, for the new states it was admitting. But the move into the Balkans would raise yet more doubts about the fit of those new states, about the burdens that, even under such limitations, they might impose on an already tired EU in its pursuit of dynamism, competitiveness and accelerated growth.

Economic life: wealth/poverty/sufficiency

The basic kinds of economic difference the new entrants of 2004 and 2007 brought to the EU demands a few pages of discussion, somewhat more discursive, as readers will find, than a presentation of tabular data but, the author hopes, better for underlining some important aspects of what expansion implies. The *CIA World Factbook* provides 2005 ratings of per capita GDP (at PPP) for a total of 233 states and state-type entities.[14]

At a $28,100 GDP per capita average in 2005, the 25-member EU as a unit ranked in 31st place among the 233. In the old 15-member EU, the weak economic links in recent years were the three southern European later entrants whose politics were, into the 1970s, a mix of non-communist authoritarianism and instability: 2005 Spain (36th, at $25,600), Greece (45th at $23,300) and Portugal (56th at $18,700). Though none were rich at all by northern European standards, they were hardly mired in poverty. Compared with the state that has posed the EU's most problematic long-time admissions issue, Turkey, in 95th place, with a per capita GDP of $8,400, they were comfortable indeed.

It is in this frame that the 2004 expansion to include ten states, eight post-communist states plus the compact island countries of Cyprus and Malta, and the latest extension of the EU in 2007 to include Bulgaria and Romania, must be appreciated. The eight-member post-communist class of 2004 is well ahead of Turkey in GDP per capita. It ranges from rich Slovenia (50th, $21,500) to poorer and much larger Poland (73rd, $13,100): the eight-country average is $16,560, poorer then than Portugal, whom only Slovenia and the Czech Republic exceed.

But these modest figures put the eight well ahead of the two recent Balkan arrivals. Of the 233, Bulgaria is placed 89th with $9,600, and Romania 101st with $8,100. We are then dealing with two states whose per capita GDP is at about one third of the 25-state EU average. One of them, Romania, has a population of 22 million, and hence a demographic potential impact exceeding all the post-communist entrants save Poland. These states are closer to Turkey geographically, and they are also closer to it on the basis of the numbers than to the East Central European and Baltic states joining in 2004.

Beyond the new eastern and southern borders, the 2007 EU looks out at a number of states whose possible admission is a matter of discussion or extended preparation, but whose actual entry any time soon is subject to considerable uncertainty. These states represent a persistent legacy of communism, and before that, lagging economic and civic development, of a variety perhaps more acute in some cases than Bulgaria and Romania, as well as negative neighbourhood effects having to do with their location in troubled political space bearing the marks of the dissolution of the USSR and the old Yugoslavia.

First in this area are the states comprising the Western Balkans. Made up of the five ex-republics, excluding EU member Slovenia, of Yugoslavia plus Albania, they range in per capita GDP from a high of $12,400 for Croatia to Montenegro's $3,800 – 105th and 153rd among the *Factbook*-rated 233 countries.

Croatia is the outlier in this set. In income, it is well ahead of the others and, in terms of admissions prospects in the EU's rather labyrinthine procedures, much more favourably situated. It is also the only post-communist state in the area that is Western in its heritage: Roman Catholic, 'Habsburg' rather than Ottoman, arguably Central European, or Dalmatian/Adriatic, rather than Balkan. It is, in fact, now the only post-communist state Western, in the sense employed here, that is not in the EU. Croatia fell on the wrong side of a thin line that separates it from the Slovak Republic, whose troubled post-divorce politics cleared up just enough in the pre-2004 run-up to allow for its admission along with the Czech Republic, while political problems different in nature but of equal intensity made the same impossible for Croatia.[15]

These six states average a per capita GDP of $6,843; subtracting Croatia, the other five fall to $5,300: figures respectively 23 per cent and 19 per cent of the 25-state EU average. On such numbers, if for no other reason, the Western Balkans are likely to remain on Brussels' back burner for some time and thus outside an expansion-fatigued EU.

Even less immediate are prospects of a set of states further out, whose strategic location lies between the world of recent EU members and aspirants in the West, and Russia in the East: Belarus, Ukraine and Moldova.[16] From the economic standpoint of Brussels, this is just as well: these three occupy places 112, 115 and 186 among the 233, with per capita GDP respectively of $7,100, $7,000 and, for the internally divided and near failed-state Moldova, an abysmal $1,900. The Belarus and Ukraine average is about $1,000 less than the Western Balkans' average, Croatia included. Each of the three is, beyond its relative poverty, much deeper-sunk in the Russian sphere of influence in political, economic and geographic terms than other post-communist states.

Looking at the whole ensemble, and with full appreciation of the fact that figures such as GDP per capita, and rankings based on them, are subject to change and fluctuations over short periods of time and, on the basis of small refinements in reporting techniques, it is easy to see why the EU's appetite for further expansion of what has been a massively successful enterprise is, for now, largely satisfied.

Economic life: feel and quality

Critical to the pursuit of prosperity by the new members of the EU as members has been the building of economic infrastructure in an organizational sense: laws, regulations, practices, a set of new operating assumptions that distinguish their present and future prospects from their command-economy pasts, and that mark them as civilized market economies rather than parts of the wild East. This clean-up provides a base for rational activity by domestic players and, under most circumstances, a legal and regulatory arena in which foreign investors can enter without undue trepidation.

Such arenas can range widely in the degree to which they are regulated. The major issue is whether the regulations are fairly, transparently, universally applied; whether incentives to participate are equitably distributed; and whether penalties are imposed when warranted, according to the law, without fear or favour. But ways of doing this differ – the US is not Europe, the Anglo-Saxon way of doing things economic differs persistently along many dimensions from the continental European way. A good deal of this book, and others like it in recent years, deals with the propensity of ex-communist EU countries to follow one or the other of broad Western models of market economy, different judgments about competition policy, safety nets and so on. There is no lack of areas in which Washington, and perhaps London, differ from Brussels.

The Index of Economic Freedom (IEF), an annual product of the decidedly neo-liberal *Wall Street Journal* and the Heritage Foundation, surely tilts heavily in that American direction, but for comparative purposes will give some indication of the general ability of states to provide the business environment necessary to nurture the kind of economic success that should generate benefits for broad segments of the population.[17]

The 25 pre-2007 EU countries rank well up on economic freedom among the 150-plus countries rated. EU member and Celtic tiger Ireland, in third place, leads the global pack after Hong Kong and Singapore. The late developers in the old 15-member Union, Portugal, Spain, and Greece, rank 30th, 33rd and 57th respectively, bested by the two non-communist-past entrants of 2007, Cyprus and Malta in 16th and 24th places. In this company, the eight post-communist states stack up well indeed; Estonia best in 8th place, with a 1.75 rating on a 1–5 scale and Poland, in 41st place at 2.49 trailing. The eight together average 2.26, beating the Spanish, Portuguese and Greek scores, and well ahead of Turkey's 3.11. The 2007 latecomers lag the class of 2004, Bulgaria, 64th at 2.88 points, and Romania in 92nd with 3.19 bracket the score of Turkey, so unlikely to join them in the near future.

How does the new Balkan duo stand relative to Europe's outer neighbourhoods still excluded? For IEF purposes, the Western Balkans here amount to three ex-Yugoslav republics Bosnia-Herzegovina, Macedonia and Croatia, Serbia and Montenegro not having been rated, plus Albania, four states that average 2.83 points, and stretch from Albania in 52nd place to Bosnia's 74th. They are fairly tightly grouped, removing Croatia only raises the score to 2.85, Croatia having been rated 55th, below Albania. At an average score of 3.03, Bulgaria and Romania thus are behind these marginally more deserving states not likely to join them in the EU at any time soon. Of course, the criteria for EU gatekeeping, and its broader base of principles, are not so neo-liberal in principle as are the Heritage Foundation and the *Wall Street Journal*.

The more distant outlanders, Ukraine, Belarus, Moldova, are, on the IEF, exactly that. Their looming neighbour, Russia, itself scores 3.50, midpoint in the 'mostly unfree economies' range (3.00–3.99) and lands in 122nd place. The three group around it: Moldova (3.10) in

83rd place, Ukraine 99th (3.24), and pariah Belarus in 151st place with a dismal 4.11 score, thus not only Russia, but also the three troubled states of the Caucasus and the Central Asia republics.[18]

Corruption need not defeat an economy's growth prospects, or determine its fate in a world of diverse, interacting economies. A certain amount of corruption is expected in what are called emerging markets, though, of course, one condition for their progressive emergence is that corruption be diminished. Corruption will, under most circumstances, limit or bend investment, but it will not deter the risk-tolerant and adventurous. If the gains to be anticipated, net of the pay-offs, are large enough, one proceeds. Of course, a requirement is that corrupt rent-seekers deliver on their promises, according to prior agreement. Russia, the historical source of the old Soviet-type economy, has been, through much of its post-communist existence, extraordinarily corrupt. This has worked to limit foreign direct investment in the past but, in more recent times, FDI has increased as the strengths of the Russian economy have increased, and the corruption has taken different forms, while the potential for profit in engaging with the Russian economy has increased.

How does the broader post-communist world look? Transparency International provides what are essentially reputational ratings of corruption perception for 163 economies for 2006.[19] Among these, the EU 25 do predictably rather well on the 10-point scale, at an average score of 6.74. First place is a three-way tie of Finland, Iceland and New Zealand with scores of 9.6. Of the pre-2004 EU-15, the three southern European latecomers rank 23rd (Spain, 6.8), 26th (Portugal, 6.6), and 54th (Greece, 4.4). The 15 members of the pre-2004 Union fit, then, into the top 54 countries rated. In this same Mediterranean neighbourhood, the two island entrants of 2004, with no communist past, Malta and Cyprus, rank 28th (6.4), and 37th (5.6) respectively, both ahead of Greece, and also well ahead of Turkey (60th, 3.8).

The eight 2004 post-communist entrants average 5.13, behind Spain and Portugal but ahead of Greece. Their scores range broadly, with Poland something of an outlier. The addition of the ten new countries lowers the score for the 25-member EU to 6.74; the 25 fit in the top 61 of rated countries.

On these indications, the admission of Romania and Bulgaria is something of a stretch. Bulgaria (57th place, 4.0) and Romania (84th, 4.1) average a lacklustre 3.55, lagging well behind the Central European states, and, indeed, trailing Turkey.

However, versus the Western Balkans, for 'transparency' purposes, Croatia, Bosnia-Herzegovina, Macedonia, and Serbia-Montenegro, plus

Albania with a score of averaging 2.92, Bulgaria and Romania look distinctly better. Removing Croatia, 3.4, still a hair below the Romania–Bulgaria average, drops the average to 2.8. This, in turn is only marginally ahead of the average for the post-USSR countries located between the expanded EU and Russia. Russia gets a 121st place with a 2.5 score. Both Moldova (79th, 3.2) and Ukraine (99th, 2.8) do better, while Belarus is at the nadir, in 151st place and 2.1.

History, distant history, as well as the nature of the communist regimes they endured, has thus affected Romania and Bulgaria, making of them different entities than the post-communist lands further west. They are poor countries, poor in a sense that the previous eight admittees on the whole are not, and very much poorer than the Czech Republic and Hungary. They are not small countries demographically; Romania at 22.3 million is the second largest of the EU post-communist states after Poland, while Bulgaria's population of nearly 7.4 million is larger than five of the eight states admitted in 2004. Room must be made for them, and it may not be comfortable. Romanians and Bulgars might, as many predict, relocate legally or illegally, Schengen or not, heading for the southern EU states rather than joining Poles and Balts further north, but this will present problems of its own.

Furthermore, as EU members, they are called upon now to police a new set of southern or eastern borders on the EU's behalf as well as their own. Romania and Bulgaria face obligations to be more restrictive toward potential border-crossers, off-the-books labour from Moldova, Ukraine, Turkey and so on, countries of deeper economic problems, as data discussed above indicate, and unlikely to be invited into the EU at any time soon. Poland, notably upon its 2004 accession, faced similar obligations, on its eastern borders with Belarus and Ukraine. Habits born of the years since 1990, engaging off-the-books hard-working Belarusians and Ukrainians ready to labour for solid zloty, with willing Polish labour thin on the ground, had to be changed. As in the north, so now in the Balkan south can similar problems, at least from Brussels rule-enforcers' standpoint, be anticipated.

A fatigued Europe?

Complicating the picture further is the political fatigue and dysfunction increasingly evident among some of the generally successful countries of the 2004 expansion. Some of this is indeed a matter of the kind of afflictions that come to the fortunate: problems, not crises, 'malaise' is the word frequently used, but problems nonetheless.[20] Polish policies and rhetoric in the Kaczynski era combine a Euroscepticism and crankiness about 'outsiders' rules', not totally unjustified, but not particularly discriminating in its targets, with a preoccupation with settling historical accounts deferred since 1990. Lowering the temperature, cutting back on the politicized reshufflings and changes in areas from national security to banking and public finance would please Brussels, but over the longer run probably work better for Warsaw as well. Czechs lived with political deadlock for more than a year before uncertainly moving towards a solution in January 2007, a peaceful deadlock in the Czech manner, but hopefully now giving way to progress on numerous frozen issues. Hungary's people learned that their recently re-elected government had lied to them about the economy, to stay in office, deplorable but not extraordinary, though short-lived riots in Budapest were.

These signs of political distemper show that some new EU members are vulnerable to inward-looking concerns and temptations that might hamper their ability to make their own distinct contributions to the Union, including their thoughts on the knotty problems of further expansion. The new members are taking care of business in what might be the most critical way; they are growing economically at impressive rates for the continent.[21] But contributions in the area of political innovation or imagination are presently quite limited,[22] although in the face of Romanian and Bulgarian accession they have not shown signs of erecting barriers in the manner that the UK, Ireland and Sweden, the most welcoming states to the class of 2004, might be doing.[23]

On the whole, the EU expansion prior to that of Romania and Bulgaria, and leaving aside the issues of Turkey, the Western Balkans, and the post-Soviet states east of Poland when and if these are squarely posed, has been successful, and good in a basic sense for the old 15-member core as well as for the 2004 newcomers. The anticipation of membership shaped and disciplined political and economic life and organization, both among those relatively sure of entry and those for whom it did not seem a 'one deal'. Indeed, even some of the policy problems and choices made in the new Europe reflect issues encountered earlier in the histories of the 15, and they are being handled on the whole within the same peaceful and reasonably orderly parameters. An *Economist* leader in autumn 2006, in taking a somewhat critical view toward the Visegrad states versus the post-Soviet Baltics, actually made the point:

> Central European countries have tended, consciously or not, to look to Austria, and so politicized their civil services and encourage cosy links between business and government. (The Baltic states, by

contrast, have looked to the more open, transparent Nordic countries, such as Finland – with spectacular results.)[24]

Things could, as most would agree, be a lot worse than they are if a major point of difference emerging among members of the class of 2004 amounts only to adopting one or the other of the two broad variants of employment, tax and welfare models prevalent among the continental members of the EU.

The vexing problem of European energy dependence on Russia has emerged into sharper relief as prices have risen, and with them Russia's wealth. This, in turn, has contributed to Russia's adoption of a more assertive, sharp-elbowed manner, even as it assures its customers in old Europe that it is doing nothing of the sort. The addition of ten post-communist states has, on the whole, done little to stiffen the spine of the EU, as some hoped it might. Poland and the three Baltic states have been more directly affected by being bypassed by the Russo-German Baltic pipeline project, and more inclined than the other new states to complain about it to a Brussels that seems tone-deaf, as Berlin, to what this routing implies about Russian and German respect for their security concerns.[25] Czechs, Slovaks and Hungarians, as dependent on Russian energy but less affected geographically, have been quieter, and one can surely expect no loud noises from Romania and Bulgaria in future intra-EU discussions on the topic.

In the thick of elite and public discussions of energy policy, with attention-focusing energy summits, with Russia's 2006 presidency of the G-8 to concentrate minds, old Europe's attitude toward Russia about which, with varying degrees of justification and sympathy, Washington worried during the Cold War with the USSR, remains a mix of accepting realities, de-emphasizing dangers and wishing for the best. A *Financial Times*/Harris poll in mid-2006 found that, on average, 53 per cent of British, French, Italian, German and Spanish respondents saw Russia more as partner than a threat.[26] In the face of indications such as this, it seems likely that divisions in the EU will persist with Poland and maybe others having recourse to vetoes of the sort advanced in late 2006 to block EU–Russia talks on a number of issues, disturbing some old Europe EU members as much as they do Moscow.[27]

The stubborn fact, the elephant in the room, is less energy dependence itself than a kind of subjective EU impotence in certain areas. Without revisiting America = Mars, Europe = Venus-type notions, it is not totally off the mark to say that much of old Europe on the whole is doubtful, not assertive, neither possessed of, nor willing to work to possess, the military or coercive resources required for it to be treated as other than an entity it is, across a fair range of issues, safe to offend.[28] Putin's Russia, from time to time, does so. Some of the new Europe, Poland, notably, the Baltics secondarily though hindered by their minimal size, react more sharply, driven by different visions of what is appropriate. But they lack resources to alter the balance. Over time, all else remaining equal, they, too, for good or ill, will probably become more 'European' rather than less in these areas where economic capacity and interdependence intertwine with more traditional concepts of national security.

With respect, finally, to the more strictly economic issues of growth, flexibility, competitiveness, of social justice versus efficiency and related hard choices, issues that concern all EU states even as they divide them, what is there to be said about 2004, and especially here about 2007, in the light of 2004? First, the states added in 2004 included both leaders and laggards in terms of pre-accession experience and records. Poland led with the original edition of shock therapy, and balanced privatization policies creatively between the risky state sector and the fostering of green-field private-sector enterprise. Hungary, well ahead in 1990, found the transition issues it had to resolve a somewhat harder go. The Czech Republic was strong in some areas, disappointing in others, while Slovakia was luckier than it might have been. Up north, Estonia created more opportunities than the rest of the Baltics, or similar-scale and initially more-advantaged Slovenia. On the whole, still not strong enough in terms of their contribution to total EU GDP to pull the body in the more or less Anglo-Saxon direction of favouring growth and competitiveness now as the key to financing more justice and equity in the future, they are themselves still divided. So, of course are the earlier 15.

Second, the addition of Romania and Bulgaria, though it is very early indeed to judge, shows no sign of bringing new elements of innovation and experimental *elan* into the EU, fostered by the relative poverty of their 30 millions. Their own post-communist histories show few of the qualities that might see them pointing in any new directions, providing, by virtue of new ways of grappling with their own legacies of poverty, demonstration effects of new policies that some of 25 other club members might find attractive. On the other hand, their accession is being handled by the Union quite well, a reminder that it is still, from most viewpoints, a very successful enterprise.

This is the basis, then, for a degree of moderate optimism, on which it seems reasonable to conclude this chapter.

Notes

1 An earlier consideration of some of these issues by the current author is Walter D. Connor, 'Europe West and East: Thoughts on History, Culture, and Kosovo', in Zvi Gitelman *et al.* (eds), *Cultures and Nations of Central and Eastern Europe; Essays in Honor of Roman Szporluk* (Cambridge: Harvard University Press, for the Ukrainian Research Institute, 2000): 71–88.

2 One recent rendering of the line, and a discussion of the civilizational divide in a broader context, can be found in the controversial book by Samuel Huntington, *The Clash of Civilizations and the Remaking of World Order* (New York: Touchstone/Simon and Schuster, 1997).

3 A relatively recent, region-wide treatment of the social and political impacts of Orthodoxy is Victoria Clark, *Why Angels Fall: A Journey Through Orthodox Europe from Byzantium to Kosovo* (New York: St. Martin's Press, 2000).

4 Schmemann, *New York Times*, 4 April 1999: 1. (It is surely worth noting that the West, and particularly the US, received virtually no credit in the world of Islam for this, or for the earlier intervention in Bosnia in 1995 in favour of the Moslem Bosniaks versus Catholic Croats and Orthodox Serbs.)

5 Kaplan, *New York Times*, 7 April 1999: A21.

6 *Financial Times*, 10 November 2006: 15.

7 The best statements of this position are those of Michael Mandelbaum. See his 'NATO Expansion: A Bridge to the Nineteenth Century' (Occasional Papers Series, Center for Political and Strategic Studies, Chevy Chase, MD), June 1997, and *The Dawn of Peace in Europe* (New York: Twentieth Century Fund, 1996).

8 Schmemann, *New York Times*, 4 April 1999: 1.

9 An early assessment of post-communist states' welfare aspirations, policies, and financing thereof, well before EU expansion was broached as a practical matter, is available in E.B. Kapstein and M. Mandelbaum (eds), *Sustaining the Transition: The Social Safety Net in Postcommunist Europe* (New York: Council on Foreign Relations, 1997), see especially Mark Kramer's chapter, 'Social Protection Policies and Safety Nets in East Central Europe: Dilemmas of the Postcommunist Transformation': 46–122.

10 *Economist*, 14 January 2006: 56.

11 *Economist*, 14 January 2006: 56.

12 'EU Entry Stirs Hopes', *The Warsaw Voice Online*, Weekly Newsmagazine.

13 *Ibid.*

14 See the *Factbook* data at www.cia.gov/cia/publications/factbook/rankorder

15 Both Slovakia and Croatia, emerging from communism, found themselves burdened by 'memories' of brief periods of national independence and status – the Tiso regime in Slovakia, the Ustasha state in Croatia – wherein roughly from 1939 or 1941 to 1944–45, they were liberated from the deeply-resented domination/tutelage, respectively, of the Czechs and the Serbs. Unfortunately, these fascist, decidedly anti-Semitic regimes were Nazi puppet states. Released from the constraints of their (quite different) communist domination, both peoples were to find, in the 1990s, that the West's collective 'reading' of these fondly-remembered periods was very different – and were to take some time to 'adjust' to this reality.

16 A call in late 2006 for the EU to in some sense 'embrace ' these countries – as well as the three that make up the post-Soviet Caucasus (see *Financial Times*, 12 December 2006) does not look like a likely prospect.

17 For the Index, see http://www.heritage.org/index

18 In the Caucasus, Armenia and Georgia, the two Christian-heritage, largely 'oil-free' states, rank in 27th and 68th place on the IEF, in a rough sense well ahead of where their GDP/pc might have been expected to place them – Armenia at $4,800 and Georgia at $3,400 were 133rd and 157th in the GDP *Factbook* rankings.

19 The TI ratings are to be found at http://www.transparency.org/news_room/in_focus/cpi2006

20 See *Financial Times*, 6 October 2006: 15.

21 As *Economist* noted (16 December 2006: 50) Latvia and Lithuania towards the end of the year were experiencing GDP growth of more than 10 per cent.

22 See Stefan Wagstyl on 'the sick man of the new Europe,' *Financial Times*, 27 September 2006: 13.

23 *Economist*, 28 October 2006: 67.

24 *Economist,* 14 October 2006: 12.

25 See *Financial Times*, 12 July 2006: 6; former Polish defence minister Radek Sikorski was not *completely* 'over the top' in pointing out parallels between the Russian–German direct Baltic pipeline project, and Molotov–Ribbentrop dealings in August 1939. Particularly 'egregious' (*Financial Times*, 4 April 2006: 14) was Gerhard Schroeder's taking the Chairmanship of the Gazprom-led joint venture – a move he then defended in a new book accusing critics of treating German–Russian deals differently from German–American (see *New York Times*, 12 December 2007: A7).

26 *Financial Times*, 15–16 July 2006: 3.

27 See *Financial Times*, 13 November 2006: 3.

28 See Anne Applebaum in *Washington Post*, 19 December 2006: A29.

9
Economic Freedom, Confidence and Growth

Steve H. Hanke

Prior to the nineteenth century, life in most parts of the world was brutish, dangerous and short. It still is in 'poor' countries but is much less so in the 'rich' ones. Indeed, life expectancies vary greatly between the developed and the less developed parts of the world. To fight the scourge of poverty and associated low life expectancies, economic growth is essential. This explains why economists have always been acutely interested in the process of economic development.

The main focus of older models of economic growth was on physical resources. In these formulations, output flowed from combinations of various inputs: land, labour and capital. In principle, then, it seemed logical to conclude that faster growth would result from infusions of additional inputs, chiefly capital, or better use of existing inputs, often thought to require government economic planning. In practice, however, such prescriptions have often been disastrous. Newer 'endogenous growth' models have identified many other variables that contribute to differences in growth rates: knowledge spillovers resulting from increases in the stock of physical capital, technology transfers, and human capital investment. Yet, even these sophisticated formulations often fail to explain observed patterns of development.

Most recently, some students of economic growth have returned to first principles. As a way of understanding the development process, they have focused on the nature of institutions and the structure of rules and norms that constrain economic behaviour. In doing so, they have rediscovered an insight contained in the works of Richard Cantillon (1680–1734), Adam Smith (1723–90) and Jacques Turgot (1727–81): economic liberty is a crucial precondition for sustained, vigorous economic growth.

Matrices that serve as proxies for economic freedom have recently been developed and are widely used. For example, the *Heritage*

Foundation and the *Wall Street Journal* jointly publish an annual volume, the *Index of Economic Freedom*, which now incorporates 157 countries. The *Economic Freedom of the World*, which includes 130 countries, is published by Canada's Fraser Institute. And the World Bank issues an annual, *Doing Business*, which reports on the ease of doing business in 175 countries. Data from these annuals on economic freedom show that there is a strong positive linkage between measures of economic freedom and economic growth (Hanke and Walters 1997).

This is not to deny that abundant natural resources, a highly skilled labour force, and ready availability of new technologies might enhance growth. But these factors are neither necessary nor sufficient. If resource endowments determined a national economy's fate, Venezuela would be rich while Hong Kong and Singapore would be poor, and South Korea would be as destitute as North Korea. Moreover, East Germany's highly skilled labour force should have enabled it to keep pace with West Germany before the Iron Curtain fell. And if access to sophisticated technology guaranteed prosperity, perhaps the Soviet Union would still exist.

There is considerable agreement, therefore, about the desirability of economic freedom. But what are the elements that produce such a liberal economic order? The following menu is quite encompassing:

Private property and contract rights should be established The following criteria should guide the establishment of private property: universality, exclusivity and transferability. Universality guarantees that all resources are either owned or ownable by a private person or entity. Exclusivity guarantees that those who own property have the exclusive right to use their property as long as that use does not harm other property owners. And transferability guarantees that owners can freely transfer their property rights.

Fiscal order and transparency should be established To establish control over public spending and reduce waste, fraud and corruption, governments should publish a national set of accounts that includes a balance sheet of its assets and liabilities, and an accrual-based annual operating statement of income and expenses. These financial statements should meet international accounting standards and should be subject to an independent audit.

Budget deficits and government spending should be kept under control One way to achieve control over the scope and scale of government is to require 'super majority' voting for important fiscal decisions: taxing, spending and the issuance of debt.

Inflationary pressures should be kept under control   To encourage economic development, inflation rates should be kept low and predictable. For many developing nations, this inflation objective can best be achieved by abolishing their central banks and replacing them with currency boards that issue fully convertible, stable, domestic currencies, or by simply doing away with domestic currencies and replacing them with convertible stable foreign currencies (Hanke 2002a; 2002b).

The advantages of open international trade should be exploited   Liberal trade policies facilitate the efficient allocation of resources and stimulate economic growth. This is particularly true in small economies, where real competition can only be obtained by allowing foreign producers to compete freely in domestic markets.

Complex tax systems and excessive tax rates should be avoided   Complex tax systems coupled with excessive tax rates distort behaviour and create large disincentives to economic activity, while yielding little revenue.

Subsidies and tax incentives for private industry should be avoided   Subsidies and tax incentives that are designed to achieve particular objectives may or may not actually assist in obtaining those goals. One thing is certain: they distort economic choices and resource allocation, and retard economic growth.

Privileges and immunities should be avoided   For example, state-created monopoly privileges and immunities for unions, such as exclusive representation, compulsory union membership, and immunity from antitrust laws, should be avoided. Privileges and immunities distort markets and act as a drag on economic growth.

Price controls should be avoided   Price controls, including interest rate ceilings, cannot be justified on economic grounds. They tend to vitiate the signalling role that prices should play. Hence, price controls impede the movement of resources from lower-valued to higher-valued uses and result in resource misallocation and slower economic growth.

Market interventions and restrictions on competition should be avoided   Market intervention and restrictions on competition, such as the use of marketing boards, result in the politicization of economic life, inefficient enterprises, resource misallocation, and the retardation of economic growth.

State-owned enterprises should be privatized   State-owned enterprises are inefficient. For example, sales, adjusted profits, and productivity per employee are lower for nationalized enterprises than they are for private firms. Taxes paid per employee are lower, sales per dollar of investment are lower, profits per dollar of assets are lower, wages and operating costs per dollar of sales are higher, sales grow at a slower rate, and, with few exceptions (petroleum), state-owned enterprises for which accounts are presented properly generate accounting losses that are passed on to taxpayers.

Unclear boundaries between public and private activity should be avoided When boundaries between the public and private sector are unclear, it is symptomatic of poorly defined property rights. Ill-defined property rights distort resource allocation and retard economic growth. Government bailouts of insolvent private firms are but one example of unclear boundaries between public and private activity.

The manipulation and repression of private capital markets should be avoided The manipulation and repression of private capital markets distort the savings and investment process, retard foreign direct investment, promote capital flight, and generally act as a drag on economic growth.

To be successful in achieving high scores for economic freedom, confidence and credibility are of primary importance. As Keynes argued in *The General Theory*:

> The *state of confidence*, as they term it, is a matter to which practical men always pay the closest and most anxious attention. But economists have not analyzed it carefully and have been content, as a rule, to discuss it in general terms. In particular it has not been made clear that its relevance to economic problems comes in through its important influence on the schedule of the marginal efficiency of capital. There are now two separate factors affecting the rate of investment, namely, the schedule of the marginal efficiency of capital and the state of confidence. The state of confidence is relevant because it is one of the major factors determining the former, which is the same thing as the investment demand schedule.
>
> There is, however, not much to be said about the state of confidence *a priori*. Our conclusions must mainly depend upon the actual observation of markets and business psychology (Keynes 1936: 148–9).

Most economists have ignored this passage in *The General Theory*, because confidence is difficult to define, quantify and measure, and is therefore difficult to insert into any formal abstract model. Yet, it is clearly unsatisfactory to confine analysis only to definable and quantifiable magnitudes simply because they can be encapsulated into a neat definition or measured by government statisticians.

Contrary to Keynes, there is much to be said a priori about the state of confidence. For example, it seems likely that confidence is determined by the general credibility of government policy. Confidence is enhanced when governments make credible commitments to implement liberal economic reform programmes. A commitment is made more credible the more one binds oneself to the achievement of an objective. At the extreme, on a battlefield when a commander orders his troops to burn all bridges behind them to cut off avenues for their retreat, his enemies will be confident that his intentions are to fight to the last man.

A credible commitment is something that many politicians are reluctant to entertain. That said, there have been numerous cases in which politicians have made credible commitments to adopt liberal economic policies. These have involved commitments at the strategic level to the entire menu of reforms outlined above, but at the same time, only fighting at the tactical level those battles that can be won. In consequence, reform momentum was created, success was built on success, and dramatic increases in economic freedom and prosperity resulted regardless of the type of political regime or the ideology of the political party that embraced reforms.

Several examples support this conclusion. In 1965, Singapore gained its independence when it was expelled from a two-year federation with Malaysia. At that time, Singapore was backward and poor, a barren speck on the map in a dangerous part of the world. Its population was made up of a diverse group of immigrants with a history of communal tensions. However, Singapore had a leader with clear ideas on how to modernize the country. Lee Kuan Yew ruled out passing the begging bowl and accepting foreign assistance of any kind. Instead, he embraced stable money and first-world competition. Stable money was initially achieved with a currency board. Competition was attained by light taxation, minimal regulation of business and free trade. In addition, Lee Kuan Yew insisted on personal security, public order and the protection of private property. To accomplish his objectives, his central principle for organizing a 'small' government was to run a tight ship with no waste or corruption. To implement that principle, Lee Kuan Yew appointed only first-class civil servants and paid them first-class wages. Today, Singapore is one of the freest, most flexible and prosperous economies in the world. Indeed, both the 2007 Index of Economic Freedom (Kane *et al.* 2007) and the Economic Freedom of the World, 2006 Annual Report (Gwartney *et al.* 2006) rank Singapore as the second freest economy, and, in terms of the ease of doing business, Singapore is ranked first (World Bank 2006).

Hong Kong, along with Singapore, ranks as one of the world's freest economies. Indeed, it ranks first on the two economic freedom metrics mentioned in the preceding paragraph and fifth in terms of the ease of doing business (World Bank 2006). Established as an *entrepôt* free port, Hong Kong has achieved its status as one of the freest economies in the world by making a credible commitment to stable money via a currency board, free trade, free markets, low taxes, non-intervention and personal liberty through the application of the rule of law. What makes Hong Kong so interesting is that it attained its economic freedom and prosperity in the absence of democracy. Ceded by China to the British Crown in 1841, Hong Kong became a British Crown Colony, not a representative democracy. It remained a colony until 1 July 1997, when it became a Special Administrative Region of the People's Republic of China. Hong Kong illustrates that a representative democracy, while perhaps desirable, is not a precondition for the application of the rule of law and attainment of freedom in the economic sphere.

On this important point, it is worth quoting Friedrich von Hayek at length:

> But to call 'law' everything that the elected representatives of the majority resolve, and to describe as 'Government under the Law' all the directives issued by them – however discriminating in favour of, or to the detriment of, some groups of individuals – is a very bad joke. It is in truth lawless government. It is a mere play on words to maintain that, so long as a majority approves of acts of government, the rule of law is preserved. The rule of law was regarded as a safeguard of individual freedom, because it meant that coercion was permissible only to enforce obedience to general rules of individual conduct equally applicable to all, in an unknown number of future instances. Arbitrary oppression – that is coercion undefined by any rule by the representatives of the majority – is no better than arbitrary action by any other ruler. Whether it requires that some hated person should be boiled or quartered, or that his property should be taken from him, comes in this respect to the same thing. Although there is good reason for preferring limited democratic government to a non-democratic one, I must confess to preferring non-democratic government under the law to unlimited (and therefore essentially lawless) democratic government. Government under the law seems to me to be the higher

value, which it was once hoped that democratic watchdogs would preserve (Hayek 1984: 354).

Estonia is another country that has made a credible commitment to liberal economic reforms. Estonia, where the author witnessed the birth of such a pre-eminent commitment, merits attention because it has the highest economic freedom ranking of any former communist country. It ranks twelfth on both of the standard measures for economic freedom. The USSR State Council conceded Estonia's fully independent status on 6 September 1991. The economy was in shambles and the Estonians were left to use the hyperinflating Russian ruble. At the invitation of the Estonian parliament, in a presentation on 5 May 1992, the author laid out a blueprint to replace the Russian ruble with a freely convertible Estonian kroon, linked to the German mark at a fixed rate and fully backed by mark, and gold, reserves (Hanke *et al.* 1997 [1992]). The parliamentarians wasted little time in committing to the proposed currency board blueprint. On 24 June 1992, the ruble was out and a currency board-issued kroon was in. Building on this initial success, Estonia has steadfastly continued to embrace a liberal reform agenda.

In closing, it is worth stressing that there is often a wide gap between a government's rhetoric and the reality of its reforms. For example, many governments in the former Soviet Union, Eastern Europe and Latin America have come to power on liberal reform platforms, only to be swept aside in the next election. Why? The common thread running through all these cases is that reform reality has not matched reform rhetoric (Havrylyshyn 2006). Indeed, commitments to reform have not been credible, reforms have been narrow and superficial, economic freedom has not been significantly enhanced, state-imposed burdens on doing business have remained onerous, and most importantly, the scope and scale of government activity has not been dramatically reduced. In consequence, corruption has gone unchecked and remains a systemic problem. All this amounts to a recipe for superficial reformers to discredit themselves, their political parties and the ideas they have masqueraded behind.

References

Gwartney, J., Lawson, R. and Easterly, W. (2006) *Economic Freedom of the World: 2006 Annual Report* (Vancouver: Fraser Institute).

Hanke, Steve H. (2002a) 'Currency Boards', *Annals of the American Academy of Political and Social Science*, 579, January–February: 87–105.

Hanke, Steve H. (2002b) 'On Dollarization and Currency Boards: Error and Deception', *Journal of Policy Reform*, 5(4): 203–22.

Hanke, S.H., Jonung, L. and Schuler, K. (1997) [1992] *Monetary Reform for A Free Estonia: A Currency Board Solution* (Stockholm: SNS Förlag).

Hanke, S.H. and Walters, S.J.K. (1997) 'Economic Freedom, Prosperity, and Equality: A Survey', *Cato Journal*, 17(2), Fall: 117–46.

Havrylyshyn, O. (2006) *Divergent Paths in Post-Communist Transformation: Capitalism for All or Capitalism for the Few?* (New York: Palgrave Macmillan): 255–76.

Hayek, F.A. (1984) [1978] 'Whither Democracy?', in C. Nishiyama and K.R. Leube (eds), *The Essence of Hayek* (Stanford, CA: Hoover Institution Press): 354.

Kane, T., Holmes, K.R. and O'Grady, M.A. (2007) *2007 Index of Economic Freedom* (Washington, DC, and New York: Heritage Foundation and Dow Jones & Company, Inc.).

Keynes, John Maynard (1936) *The General Theory of Employment, Interest and Money* (London: Macmillan): 148–9.

World Bank (2006) *Doing Business 2007: How to Reform* (Washington, DC: World Bank).

Part III

Key Factors in the Search for Growth and Security

10
Public Finances and Structural Reforms in the US and the EU: Lessons for the New Member States

Filip Keereman and Siegfried Steinlein[1]

Introduction

The new EU member states in Central and Eastern Europe have successfully mastered the transition from planned to market economies. They have made great and impressive progress in reforms and growth. Nevertheless, although there is considerable diversity, their average living standard still lags significantly behind the EU average. Hence, there remains a considerable need for further fiscal and structural reforms to advance their economies. In searching for future economic policy orientations and best practices, Central and Eastern European countries might be tempted to look across the Atlantic rather than closer to home. This reaction seems at first sight natural, in particular if per capita income and growth figures over recent years are compared between the EU and the US. This contribution tries to put things into perspective by pointing at the strong accession-related catching-up process experienced by the new member states and the opportunities offered by the EU policy framework. It puts a special focus on the relation between budgetary consolidation as privileged by the Stability and Growth Pact and structural reforms as emphasized by the Lisbon agenda.

The chapter is structured as follows. First, the EU-15 per capita income performance is compared with the US and the role of productivity, labour markets and the business environment is highlighted. The chapter then looks at the new member states' catching-up experience relative to the EU-15 and argues that the accession process has acted as a catalyst for the success in catching-up. In the third section, the challenges are sketched for a continuation of the catching-up story and a repetition of the successes so far. The Lisbon agenda is the subject of the fourth section, explaining the disappointing results until now and the revamping of the process in order to do better. It looks also at the US for comparison and draws attention to the importance of both budgetary consolidation and structural reforms. The relation between budgetary consolidation and structural reforms from the angle of the Stability and Growth Pact is then examined, followed by analyses of that relation in practice. Finally, the main conclusions are presented.

Per capita income and productivity performance in the US and the EU: some stylized facts

Comparing US and EU per capita income performance and looking at some stylized facts over recent decades could tempt Central and Eastern European countries to look across the Atlantic rather than closer to home when designing their fiscal policies and structural reforms.

In terms of per capita income the EU is lagging behind the US ...

In terms of economic performance, the EU significantly lags behind the US. GDP per capita is about 70 per cent of the US level in the 15 old member states (see Figure 10.1), and in the 10 new member states that joined the EU on 1 May 2004, the gap is even greater. Until the early 1980s, the old member states were catching up, reaching about 75 per cent of US GDP per capita, but have since lost some ground, particularly during the 1990s when the US economy received a boost from the information and technology sector. Starting from low average income levels, the new member states are engaged in a steep and steady catching-up process, but the road to full real convergence is still long.

However, behind these aggregate figures are wide differences at the state level in the US and at the national level in the EU. Leaving aside the upper extremes both in the US (District of Columbia) and in the EU (Luxemburg), the richest region in the US has an average income per capita that is almost two-and-a-half times that of the poorest (Delaware versus Mississippi in 2005). In the EU, taking the old and new member states together, the difference is even larger, with Ireland almost three times as rich as Latvia. By contrast, within each EU subgroup the difference is less than twofold. It is also noteworthy that the richest EU countries surpass the per capita income of the poorest US states.

Furthermore, a note of caution is in order as this kind of international comparison might suffer from differences in statistical and national accounts methodologies or in economic structures. Through a more widespread use of hedonic prices, US national accounts recognize better qualitative and productivity improvements that are then reflected in

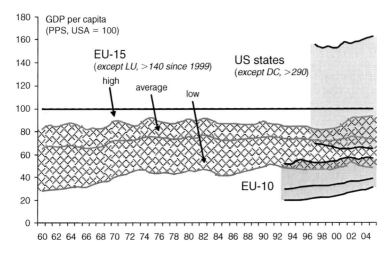

Figure 10.1 Relative economic performance in the EU and the US
Sources: Eurostat, US Department of Commerce (BEA)

higher GDP growth. With respect to economic structures, the US is notably more market-oriented and hence a larger share of goods and services is traded for a price in the market with the consequence of being captured in national accounts.

... because of lower labour utilization and productivity ...

Despite measurement difficulties and regional differentiations, the assessment of economic performance swings overall undoubtedly in favour of the US. The discrepancy in per capita income is due to a lower utilization of labour, lower employment and, in the old member states, fewer hours worked, and a lower hourly productivity (see Figure 10.2) in the EU. Comparing 2005 to 2000, only the new member states, admittedly starting from low levels, succeeded in making significant progress towards closing the income gap with the US. In the old member states, better labour utilization is offset by a relative deterioration of productivity.

... rooted in particular in labour market rigidities ...

The US scores particularly well on the labour market front with an unemployment rate that has declined to less than 5 per cent, while it is still 7.5 per cent in the old member states of the EU (see Figure 10.3). In the new member states, the high unemployment of about 11 per cent is linked to the restructuring process of the centrally planned economy to a market economy. The achievement of the US is particularly remarkable

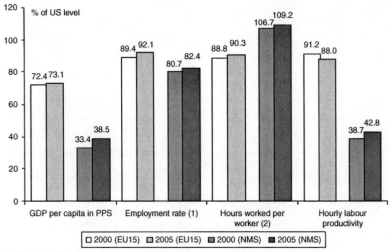

Figure 10.2 Decomposition of EU GDP per capita relative to the US
Source: Eurostat

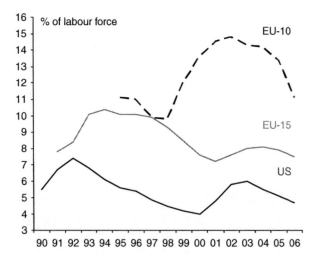

Figure 10.3 Unemployment in the EU and the US
Source: Eurostat

in comparison to the EU-15, when the demographic pressures on the labour market are brought into the picture. Between 1960 and 2000, about 68 million jobs were created in the US, compared to a mere 25 million in the EU-15, leading to a much better absorption of the increasing population in the US, +99 million, than in the EU-15, +63 million. Since 2000, the situation has been improving in the EU with a stronger employment creation in the EU-15 than in the US, about 12.5 million against 10 million, reflected also in the relative improvement of the employment rate (see Figure 10.2).

... and a better business environment in the US ...

The US is doing better in terms of productivity and growth because of a stronger performance in product, labour and financial markets for which, respectively, the following indicators have been used: starting a business, rigidity of employment and getting credit (Figure 10.4). For instance, it takes less than 10 days to set up a business in the US, while in most EU countries several more days are needed. Similarly, economic performance seems to be helped by a lower degree of labour market rigidity and the US is characterized by easier hiring/firing rules and greater wage flexibility compared with the EU member states. Access to credit also facilitates economic activity, and in this domain the US occupies a rank near the top.

... but better social coherence in the EU

However, in terms of social cohesion, the US does not score so well, here illustrated with the degree of income inequality and the provision of healthcare services (see Figure 10.5). In line with Kuznets' inverted U-shaped curve (Kuznets 1955), after having reached a certain level of development, richer countries should experience less income inequality, because society is likely to pay more attention to social issues. Plotting the EU member states, there indeed appears to be a slightly negative relation between income and inequality, implying that the higher GDP per capita, the lower income dispersion. In the US, a relatively rich country, there is however a degree of income dispersion similar to the least affluent countries in the EU. Related to social coherence, the US is, for example, also not ranked high in the provision of healthcare services. It has a very high per capita expenditure on healthcare, but its provision of services is at the level of countries that spend, in relative terms, less than half compared with the US. This testifies to the high cost of the present US healthcare system, which delivers high quality services, but not to all.

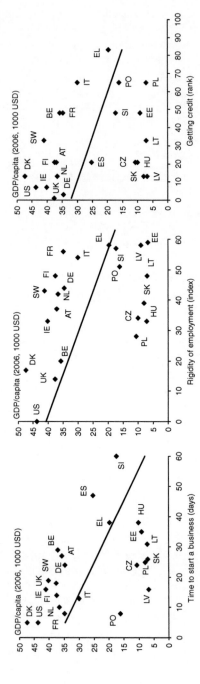

Figure 10.4 Business conditions in the US and the EU
Source: World Bank

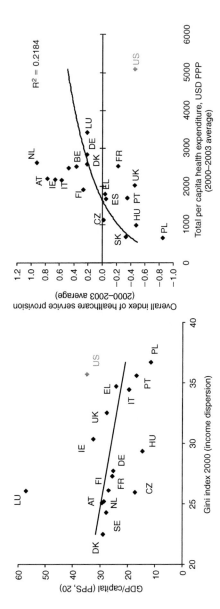

Figure 10.5 Social conditions in the US and the EU

Note: The overall index of healthcare services is based on countries' relative performance in the following four categories: density of practising physicians per 1000 inhabitants, density of practising nurses per 1000 inhabitants, number of computed tomography scanners per million inhabitants, and number of magnetic resonance imaging units per million inhabitants.

Source: Eurostat, OECD

Catching-up experience of the new member states so far

In addition to a different emphasis on equity and social coherence in the US and the EU, one also has to keep in mind that the new EU members have fared quite well by joining the EU. By orienting themselves towards the EU economic policy framework, the new member states benefited both in terms of growth and macroeconomic stabilization.

Impressive per capita income growth ...

From an economic perspective, it is better to look at EU accession as a dynamic process rather than a discrete event in time. Preparing for enlargement took several years and, when joining the Union, the Central and Eastern European EU-10 had successfully transformed their economies from central planning to functioning free markets over one-and-a-half decades. Their desire to comply with the macroeconomic and structural criteria for EU accession, the economic part of the so-called Copenhagen criteria, served as a catalyst for change: they guided macroeconomic and fiscal stabilization efforts and structural reforms. Hence, transition- and enlargement-driven reforms went hand-in-hand and were mutually reinforcing. Numerous pre-accession assistance initiatives by the Union helped in the process.

As a consequence, developments before and after enlargement have already led to strong, real catching-up. Per capita incomes are much closer to EU-15 levels now than they were back in 1997, the year in which enlargement prospects crystallized in the Commission's Agenda 2000. After the output collapse in the early years of transition, growth rates in the EU-10 have consistently been higher than in the EU-15, although growth has, on average, also been more volatile. As a result of stronger growth, per capita income in the EU-10 rose from an average of 44.7 per cent of the EU-15 level in 1997 to 52.6 per cent of this level in 2006 (Table 10.1).

Per capita income figures also illustrate the diversity among the new EU member states after enlargement. In 2006, these figures ranged, in purchasing power parity, from 44.9 per cent of the former EU-15 average in Latvia and 45.9 per cent in Poland to 75.6 per cent of the EU-15 average in Slovenia and even 82.1 per cent in Cyprus. Four countries, the Czech Republic, Cyprus, Malta and Slovenia, have already achieved income levels surpassing the least affluent EU-15 country – Portugal, at 66.1 per cent of the EU-15 average. Particularly impressive catching-up took place in the Baltic countries but also in Hungary and Slovenia, in spite of the fact that the latter two countries already had a comparatively

Table 10.1 Catching-up by the new member states

Countries	GDP per capita		Average of real GDP growth
	(% of EU-15, PPS)		(in %)
	1997	2006	1997–2006
CZ	62.8	68.0	2.8
EE	35.8	55.2	7.6
CY	72.7	82.1	3.7
LV	29.8	44.9	7.6
LT	33.4	48.1	6.5
HU	46.4	57.8	4.4
MT	69.0	68.4	2.6
PL	40.1	45.9	4.2
SI	64.5	75.6	4.1
SK	43.4	52.7	4.2
EU-10[a]	44.7	52.6	4.1
BE	106.8	109.0	2.3
DK	113.4	112.5	2.1
DE	105.8	101.6	1.5
EL	64.4	77.6	4.1
ES	79.4	90.4	3.8
FR	103.6	100.2	2.3
IE	101.1	128.2	7.6
IT	104.1	93.0	1.4
LU	174.7	231.8	5.1
NL	110.7	115.9	2.5
AT	113.1	113.5	2.2
PT	69.5	66.1	2.2
FI	99.4	102.0	3.8
SE	104.7	106.0	3.1
UK	101.7	108.6	2.8
EU15[a]	100.0	100.0	2.3

Note:[a] = weighted average
Source: Eurostat

high per capita income in 1997. In general, countries with the lowest initial per capita incomes tended to grow fastest.

... and macroeconomic stabilization

Again, to a substantial extent motivated by the Copenhagen enlargement criteria, the EU-10 had already succeeded in broad macroeconomic stabilization of their economies when they joined the Union. Nevertheless, Euro adoption will require further progress in nominal convergence. The recent integration of the EU-10 into the union-wide economic policy coordination, and budgetary surveillance procedures, help to reinforce economic policy discipline and to achieve this goal. Inflation and interest rates in the EU-10 have fallen towards EU-15 levels and have in all cases entered the single-digit range. These favourable trends reflect a clear orientation of monetary and exchange rate policies. Inflation expectations declined and risk premium on interest rates narrowed, partly driven by convergence in financial markets in the expectation of Euro adoption.

The development of public finances has varied widely across the EU-10. In the former centrally planned economies, budget balances were strongly affected by transition-related reforms such as bank restructuring operations. Some countries, in particular the Baltic members, made progress in reducing their fiscal deficit between 1999 and 2006, while the position of others remained basically unchanged or deteriorated. Estonia was exceptional in regularly registering a budget surplus, and the two other Baltic countries had deficits well below the Maastricht threshold of 3 per cent of GDP. Slovenia also featured a deficit below the threshold. The deficit of the other countries exceeded the Maastricht value by varying margins, while Hungary had the highest deficit, 9.2 per cent of GDP in 2006. Cyprus and Malta had deficits above the Maastricht threshold, but in the meantime have addressed the situation. Except for Hungary, Cyprus and Malta, public debt ratios in 2004 were below 60 per cent of GDP in all EU-10 countries. Estonia had a very low public debt, less than 5 per cent of GDP.

In short: reforms and accession have paid off

The policy lessons from this convergence experience so far are obvious: macroeconomic and structural economic reforms, transition-related and EU-accession-oriented, have clearly paid off. However, they also show that there remains a substantial need for further convergence.

Catching-up opportunities ahead

Past accession-related catching-up experiences bode well for the future. As real, financial and institutional integration continues and EU transfers increase substantially, growth rates in the EU-10 are likely to remain higher than in the EU-15 if the right conditions can be created. The EU's economic policy framework is suited to act as a catalyst, in a similar way as the accession framework did before, and assist the new members in achieving these favourable conditions. In addition to central bank independence and a stable monetary framework, the main pillars of the EU approach are the Stability and Growth Pact and the revamped Lisbon agenda. In addition, Euro adoption can create a new focal point for further structural reforms while providing for macroeconomic and fiscal discipline. Despite a strong EU policy framework, appropriate domestic policies are key to success.

The ultimate goal is Euro adoption ...

The Euro will have many microeconomic and macroeconomic benefits for the EU-10. On the microeconomic level, to the benefit of entrepreneurs and consumers, it will eliminate currency fluctuations, reduce economic uncertainty and transaction costs, and increase price transparency and competition. Through all this, it will further foster integration into the Single Market, and enhance trade and foreign direct investment. On the macroeconomic level, membership in the Euro area will ensure monetary credibility and lower inflation and interest rates, provide for strong policy discipline, and increase the resilience against economic shocks from outside the Union. Enhanced macroeconomic stability is a necessary condition for smooth convergence. In light of all these advantages, none of the new EU member states has wanted an opt-out from the adoption of the Euro: they all committed themselves to the sustainable fulfilment of the associated conditions so as to enjoy fully its micro- and macroeconomic benefits.

Furthermore, the full participation of the EU-10 in the Single Market and their ultimate accession to the Euro area will have positive effects not only for these economies, but also for the EU as a whole. Building on the already high openness of the EU-10 and the achieved progress in domestic liberalization, still stronger linkages in goods and services trade, intensified FDI and capital mobility, and successively reinforced labour mobility will enhance competition and lead to more efficient resource allocation and specialization patterns across the Union. While successful catching-up of the EU-10 will restore greater economic coherence, these effects promise to give additional impetus to the EU's growth potential, albeit that economic restructuring will be required on the way.

... thus promoting sound domestic policies

As when the new members were on their way to accession, the post-accession EU economic policy framework offers superb opportunities for growth and convergence. However, it still leaves considerable leeway to domestic policies and the keys to success will lie at home, including in the domestic compliance with the European rules and their underpinning with good national institutions. The importance of domestic policies has been demonstrated by the different growth experience resulting from different policies of longer-standing converging EU members – Greece, Ireland, Portugal, and Spain. Valuable lessons can be learnt from these countries on how domestic policies can get it either awfully wrong or wonderfully right (for a discussion, see, European Commission, 2006c: 47).

The most obvious example of wrong domestic policies is certainly a fiscal policy that uses foreign resources to finance high public consumption, thus combining a high current account deficit with a high fiscal deficit. Hungary is the most prominent case in this respect in the EU at the moment. Being in such a situation means paying high interest rates and playing with investor confidence: the loss of it can easily lead to sharp foreign capital inflow reversals – with quite adverse consequences for growth. But even if public finances are more favourable, as in the Baltic States, there is still the possibility that the private sector uses foreign resources sub-optimally. This could be the case in a scenario of private sector over-exuberance. Overly optimistic expectations on profitability could lead to unproductive investment – for example, in real estate – and over-estimated income prospects could raise household consumption and debt to unsustainable levels. Both could be fuelled by rapid credit expansion and increased capital inflows from abroad. In this scenario, it would mostly be the savings and investment patterns in the private sector that would make a high current account deficit unsustainable. In order to realize the ultimate goal of Euro adoption and ensure the sustainability of the catching-up process, fiscal policy and structural reforms have a crucial role to play. Budgetary consolidation and structural reforms can go hand-in-hand and compatibility is helped by the EU policy framework. This is explained in greater detail in the remainder of the chapter.

The Lisbon process

At the end of the 1990s, the US had increased its lead on the EU in terms of income per capita (Figure 10.1) thanks to impressive productivity gains realized through progress in the information, technology and communications domain. In order not to lag further behind, the EU launched the Lisbon process in 2000 with the aim 'to become [by 2010] the most competitive and dynamic knowledge-based economy in the world, capable of sustainable economic growth with more and better jobs and greater social cohesion' (European Council 2000). To that end, a comprehensive strategy was developed with economic, social and environmental pillars.

The mid-term review of the Lisbon Strategy

Not much progress was realized towards the Lisbon targets and a 'mid-term review' (Kok 2004; European Commission 2005a; Dierx and Ilzkovitz 2006; Pisani-Ferry and Sapir 2006) pointed at insufficient implementation of reforms, which stemmed primarily from weak national ownership and an inefficient governance framework. There was a proliferation of sectoral targets with not enough focus on the principal Lisbon objectives. The Strategy lacked credibility because targets were multiple and overambitious and national ownership was poor because national politicians did not feel involved. Also, the so-called 'open method of coordination' failed to deliver results with its reliance on peer pressure and without a sanctioning mechanism if targets were not met (Box 10.1). Finally, it was felt that the benefits of structural reforms were badly communicated to the public, which often only saw the short-term costs but failed to appreciate the medium-term benefits.

The revamped Lisbon process

Based on the mid-term assessment, the spring 2005 European Council relaunched the Lisbon process. Growth and job creation are now the two principal objectives, while the social and environmental objectives became dimensions of them in an effort to maximize synergies.

On the basis of 'Integrated Guidelines', National Reform Programmes were, for the first time, submitted in autumn 2005. Their assessment by the Commission was forward-dated to the spring European Council of the following year. At the same time, the Commission presented a Community Lisbon Programme, which added an EU-wide dimension in order to maximize synergies with the national reform effort. In this context, actions are planned in the domain of, for example, the support of knowledge and innovation in Europe, the completion of the Internal Market for services, the removal of obstacles to academic mobility, the development of a common approach to economic migration (European Commission 2005c). In its Conclusions concerning the challenges presented in the National Reform Programmes, the spring 2006 Council (European Council 2006), stressed four priority actions: (1) investment in knowledge and innovation, (2) unlocking the business potential, especially of small and medium-sized enterprises (reduction of red tape), (3) employment of priority categories (young and older workers, women, minority groups); and (4) the definition of an Energy Policy for Europe.

Box 10.1   Governance is important

As structural reforms touch on sensitive issues of national competence – such as social benefits, education, innovation and pensions – a new soft form of coordination was required contrary to
domains such as public finance surveillance or competition policy,
where there is an EU competence. The 'open method of coordination', as the approach was called at the Lisbon Summit in 2000,
aims at centralizing targets, timetables, benchmarks and indicators
while respecting differences in national preferences and economic
structures. A central role in the monitoring of the Lisbon process
continues to be played each year by the Spring European Council.
It identifies the policy priorities that lead to medium-term recommendations. A full review of the policy priorities is undertaken
every three years. In autumn of each year, the member states report
on the implementation of the policies: the Commission then assess
the report and this assessment is submitted to the following year's
Spring European Council.

In light of the unsatisfactory implementation, the governance of
the process was further modified, giving a greater responsibility
and more ownership to the country level. In autumn 2005, member states presented their reform challenges in National Reform
Programmes and streamlined their implementation reporting
(for the first time, in autumn 2006). A greater involvement of
stakeholders such as parliament and social partners should
increase national ownership. The new arrangement continues to
rely on an annual policy cycle, with a pivotal role for the Spring
European Council, and has a three-year horizon until 2008,
when the set-up will be reviewed.

By 15 October 2006, member states had reported on the measures
taken in response to the challenges indicated in the previous year's
National Reform Programme and the four priority actions identified by
the Council. The Commission reviewed in its Annual Progress Report
(European Commission 2006b) the implementation of the measures
and found that the reform process is bearing fruit. However, there is
still scope for stronger action in areas such as long-term sustainability
of public finances, labour market reform, R&D, climate and energy
policies, as well as competition.

Budgetary consolidation and structural reforms in the Lisbon process

The emphasis of the Lisbon process is on structural reforms, but this is not at the expense of fiscal sustainability (Box 10.2). Indeed, the Stability and Growth Pact clearly privileges budgetary consolidation, and the reform of the Pact in 2005 did not change that. The new member states are fully integrated in the relaunched Lisbon process. Pursuing the Lisbon agenda, with its focus on reforming product, labour and financial markets, while paying attention to macroeconomic stability, will assist them in their catching-up process. Drawing up National Reform Programmes promotes greater and broader national reform ownership, as does better alignment of other national expenditure programmes, such as for the use of EU structural funds, with the Lisbon objectives. Enhanced labour, product and financial market flexibility will have to substitute for the exchange rate instrument after Euro adoption. Lisbon, therefore, also prepares for a successful Euro area participation.

Some of the measures possible in the US are more sensitive in the EU

Despite the efforts made under the Lisbon agenda, the EU remains trailing behind the US in terms of per capita income. This had led some in the new member states to suggest taking over more of the US economic policy model, and in particular downsizing government involvement in the economy. In the US, various tax-cutting episodes have lowered the burden of the public sector on the economy as measured by government revenues as a share of GDP. The revenue ratio[2] increased from 30 per cent of GDP at the beginning of the 1970s to about 34 per cent of GDP in 2000, but then declined by about 4 percentage points in the following three years to the level observed at the start of the period under examination (Figure 10.6). In the EU, a clear upward trend is discernable in the revenue ratio (from 36 per cent of GDP to about 45 per cent of GDP), leading to an average burden of 43 per cent of GDP for the EU compared to 31 per cent of GDP for the US in the whole period.

Different political priorities, social sensitivities and expenditure developments are the background to these divergent revenue trends. However, the government deficit was about the same for both the US and the EU in the period 1970–2005; namely, around 3 per cent of GDP. By contrast, US growth was significantly higher than in the EU (3.1 per cent versus 2.5 per cent) and some might want to attribute this to the lower weight of the public sector in the overall economy. There is

Box 10.2   Structural reforms and budgetary consolidation in the Integrated Guidelines for Growth and Jobs (2005–08)

The Integrated Guidelines (European Commission 2005b) contain 24 guidelines regrouped in three sections (macroeconomic policies, microeconomic reforms, and employment measures) of which the following are the most relevant for the relation between structural reforms and fiscal prudence:

Guideline No. 1
[...] As long as this [medium-term budgetary] objective has not yet been achieved, [Member States] should take all the necessary corrective measures to achieve it. [...]

Guideline No. 2
[...] in view of [...] ageing populations, undertake a satisfactory pace of government debt reduction [...], reform pension and health care systems. [...]

Guideline No. 3
[...] redirect the composition of public expenditures towards growth-enhancing categories [...]

Guideline No. 7
To increase and improve investment in R&D [...] through more effective and efficient public expenditure on R&D [...] and making better use of incentives to leverage private R&D [...]

Guideline No. 13
[... reduce] state aid that distorts competition [...]

Guideline No. 16
To expand, improve and link up European infrastructure and complete priority cross-border projects [...]

Guideline No. 23
Expand and improve investment in human capital [...]

Guidelines 1, 2, 3 and 13 emphasize fiscal prudence or advocate measures with a favourable budgetary impact, while guidelines 7, 16 and 23 imply a budgetary cost.

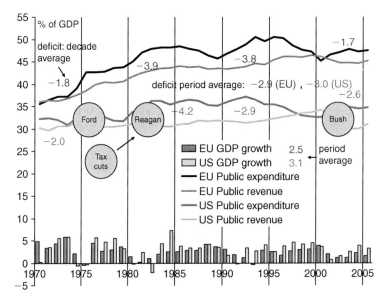

Figure 10.6 Public finance and growth in the US and the EU
Source: Eurostat

some evidence for this statement in Figure 10.7, suggesting an overall negative relation between public revenues and GDP growth. However, the unfavourable growth and per capita income comparison from the perspective of the EU is offset by greater social cohesion in the EU, to which, apparently, the government contributes. Furthermore, it has to be borne in mind that most of the difference in the headline growth performance between the EU and the US is due to the difference in population growth. Indeed, real per capita GDP growth in the US, as well as in the EU-15, averaged about 2.0 per cent per year between 1970 and 2006.

Besides different social priorities, budgetary reforms seem to be more sensitive in the EU context with its higher emphasis on medium- and long-term sustainability of public finances. For instance, while there are differences at the country level and over time, tax cuts aiming at reducing the weight of the government in the economy or as a discretionary countercyclical device are generally more difficult to implement in the EU policy framework, unlike in the US, which experienced three episodes of large tax reductions (Figure 10.6) in the period under consideration. In 1975, 1981 and 2001–03, under presidents Ford, Reagan and G.W. Bush, significant tax cuts were implemented to the order of

228

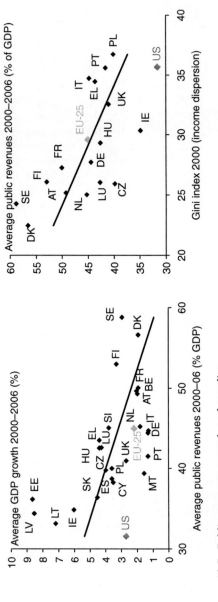

Figure 10.7 Public revenues, growth and equality
Source: Eurostat, OECD

1 per cent of GDP, 1.4 per cent of GDP and 2 per cent of GDP respectively (Meeropol 2001; Bieńkowski 2006). Although the political motivations differed among these three tax-cutting episodes, they were all implemented in the context, or against the background, of recessions.

These tax-cut episodes were accompanied by widening deficits, admittedly not only because of the tax cuts but also because of rising expenditures linked to adverse cyclical conditions and/or new political priorities. As a share of GDP, the fiscal position of general government deteriorated by 4.2 per cent between 1974 and 1975, by 3.4 per cent between 1981 and 1983, and by 6.4 per cent between 2000 and 2003. There is a debate about the self-financing capacity of tax cuts (for an overview, see Hayward 2006). Some, based on the Laffer curve, argued the tax cuts would lead to higher tax revenues generated by stronger growth ensuing from the smaller burden of the government on the economy. Others were less sanguine and presented estimates that only 20 per cent would be earned back or that it takes several years, up to seven, to recuperate a part, about 70 per cent, of the revenue loss. Without attempting to disentangle the impact of the cycle, tax-cut reversals, and a possible earn-back effect, the broad picture of revenue and deficit developments in the years following the major tax cuts shows that government revenues as a share of GDP started to rise again after a few years in the US. However, the fiscal deficits remained wider much longer, except in the aftermath of the tax cuts implemented by the Ford administration when the deficit returned to the ex-ante situation after five years. In the 1980s, under President Reagan, and since 2001 under President Bush, US fiscal deficits were on average larger compared with those observed in the same period in the EU.

More attention to structural reforms in the revamped Stability and Growth Pact

While perhaps less problematic in the US context, large tax cuts in the EU policy framework are more sensitive because of the necessity to maintain a sound budgetary position in order to preserve the smooth functioning of European Monetary Union. This is reflected, among other things, in the EU Treaty requirement to observe a 3 per cent of GDP ceiling for the general government deficit.[3] It had led many observers (see, for example, Beetsma and Debrun 2003) to criticize the Stability and Growth Pact for hampering structural reforms with short-term budgetary cost but long-term benefits for growth. These issues were particularly relevant for the new member states that entered the EU on 1 May 2004. Several of them had deficits in excess of 3 per cent of GDP reference value. At the same time, these countries faced a significant catching-up effort to which public finances are called to contribute. As a consequence, it was judged inappropriate to oblige the new member states that entered the EU on 1 May 2004 to correct the excessive deficit in the year following its identification – that is, 2005 – as would normally have been the case.[4] The 2004 Update of the Broad Economic Policy Guidelines (European Commission 2004) endorsed by the European Council on 17–18 June 2004, suggests therefore paying attention to 'country-specific circumstances, in particular to: initial budgetary positions, ongoing structural shifts in the economies and the possible risks resulting from current account imbalances and strong credit growth. It could be appropriate, from an economic point of view, to allow for a multi-annual adjustment period in some cases when correcting a deficit of more than 3 per cent.'

While the old Stability and Growth Pact already allowed for this, its reform in 2005 (European Council 2005) was seized as an opportunity to articulate better how to take account of structural reforms in budgetary surveillance. This had to occur both in the corrective arm of the new Pact, the excessive deficit procedure, and in the preventive arm, including the evaluation of the stability and convergence programmes submitted by member states on an annual basis. Regarding the corrective arm, in deciding whether a deficit beyond 3 per cent of GDP is excessive, 'all relevant factors' have to be considered, which include structural reforms related to the Lisbon agenda, such as policies fostering research and innovation, subject to the condition that the deficit remains close to the reference value and the excess over the reference value is temporary.[5] These relevant factors will be taken into account in all steps subsequent to the decision of categorizing a country as having excessive deficit in making the recommendation on how to correct the deficit. However, they are not considered for the abrogation of the excessive deficit. Systemic pension reforms were particularly emphasized. They weigh on the government balance in the short term, while enhancing long-term fiscal sustainability. This is recognized in the new Pact, which allows taking into account in all steps of the excessive deficit procedure the net cost of the implementation of a mandatory fully funded pension system,[6] again subject to the condition that the deficit remains close to the reference value and has been declining.

With respect to the preventive arm[7] of the Stability and Growth Pact, the achievement of a country-specific structural budgetary balance in the medium term is foreseen. Major structural reforms, for example, in the domain of healthcare, pensions, labour markets, that have a verifiable impact on the long-term sustainability of public finances can provide a justification for a deviation from this medium-term objective of the structural balance or the adjustment path towards it. Again, special attention is paid to systemic pension reforms. As under the corrective arm of the Pact, there are limitations: the deviation from the medium-term objective due to major structural reforms should be temporary and in any case a 'safety margin' against breaching the 3 per cent of GDP reference value should be observed.

So far, already one occasion has occurred in which use has been made of the exceptions foreseen in the new Stability and Growth Pact. Lithuania was granted a deviation from the requirement to implement a structural adjustment effort of 0.5 per cent of GDP per year because it had introduced a fully funded pension system while respecting the limiting conditions, in the form of safety margin against breaching the 3 per cent of GDP ceiling and temporariness of the deviation.[8]

The fiscal consolidation required by the Stability and Growth Pact does not necessarily conflict with the catching-up related spending needs of the new member states, if rationalization options are sufficiently taken into account in a medium-term fiscal framework. The existence of such options is suggested by the relatively large size of government in relation to per capita income in some new member states, compared with more advanced EU members and certainly compared with the United States, and the very diverse expenditure structures among them. The Stability and Growth Pact offers a medium- and long-term orientation for fiscal policies that limits the scope for short-term measures that might not take long-term sustainability considerations sufficiently into consideration, such as unfunded tax cuts without sufficient growth-enhancing effect. These rule-based limitations for policy action might be quite propitious for the new member states where political 'budget cycles' are still relatively pronounced against the backdrop of a relative short experience of the electorate.

The trade-off between structural reforms and budgetary consolidation in practice

The possible trade-off between structural reforms and budgetary consolidation has been empirically analyzed at a conference organized by the European Commission's Directorate General for Economic and Financial Affairs in December 2005 (Deroose *et al.* 2006). Drawing general conclusions is difficult because of the great variety of approaches followed by the papers presented at the conference, but it appears that, in the long term, many structural reforms are beneficial for public finance. However, short-term costs cannot be easily dismissed with the magnitude of the impact varying considerably depending on the sector, for example, labour market versus product markets; or the design of the reform, for example, parametric versus systemic pension reforms. Also, the impact of budgetary retrenchment on the likelihood of structural reforms depends on the type of reforms. Labour market reforms are possibly delayed when there is a need for budgetary retrenchment, but such a trade-off is not evident for product or financial market reforms as well as for pension reforms.

One can also look at the experience with the revamped Lisbon agenda to gauge how member states dealt with the possible existence of a trade-off between structural reforms and budgetary consolidation. In the following, this is done by examining the challenges as presented in the National Reform Programmes submitted in 2005 (European Commission 2006a) and the implementation measures reported in the subsequent year as assessed in the Annual Progress Report (European Commission 2006b) and leading to a Council Recommendation.[9] In Table 10.2, the presented reform areas are listed with a tentative indication of the likely direction of the fiscal impact in the first column. A minus sign suggests a budgetary cost, for example, in the reform area 'utilization of labour', a cut in social security contributions to tackle structural unemployment; a positive sign improves the budget, for example, healthcare reform to foster public finance sustainability; and a zero is for neutral measures, for example, adopting legislation to enhance the business environment. While, in each reform area, one can think of measures with opposite budgetary effects, as well as of differences through time and across countries, the chosen sign should reflect the dominant tendency. From the second column in Table 10.2, figures under 'total', it appears that R&D and a better utilization of the labour supply are top challenges for most member states, while short-term budgetary stabilization is perceived to be less of an issue. Indeed, 24 countries report that R&D is important for them, while only 5 indicate short-term budgetary stabilization. With respect to implementation, the reform areas of strength and weaknesses can be derived from the Council Recommendation.[10] Only the weaknesses are reported in third column; implementation failures are most notable in the domains of labour utilization, education and long-term sustainability of public finances.

With respect to challenges, member states do not seem to be particularly concerned by a trade-off between structural reforms and fiscal orthodoxy. Indeed, some structural reforms with negative budgetary impact – for

Table 10.2 The Lisbon process and structural reforms versus fiscal consolidation

Number of member states (as % of total EDP or non-EDP countries)	Budgetary Impact	Challenge (2005)			Implementation weakness (2006)		
		Total	EDP[a]	Non-EDP	Total	EDP[a]	Non-EDP
R&D, innovation	–	24	11(92)	13(100	10	7(70)	3(20)
Utilization of labour (labour supply and/or structural unemployment)	–	23	10(83)	13(100	20	9(90)	11(73)
Business environment/entrepreneurship	0	22	11(92)	11(85)	4	0(0)	4(27)
Sustainability of public finance	+	20	10(83)	10(77)	13	6(60)	7(47)
Education and skills (including Lifelong Learning)	–	20	10(83)	10(77)	16	8(80)	8(53)
Sustainable development	0	18	8(67)	10(77)	9	4(40)	5(33)
Competition	0	14	7(58)	7(54)	9	4(40)	5(33)
Infrastructure	–	13	6(50)	7(54)	2	2(20)	0(0)
ICT	0	11	8(67)	3(23)	2	2(20)	0(0)
Efficiency of public administration/services	+	8	5(42)	3(23)	1	1(10)	0(0)
Short term budgetary stability	+	5	2(17)	3(23)	3	1(10)	2(13)

Note:[a] = excessive deficit procedure (EDP). There were 12 countries in EDP in 2005 and 10 in 2006.
Sources: National Reform Programmes (European Commission 2006a) and Annual Progress Report (European Commission 2006b)

example, labour utilization – are considered more important than long-term sustainability of public finances, which in turn receives a higher priority than some other structural reforms such as competition. Nevertheless, countries with fiscal difficulties, here represented as being in excessive deficit procedure (EDP), are somewhat under-represented in the reform categories implying a budgetary cost and over-represented when reforms improve the fiscal situation or when the impact is neutral (see percentage figures in brackets in second column). This suggests that there may be some form of prioritization, which is, however, not all-determining, as the differences in the percentage shares are not significant.

With respect to implementation, most weaknesses appear in domains where reforms are costly for the budget, for example, utilization of labour, education. Furthermore, taking measures seems particularly difficult in EDP countries, as suggested by the higher percentage figures in brackets for EDP countries in the third column. This suggests that a difficult fiscal situation could delay structural reforms that weigh on the budget. The point is further illustrated with the good implementation score for business environment/entrepreneurship where measures are rather neutral for the budget and thus 'easy' to implement for EDP countries. However, EDP countries are also relatively well represented with a large implementation gap in areas without negative consequences for the budget such as sustainable development, competition and sustainability of public finances. A rationalization of this finding would be that a difficult fiscal situation reduces the 'political capital' of governments to press ahead with measures of any kind against the opposition of interest groups.

Summarizing, the existence of a trade-off between structural reforms and budgetary consolidation is not clear-cut. At the level of challenges formulated under the Lisbon agenda, member states do not seem to sacrifice one for the other. However, measures in some domains might be more difficult to implement when a country is in a difficult fiscal situation.

Conclusions

In terms of per capita income, the EU lags behind the US. As a consequence, some new member states are looking at the US for guideposts for steering domestic economic policies and fostering catching-up. However, one should put things in perspective and not forget that Central and Eastern Europe has fared quite well by orienting its reforms towards the EU benchmark. The process of EU accession acted as a strong catalyst and policy anchor for macroeconomic stabilization, fiscal consolidation, and structural reforms, and enabled a unique transition success story. Chances that this success story can be continued are good if the reform momentum is kept up and if it is revived in those cases where reform fatigue has crept in.

The EU economic policy framework offers the right vehicle for moving ahead. Its macroeconomic policy component includes the objective of ultimately adopting the Euro and the criteria for doing so. Euro adoption can act as a focal point for macroeconomic stability and fiscal discipline while providing reform incentives, notably to enhance competitiveness and adaptability through labour and product markets when the exchange rate instrument is no longer available. The renewed Stability and Growth Pact guides fiscal policy towards the objective of fiscal sustainability while leaving sufficient leeway to implement structural reforms. It sets precise rules how to deal with structural reforms that have a budgetary cost. Hence, some measures applied in the US cannot be transposed in an unqualified way to the EU context. There is, for example, a reluctance to implement unfunded tax cuts in the EU because of the Stability and Growth Pact requirements.

With respect to structural reforms, the EU framework has been continuously evolving in search of best practices amongst the policies of EU member countries but also of other advanced industrialized countries including the US. This resulted in the reformed Lisbon process, which fosters the creation of jobs and growth, and fosters successful participation in the Euro area. Any trade-off between budgetary consolidation and structural reforms does not seem to be dramatic, although in practice it appears that in countries with a weaker fiscal position, and under close budgetary surveillance by the EU, some measures may be delayed.

Notes

1   The views expressed in this chapter represent exclusively the positions of the authors and do not necessarily correspond to those of the European Commission. This paper benefited from comments and suggestions by A. Dierx, H. Feddersen, N. Lubenets and participants in the conference 'US Economic Experience and Its Applicability to Poland and the EU'. This conference was held in Warsaw on 16 October 2006 and organized by the US Economy Research Center of the Warsaw School of Economics under auspices of the National Bank of Poland. We are grateful to J. Nagant for technical assistance.

2   For reasons of comparability, the public finance data reported are based on Eurostat's ESA95 methodology. Compared with the data of the US Bureau of Economic Analysis, the share of the government is somewhat higher in

Eurostat's approach, but the changes are similar. Overall, the message is independent of the statistical method used.

3   In exceptional circumstances, it is possible to exceed this ceiling as foreseen in Article 2 of Council Regulation (EC) No. 1467/97 of 7 July 1997 on speeding up and clarifying the implementation of the excessive deficit procedure, OJ L 209, 2.8.1997, p.6. Regulation as amended by Regulation (EC) No. 1056/2005 (OJ L 174, 7.7.2005, p.5), available at: http://europa.eu.int/comm/economy_finance/about/activities/sgp/main_en.htm

4   In 'special' circumstances, further delays are possible. Article 3(4) of Council Regulation (EC) No. 1467/97 of 7 July 1997 on speeding up and clarifying the implementation of the excessive deficit procedure, OJ L 209, 2.8.1997, p.6. The 'special' circumstances referred to here are to be distinguished from the 'exceptional' circumstances that characterize a severe economic downturn.

5   Articles 3, 4 and 6 of Council Regulation (EC) No. 1467/97 of 7 July 1997 on speeding up and clarifying the implementation of the excessive deficit procedure, OJ L 209, 2.8.1997, p.6. Regulation as amended by Regulation (EC) No. 1056/2005 (OJ L 174, 7.7.2005, p.5), available at: http://europa.eu.int/comm/economy_finance/about/activities/sgp/main_en.htm

6   Articles 5 and 7 of Council Regulation (EC) No. 1467/97 of 7 July 1997 on speeding up and clarifying the implementation of the excessive deficit procedure, OJ L 209, 2.8.1997, p.6. Regulation as amended by Regulation (EC) No. 1056/2005 (OJ L 174, 7.7.2005, p.5), available at: http://europa.eu.int/comm/economy_finance/about/activities/sgp/main_en.htm

7   Articles 2a and 5 of Council Regulation (EC) No. 1466/97 of 7 July 1997 on the strengthening of the surveillance of budgetary positions and the surveillance and coordination of economic policies, OJ L 209, 2.8.1997, p. 1. Regulation as amended by Regulation (EC) No. 1055/2005 (OJ L 174, 7.7.2005, p. 1), available at: http://europa.eu.int/comm/economy_finance/about/activities/sgp/main_en.htm

8   Council Opinion on the updated Convergence Programme of Lithuania, 7381/06, Brussels, 14 March 2006, available at: http://ec.europa.eu/economy_finance/about/activities/sgp/country/lithuania_en.htm

9   Council Recommendation on the 2007 update of the broad guidelines for the economic policies of the member states and the Community and on the implementation of member states' employment policies, COM(2006) 816 final, Brussels, 12.12.2006, available at: http://ec.europa.eu/growthandjobs/annual-report-1206_en.htm

10   Issues in the Council Recommendation mentioned under 'progress' and 'points to focus on' are included in strengths and weaknesses, respectively.

References

Beetsma, R. and Debrun, X. (2003) 'Reconciling Stability and Growth: Smart Pacts and Structural Reforms', IMF Working Paper, 03/174, September, available at: http://www.imf.org/external/pubs/cat/longres.cfm?sk=16792.0

Bieńkowski, W. (2006) 'The Economic Policy of George W. Bush: A Continuation of Reagonimics?', in *Reagonomics Goes Global; What Can the EU, Russia and*

Other Transition Countries Learn from the US?, W. Bieńkowski, J.C. Brada and M.-J. Radło (eds) (New York: Palgrave Macmillan).

Deroose, S., Flores E. and Turrini, A. (eds) (2006) 'The Budgetary Implications of Structural Reforms', Proceedings from the ECFIN Workshop Brussels, 2 December 2005, Economic Papers, 248, available at: http://ec.europa.eu/economy_finance/publications/economic_papers/2006/economicpapers248_en.htm

Dierx, A. and Ilzkovitz, F. (2006) 'Economic Growth in the EU: Challenges for Euro Area and New Member States', Paper presented at the ICEG EC Annual Conference, Budapest.

European Commission (2004) 'The 2004 Update of the 2003–05 Broad Economic Policy Guidelines', Brussels, 7 April 2004, COM(2004)238, available at: http://ec.europa.eu/economy_finance/publications/european_economy/broadeconomypolicyguidelines2004_en.htm

European Commission (2005a) 'Working Together for Growth and Jobs. A new start for the Lisbon Strategy', 2 February 2005, COM (2005)24, available at: http://ec.europa.eu/growthandjobs/key/index_en.htm

European Commission (2005b) 'Integrated Guidelines for Growth and Jobs (2005–08)', 12 April 2005, available at: http://ec.europa.eu/growthandjobs/key/index_en.htm

European Commission (2005c) 'Communication from the Commission to the Council and the European Parliament, Common Actions for Growth and Employment: The Community Lisbon Programme', Brussels, 20 July 2005, COM(2005)330, [SEC(2005) 981], available at: http://ec.europa.eu/growthandjobs/pdf/COM2005_330_en.pdf

European Commission (2006a) 'Time to Move Up A Gear', 2006 Annual Progress Report on Growth and Jobs, 25 January 2006, available at: http://ec.europa.eu/growthandjobs/annual-report_en.htm

European Commission (2006b) 'Communication from the Commission to the Spring European Council – Implementing the Renewed Lisbon Strategy for Growth and Jobs, A Year of Delivery', Brussels, 12 December 2006, COM(2006) 816final, available at: http://ec.europa.eu/growthandjobs/pdf/1206_annual_report_en.pdf

European Commission (2006c), 'Enlargement, Two Years After: An Economic Evaluation', European Economy Occasional Paper, 24, May, available at: http://ec.europa.eu/economy_finance/publications/occasional_papers/2006/occasionalpapers24_en.htm

European Council (2000) 'Presidency Conclusions', 23 and 24 March 2000, Lisbon, available at: http://www.consilium.europa.eu/ueDocs/cms_Data/docs/pressData/en/ec/00100-r1.en0.htm

European Council (2005) 'Improving the Implementation of the Stability and Growth Pact', Presidency Conclusions, Brussels, 22–23 March, available at: http://europa.eu/european_council/conclusions/index_en.htm

European Council (2006) 'Presidency Conclusions', 23–24 March, Brussels, available at: http://www.consilium.europa.eu/ueDocs/cms_Data/docs/pressData/en/ec/89013.pdf

Hayward, S. (2006) 'The Evolution of US Economic Policy in the 1980s', in *Reagonomics Goes Global; What Can the EU, Russia and Other Transition Countries Learn from the US?*, W. Bieńkowski, J.C. Brada and M.-J. Radło (eds) (New York: Palgrave Macmillan).

Kok, W. (2004) 'Facing the Challenge: The Lisbon Strategy for Growth and Employment', High Level Group chaired by Wim Kok, November.

Kuznets, S. (1955), 'Economic Growth and Income Inequality,' *American Economic Review*, 45.

Meeropol, M. (2001) 'A Tale of Two Tax Cuts; What Recent History Teaches about Tecessions and Economic Policy', *Economic Policy Institute Issue Brief*, 157, 7 May, available at: http://www.epinet.org/content.cfm/issuebriefs_ib157

Pisani-Ferry, J. and Sapir, A. (2006) 'Last Exit to Lisbon', Bruegel Policy Brief, 2, March, available at: http://www.bruegel.org/Files/media/PDF/Publications/Papers/EN_LastExitToLisbon_Paper_ElectronicDistribution.pdf

US Department of Commerce Bureau of Economic Analysis (2007). Data presented online at: http://www.bca.gov/

11

Competition and Solidarity in Higher Education – A Reform Proposal Aiming at Improving Quality and Enhancing Security: The Case of Hungary

Lajos Bokros

Introduction

For those of us who believe that tertiary education is an important factor for enhancing growth and competitiveness, the fact that only three universities outside the United States have been listed among the best twenty in the world comes as an uncomfortable realization of how much the old continent has fallen behind. One should add that the remaining three universities are Tokyo, Oxford and Cambridge. None of the famous universities of France, Germany, Spain or Italy have been listed, to mention only the countries that for centuries topped the quality list and used to be the reference point for others.

This chapter aims at investigating the causes that make the continental European universities, and especially those of Central Europe, uncompetitive in higher education with the Anglo-Saxon ones. Is it a question of ownership or management and financing? Are there some other factors that have caused these unfavourable rankings?

The author of this chapter concentrates on Hungary as a case study, but the most important shortcomings of the Hungarian higher education system very much resemble the problems that other countries have faced both in Central and Western Europe for many decades.

Higher education in crisis all over in Central and Eastern Europe

Output quality is rather low: unemployment among fresh graduates is at least twice as high as the national average and many young people work in jobs that do not correspond to the formal qualifications reflected by their degrees. Training of teachers is still widespread in circumstances where the number of children at the age of primary and secondary schooling is in sharp decline. In Hungary, more than 35 higher educational institutions offer various degrees for economists. At the same time, multinational corporations are increasingly looking for young graduates with Western degrees. There is an immense overproduction of historians, communication experts, even lawyers, but we have too few engineers, technicians, computer scientists and biotech experts.

The network of higher educational institutions is grossly oversized and drastically fragmented. In terms of quality, Hungarian higher education is nowhere near world standards: not one Hungarian university is among the best two hundred of the world.[1] If there is competition in higher education in Hungary, it is only between Szeged and Pécs and between Debrecen and Budapest, but never with any high-ranking Western European institution, let alone world-class North American or Far Eastern universities.

The low quality of higher education in Hungary is closely linked to the low quality of secondary and primary education.[2] It is, therefore, obvious that reforming public education is as important as reforming higher education. This chapter does not deal with the problems of public education. From the viewpoint of higher education reform, however, it is worth comparing the specific characteristics of both levels of education, since their differences would highlight the most important differences in the way in which they need to be reformed.

Substantive differences between public and higher education

The basic characteristics of public education in Hungary are that for specific cohorts (between age 6 and 16) participation is mandatory; in theory, all children attend school, each child attends only one school, and only for a limited period of time. Therefore, there is no excess demand. There are limits to competition, such as, small children cannot travel too far from their home, parents wish to supervise the performance of their children, and follow the activities of the school on a daily basis.

The quality of public education is vital, indeed, because opportunities in life are largely determined by the quality of primary schooling. It is at this level that it is determined whether one can get into a good secondary school and then go on to any good university. The constitutional and moral principle of equal opportunity can prevail only if the quality of primary schools is somewhat even. This requires many professional preconditions that are out of the purview of this study. Nevertheless, we point out the fact that, for equal opportunity to prevail, the state and, in Hungary, local governments or the district association of several local governments, need to spend more or less the same amount on the schooling of each and every child.

If there is no excess demand in the system, capitation financing is not dangerous because it does not loosen the hard budget constraint of the respective levels of government. Nobody attends two schools at the same time, and everybody attends school only for a limited period of time, no matter whether able to complete schooling successfully or not. It is sufficient to determine the minimum size of schools and classes as well as the minimum mandatory work load of teachers. If these conditions are met, then the school system does not become fragmented, and quality is preserved and costs are contained. Capitation financing in public education is, therefore, not only permissible, but also even desirable for societal security and solidarity to prevail.

The basic characteristics of higher education are clearly different from those of public education, in all aspects. In higher education, there are no predetermined cohorts, attendance can start at any age, it is not mandatory at all, participation of the majority of any cohort is not even desirable, it is possible to attend more than one school at the same time, there is no mandatory exit point in time either, therefore, there is a possibility for significant excess demand.

At the same time, competition can be much stronger among higher educational institutions, because, for students, the whole world is wide open today: one can travel seemingly to anywhere to get a good education; excellent students can select between unlimited offers of stipends, first and foremost in masters and doctoral programmes; and there not all institutions have an admission test and performance leads to student ranking and better opportunities only at a later stage.

The most important difference between public and higher education is the appearance of excess demand in the latter. This exists in all countries where students are not required to pay a tuition fee covering more or less the full costs of higher education. Excess demand leads to waste on two counts: on one hand, there is a need for more schools, larger infrastructure, more faculties and so on; on the other, graduates may not be able to find a job corresponding to their formal qualifications.

If a school's owner tries to limit waste by offering fewer classrooms, smaller laboratories, a less extensive library and so on, that leads to overcrowding and, hence, to deterioration in the quality of education. If the increase in student numbers does not lead to a corresponding increase in the number of good faculties, then the deterioration in the quality of education is further amplified. As a consequence, the wastage of investment in education created by graduates not being able to find jobs corresponding to their qualifications also increases. In Hungary, higher education is largely financed by capitation, as is public education. This is not only unnecessary, but also clearly detrimental to quality because universities become interested in maximizing student intake and create excess demand by themselves. Unnecessary increases in the quantity of students lead to deterioration in the quality of education. It is a vicious circle.

Twentieth-century misconceptions

Capitation financing in higher education is not just the legacy of non-market-oriented socialist systems: it has also a strong tradition in continental Western Europe. Moreover, it is regarded by many not as an obsolete legacy of the past, but rather as a valuable achievement of working-class struggle in the twentieth century. The argument is that, if students had to pay a substantial fee for higher education, then smart but poor young people could never go to university and it would be detrimental to equal opportunity.

Free university education and equal opportunities for disadvantaged people are wholly different things. Moreover, equal opportunities do not prevail to any meaningful degree in any of the post-socialist countries. The specific situation is such that it cannot prevail. When public goods and services are provided at no cost, this means only that users are not required to pay at the time and place of delivery, or, at least, not to the extent commensurate with the quantity and quality of this service. Of course, producing public services incurs costs, which is covered by the whole society, most frequently through the state budget. If something is to be provided for free at the time and place of delivery, then it is free not only for the poor people, but also for the rich. Higher education is precisely such a service. The public service nature of higher education creates excess demand and disregards social needs. Therefore, contrary to conventional wisdom, providing free higher education is inefficient from both the economic and the social point of view.

In Hungary, the obvious disadvantages of capitation financing have been mitigated by limiting the number of students admitted to places fully financed by the state, while the gates of the universities have been opened up to students willing to pay a considerable amount of some of the costs. This appears to be a reasonable strategy on the part of the state. If universities cannot survive exclusively on capitation financing, then there is a need to open up new channels of financing for them. In fact, half of those admitted to higher education in Hungary every year are now paying tuition fees, despite all the rhetoric to the contrary. Considering that some of the best state universities also have English- and even German-language courses tailored to the specific needs of basically Western European students, then it is clear that capitation provided by the public purse is losing its central role in financing quality education anyway. The medical (SOTE) and technical (BME) universities of Budapest are true market leaders in these types of programmes.

Mixed financing, although it somewhat limits excess demand, does not eliminate waste and does not necessarily improve equality of opportunities either. The quota financed by the state budget is arbitrary. It does not reflect any calculation of education needs derived from future labour market demand. Indeed, no such surveys of demand are produced in Hungary at all. To obtain a place at the university financed by the state is possible when students have good high school results (matriculate) and pass the admission test successfully. Hence, skills and knowledge do matter, but social conditions do not.[3] It is no surprise, therefore, that most university places fully-financed by the state are occupied by students coming from well-off families, because they are the ones who have not only sufficient knowledge capital brought from home, but also valuable relationship capital. The tuition fee was thus introduced in a creeping way, without allowing it to deliver positive results – that is, by reducing excess demand, improving quality and providing equal opportunities. This measure was not a reform, just an empty measure.

Is there any chance to break the vicious circle?

Reforming higher education must start with the identification of guiding principles. It must be made clear that higher education is not a citizen's right – a public service free and accessible to all – but, rather, that it is most probably available only to a minority of each age cohort, and that it is a lifetime investment with a huge cost to families and students. Moreover, its benefits, although making the whole of society richer, are enjoyed mainly by the individual, because the returns from applying knowledge capital can be earned not only from working on the home labour market, but also throughout the whole world. For this reason, the state should share the costs of higher education only for a limited period of time: for the talented, well-off – only symbolically; for the talented poor – significantly; and for the untalented – not at all.

In addition, it is important that, when choosing a school and a degree, it is the citizen who bears primary responsibility, and thus the state guarantees neither the value of the degree nor any future job and its benefits. The state can, and possibly should, mitigate the risks of a bad choice of university or degree by compelling universities to publish reliable information on job placements, and by creating an environment that leads to unfettered competition among universities no matter what form of ownership they have.

From these principles, the conditions of effective and efficient regulation can be well derived.

The tasks of higher educational institutions

For universities to be able to transmit a modern and valuable education, they must be able to produce modern and valuable knowledge. Although, in principle, there might be such a thing as quality teaching without meaningful research, it is the exception rather than the rule. Stand-alone colleges offering only a bachelor's degree might be such institutions. Therefore, it is a general requirement that, in any higher educational institution calling itself a university, the overwhelming majority of faculties should conduct research, and the results of this research should find their way into teaching without delay.[4]

There is an intensive debate among intellectuals and university leaders on what other societal functions, beyond research, must be performed by higher educational institutions. The list can be endless according to taste, but the substance of all debates is *how universities can squeeze out more funds from the state*. In Hungary, the truth is that the poorer a university is in research results, the more activities it tries to perform in order to justify the extraction of additional fiscal funds. By declaring that the government does not have any obligation to support activities other than education and research, this discussion is rendered pointless. An outstanding university will perform many auxiliary activities anyway, with or without state funding.

A critical mass of reforms

It is time to abolish all state financing based on capitation. In addition, distinguishing between student places with and without state support should be eliminated immediately. It is insufficient to break down the walls between the two financing categories, as is planned by the Hungarian government at the moment. At the level of degree education, it is vital that all students pay a tuition fee, except for a maximum 15–20 per cent of students acknowledged as being students in need by the students' union.[5] Student unions will obtain real power, as well as huge responsibility, in this way.[6]

In the case of state-owned universities, the central budget should finance the costs of creating and maintaining a basic physical infrastructure, such as classrooms, lecture halls, laboratories, library, dormitories and so on. The size and make-up of this basic infrastructure needs to correspond to the number and composition of students harmonized with future labour market demand. The benefits would far outweigh the costs as the target would be a much better education assured to fewer students. The government has to make three big decisions in this regard.

First, all higher educational institutions lacking adequate physical and human infrastructure (faculty) must be closed down. Second, it is vital to identify and upgrade so-called priority schools, which would receive additional financing, provided they can meet clearly identifiable and achievable additional requirements, to be monitored continuously by the government. Third, as state support does not cover the costs of faculty, this would have to be financed largely by tuition.[7]

It is important to observe that the new arrangement constitutes a multichannel financing regime whereby the state budget keeps covering a good part of the costs of the most important activity of universities – that is, education. But state support does not come according to frequently and unpredictably changing rules. The ministers of finance and education should sign five-year contracts with individual state universities. Financial management of state-owned universities can be made much more stable and predictable by this arrangement, and assure maintenance of the quality of the physical infrastructure. Nevertheless, state financing would not be sufficient even for education, and thus for survival, not to speak of any research. This latter would be financed by grants awarded to specific projects. Funds could come partially from the state budget, but the bulk of them should arrive from corporate coffers. Last, but not least, tuition to be paid by students would play a crucial role in financing education.

In Central and Eastern Europe a brutal question arises: how to finance non-state universities? The principle of competition with equal chances would require that all owners cover the costs of basic infrastructure by themselves. This is obvious, in the case of private universities. But there can be a huge problem with church-owned universities, which serve a growing number of students in this part of the world.

The restructuring of church-owned universities

After decades of communism, it was a natural ambition of churches of all denominations to re-establish and even enlarge the network of their schools and other institutions. In the case of universities, the first initiative was to restore faculties of theology. It soon became clear, however, that stand-alone faculties of theology could not be rationally maintained, even with very generous state support; more often than not this support is even more generous than is applicable to state-owned universities. Churches were faced with the alternative that theological faculties would either join state universities or enhance their scope and status by establishing non-theological faculties too.

It is quite lamentable that, at least in Hungary, contracts signed between influential churches and the government supported the second option. Thus, on the one hand, non-theological schools have proliferated to an even greater extent, on the other hand, their financing was left to the state budget as well.[8] Moreover, non-theological faculties of church-owned universities cannot be either rationally regulated or closed, because this would be tantamount to breaching not only university autonomy, but also church independence. It would be important to try to extend higher educational reform to church-managed universities as well. When the whole higher education system is in crisis and needs comprehensive restructuring, there can be no sacred cows.

As we have seen, for priority universities to be selected, it is necessary to analyze and review all existing universities. If a non-theological faculty of a church-owned university proves not to meet the minimum standards, then the options are either to close it or for the church itself to finance its basic infrastructure in the future.[9] In the case of non-state universities, it is irrelevant whether their output corresponds to some future labour market demand or not. If, together, maintenance support and the tuition fee cover the full cost of education, then it does not matter that much whether excess supply will be created in the labour market because there is little or no waste of taxpayers' money. Let one hundred flowers bloom.

If churches are unable or unwilling to finance the basic infrastructure of their non-theological schools, they will certainly close them. The remaining theological faculties might wish to join state universities. The government will then, indeed, support their basic physical infrastructure.[10] At the same time, students will pay tuition fees that would be used for covering the costs of human infrastructure in exactly the same way as with all other universities.

When does tuition have an impact?

The introduction of tuition fees is merely a necessary, but far from sufficient, condition of competition. For it to have a truly positive impact on university life, there is a need for further substantive reforms. It is absolutely vital that students know they can demand value for their money. As with renowned American universities, it is important that students anonymously evaluate, in writing, the courses of each and every professor before the examination takes place, the professors receiving an aggregate evaluation after the examination. This evaluation should play a key role in deciding remuneration, promotion or dismissal. In Hungary, and most other European countries, this can happen only if the public employee status of the faculty is eliminated. It is also of key significance that the rector of the university, in consideration with the norms established by the senate, has a free hand in selecting and remunerating members of faculty and staff. The internal governance of universities requires a reshuffle in this regard.

A distorted interpretation of autonomy assigning seemingly limitless freedom to departments and schools should be revisited, because it leads to suboptimal allocation of resources and downward levelling of the quality of education. If a university as a whole wants to survive in competition with higher educational institutions, it needs to foster internal competition as well. The latter cannot be restricted by factional autonomy as exercised by internal units. When it comes to internal affairs, the rector should have the final say not only in financial and employment matters, but also in academic matters, too.

Informed choice

Competition leading to continuous efforts to improve quality has a further condition, which is that students should have reliable information in advance on the quality of teaching at various universities and the marketability of the degree universities offer.

It is quite difficult to assess the value of any degree in advance as the quality of education as well as the structure and judgements of the labour market might change significantly during a long period of education. The publication of long series of factual information can certainly help in making an informed choice when selecting a university and undertaking a huge family investment. It is critical, therefore, that all universities should follow the careers of their graduates and publish aggregate information on their chances of obtaining a good job and remuneration.[11] The universities should also publish information on the number, proportion and composition of students who have successfully completed their master and doctoral courses, and received their degrees within the established time frame; the names and proportion of graduates and postgraduates who have made an internationally recognized academic career, regardless of whether they stayed with their alma mater or not; as well as the number, curricula and faculty involved in master and doctoral courses, and schools regularly and successfully accredited by international committees of accreditation, and so on.

It is quite remarkable that, in Hungary, there are a few higher educational institutions that have already started to follow the careers of their former students and regularly publish aggregate information on this subject. What is needed now is that all universities follow their example. Moreover, it is important that the government prescribe the minimum information to be published by all universities and set standards for its content.[12] For students and their parents to make an informed choice, information thus published should be reliable and comparable.

The true nature of autonomy in higher education

Transparency helps foster competition but also enhances institutional responsibility. Internal and external competition will, nevertheless, lead to much needed improvements in the quality of education, but only if the structure of incentives for university leaders is changed. For that to happen, outside governance structures for universities have to be redesigned.[13] Unlimited autonomy for universities is no longer sustainable. This concept and practice of university autonomy today in Hungary, as in many other former socialist countries, also includes the unconstrained management of fiscal resources without any substantive control by the government. This is unfortunately true, not only in the case of state universities, but also with church and, seemingly, private institutions as well. The situation in Hungary is especially difficult, because this unconstrained financial autonomy is not only guaranteed by law, but has also been explicitly strengthened and converted into a dogma by repeated decisions of the Constitutional Court.

It is vital to adopt the practice of world class Anglo-Saxon private universities, where internal self-government (senate) embodies academic autonomy while strategic decisions – primarily, but not exclusively financial ones – are in the hands of a board of trustees representing the owners (maintainers) of the university.

It has to be acknowledged that there was an attempt to come closer to this structure when the draft law of higher education was discussed in Hungary in 2005. Unfortunately, these modern requirements, one by one, fell victim to political fights and vested interests. The reflection of this, however, can still be seen in the newly created bodies, called 'Economic Councils'. Some of these might even positively influence the behaviour of universities in the event that they cooperate with well-intended and responsible university leadership. But it is moral suasion without institutional guarantees. Progress can only be made if academic autonomy and financial control are separated, and the latter becomes the competence of owners and maintainers.

After the repeated failures of reform attempts after 1990, many experts no longer believe that any significant improvement in the quality of higher education can ever be achieved in Hungary. There are many more who are convinced that, by and large, all is fine, and that we only need some modification of the parameters of regulation and financing, without systemic change. This study argues that what we need is comprehensive paradigmatic reform. This requires not only a one-off, deep restructuring of Hungarian higher education but, even more so, the fundamental revision of the structure of incentives by creating conditions for strong competition, more security and better solidarity. Readers in other Central and Western European Countries might find some similarities between their systems and that of Hungary, and such similarities might also suggest that some of the reforms proposed here could also apply in their countries.

Notes

1   Webometrics ranks the Technical University of Budapest at 258, Eötvös Loránd University at 374, and the University of Szeged at 472 in the world.
2   In Hungary, primary and secondary levels of education are called public education while higher education includes only tertiary education.
3   Of course, I do not imply that social conditions should matter at entry. On the contrary, I oppose all attempts to dilute the quality of student intake on the basis of social needs and consider it detrimental if anybody is granted almost automatic entry because of special social conditions. The problem is not that social needs are currently disregarded at entry. It is that a one-off, good performance at entry guarantees socially unjustified support for a long period. Social assistance is much in need, but not at the moment of entry. It is needed much more thereafter, during the course of obtaining higher education in the event of continuously good performance in order to achieve the successful completion of studies.

4   This time around, we do not distinguish between basic and applied research. It is understood in the widest possible terms, including all kinds of research activity such as innovation, and so on.

5   As is widely known, the Bologna process that is taking place in the EU will distinguish between three stages in higher education. Basic training leads to a bachelor's degree, masters training ends with a master's degree, and doctoral training results in a PhD. The stages and degrees form a pyramid. Most students participate in basic training, only a proportion of those obtaining a bachelor's degree go on to masters training, and only a small fraction of graduate students enter into doctoral education. The length of the training period is variable (usually $3 + 2 + 3$ years) but is limited in any case. In the American model, the overwhelming majority of undergraduate students pays towards tuition, graduates might receive some stipend but some of them still pay, and, at the doctoral level, it is typical that most students do not pay anything but receive a substantial amount of monetary support. It is quite useful for any university to offer all three levels of higher education because it can achieve a remarkable profit in basic education which can then be used to support doctoral education (cross-financing).

In continental Western Europe, until recently there was another type of financing model. One of the proud 'achievements' of the students' revolt in 1968 was that participation in basic higher education became a citizen's right, and almost all young people were admitted into a university without sitting an entry examination and without paying tuition. The clearly foreseeable result of this process was increasing overcrowding and decline in the quality of education. This is exactly the reason why this process seems to be reversing now. More and more countries, regions and universities introduce tuition fees, restore the prestige of entry examinations and restrict the number of students admitted to any level of higher education.

6   It is highly debatable whether it is the student body that is best placed to assess the financial needs of students. In most US universities, there is a separate administrative unit to assess the social conditions of students and to offer stipends and any other social support to talented but less than well-off students.

7   As we can see, the role of tuition is substantive in such an arrangement. It also means that students are required to pay a significant amount – at least, at the undergraduate level. It has a clear logic from the viewpoint of universities. Neither capitation financing nor lump sum support is adequate for covering the costs of a faculty because there is no link between the quality of service and remuneration. It is so much better if there is a virtuous circle engaging the quality of education, faculty remuneration and student demand.

8   The reason for this is quite simple: non-theological faculties of church-owned universities are performing state functions; therefore, they are entitled to receive capitation financing in very much the same way as state owned universities. This argument can be dismissed only if we deny that providing higher education is a task of the state in general. *According to the new principles, higher education is not the duty of the state.* It is not a public service to be provided free and to all. It is a major private investment based on individual choice. Although some of the important conditions of higher education

are created by the state, this by no means involves unlimited financing of non-state universities.

9   According to the rules applicable to all universities in a uniform way, current costs of education are to be covered by tuition fees in church-owned universities too.

10   In this chapter, we do not deal with the question as to whether it is desirable or not. Analyzing the situation of church endowments is outside the purview of this study. It is important to note only that in a situation where, in the absence of any meaningful endowment, almost all state activities are financed by the state budget, it is not worth discussing church-offered higher education separately.

11   The best way to achieve that is to establish an *alumni association* that keeps permanent contact with former graduates. For alumni to be interested in providing reliable information about themselves, it is necessary that they feel themselves to be involved and concerned about the fate of their former alma mater. A good alumni association fosters a two-way exchange of information. The school should provide information regularly about its life, achievements and problems too. Last, but not least, the feeling of being an insider can also open the purse of alumni, and they might contribute financially to the future maintenance of their alma mater in quite a significant way in the long run.

12   In reality, what is needed is a two-tier information system. Information published by the universities has to be aggregated and ranked not only by the government, but also by independent rating agencies. Market oriented rating of courses, degrees and universities by independent – and, preferably, international – rating agencies would immensely enhance the power of competition and change the inward looking behaviour of most, if not all, higher educational institutions. At the same time, it is worth mentioning that such an overly ambitious information system needs careful regulation, and serious and constant attention by the authorities.

13   There is an intensive debate in the international academic world as to the extent to which outside and inside governance structures of a university should be similar to those of a business enterprise (corporation). Without getting into this debate, it is worth mentioning that the practice of world-class universities might offer what we call 'best practice'. The dominant trend is that universities that are truly outstanding in international competition proudly maintain their academic autonomy so they operate as cooperatives or partnerships in this regard but, when it comes to business decisions, they are under much stricter corporate governance.

12
Growth versus Security: Choice and the Generational Difference in Preferences

Stanisław Gomułka

Introduction

The choice of an optimal economic system can be viewed as a problem linked to preferences of individuals with respect to the income that might need to be forgone in order to enjoy a desirable level of job or income security. A highly competitive, market-oriented economic system has proved to be more innovative and more efficient, thus also more productive, than any centrally planned system. Therefore, the expected lifelong income of any individual in a competitive system is higher than it would be otherwise. However, the microeconomic fundamentals of such a system rest on the widespread use of strong incentives: both positive – such as bonuses, promotions and higher status, as well as negative – such as loss of income, demotion and loss of job. The result of such an incentive system is the prevalence of high uncertainty with respect to incomes, jobs and social position.

Within a market-based system we have various regulations, customs and policies that might limit this uncertainty, even though there might be some costs of such limitations for the average level of income and its future rate of growth. The demand for security varies among individuals and societies. Therefore, the choice of such regulations and policies is typically dependent on the specific circumstances of a given country. Perhaps the most important of these circumstances is the age distribution of members of a society. The young, the poor and the unemployed dominate some societies, such as the Chinese or Indian. In those societies, the primary concern is to have jobs and ensure rapid economic growth. However, the formerly socialist countries in Central and Eastern Europe (CEE) have stable or declining populations dominated by relatively old workers and pensioners. In those countries, there is typically a sharp clash of interests between the generation of the young and entre-preneurial on the one hand, and the generation of the old and pen-sioners on the other.

The primary purpose of this chapter is to apply a growth model that could capture this conflict and help to assess the size of the gap between optimal policies for these two groups of individuals. The model may be used to interpret political election battles in Central Europe and the dif-ference in actual economic policies between Central Europe and China.

The growth model

The transition economies belong to the category of emerging econo-mies, in which the primary source of new technology is the technologies that have been accumulated by the developed economies located on the world's technology frontier area (TFA). The production relationship that might be assumed to apply worldwide is the standard constant-returns-to-scale production function, in which the index of quality T of the key inputs, capital K and labour L, is labour-augmenting:

$$Y = F(K, TL) \qquad (12.1)$$

where Y is total net output. Crucial, now, is the assumption concerning the determination of technological changes; that is, changes in T. As I argue elsewhere (Gomułka 1990), these changes in the TFA are best explained by the level of the combined research and development (R&D) activity of the entire world economy. Now, I use the stylized fact that over a long period of time, the K/Y ratios in developed countries have been fairly stable. Taking into account Equation (12.1), such stabil-ity is possible only if T has been changing over time in the same way as the ratio K/L; that is, if K/L and T have been proportional each to the other. Thus, if the stock of all the technologies present in the TFA is freely available to investors in any emerging economy, which I assume is the case, the choice of a specific T would be determined by the parallel choice of K/L, as:

$$T = a\frac{K}{L} \qquad (12.2)$$

where a is constant. While technologies of the TFA are themselves free, by Equation (12.2) an investment in fixed capital would be required to absorb and take advantage of them. Given this technology function, we have that:

$$Y = F(K, aK) = F(1, a) \cdot K = A \cdot K \tag{12.3}$$

where A is another constant. By Equation (12.3), output is proportional to the stock of physical capital. This is the so-called AK model (Barro and Sala-i-Martin 1995). In this model, the standard neoclassical law of declining marginal productivity of capital applies only in the short term. In the long term, technological changes increase the marginal productivity of capital sufficiently to ensure that this productivity is constant.

We may now proceed further by assuming that households maximize their total future utility, properly discounted and related to consumption. To simplify, people are assumed to live forever, so they maximize:

$$U = \int_{0}^{+\infty} u(c(t))e^{-(p-n)t} \, dt \tag{12.4}$$

In Equations (12.4) and (12.5), k is the K/L ratio, n is the growth rate of labour L, w is the wage rate, r is the net profit rate, $u(c)$ is the utility flow and ρ is the time preference rate.

The choice of per capita consumption c is subject to the budget constraint:

$$c + \dot{k} = w + rk - nk \tag{12.5}$$

where $\dot{k} = \dfrac{dk}{dt}$

In Equation (12.5), $\dot{k} + nk$ is the investment expenditure per worker, and therefore the difference between total income $w + rk$ and that expenditure investment is the income left to finance consumption, c. The Euler's first-order maximization condition implies that:

$$r = \rho + \Theta \, \frac{\dot{c}}{c} \tag{12.6}$$

where $\Theta = -\dfrac{u''c}{u'}$, so it is the elasticity of the marginal utility u'. Following Barro and Sala-i-Martin (1995), let us consider a utility function for which Θ is a constant, a number between 0 and 1. This function has the form:

$$u(c) = \frac{c^{1-\Theta} - 1}{1 - \Theta} \tag{12.7}$$

We may note that if Θ is zero, then $u(c) = c-1$, so welfare is proportional to consumption and marginal utility u' is constant. If $\Theta = 1$, then $u(c) = lnc$, so in this case the marginal utility u' is inversely related to c. We assume further that firms select k so as to maximize profits, or the difference between output AK and the sum $rK + wL + \delta K$, where δ is the depreciation rate. The first-order maximization condition implies that:

$$r = A - \delta \qquad (12.8)$$

Combining Equations (12.6) and (12.8) gives us the growth rate of consumption along the optimal path:

$$\frac{\dot{c}}{c} = \frac{A-\rho-\delta}{\Theta} \qquad (12.9)$$

Along such a path the growth rate $\dfrac{\dot{c}}{c}$ is thus constant. Therefore, the growth rate of the *k-ratio* must be the same constant. Hence:

$$\frac{\dot{k}}{k} = \frac{A-\rho-\delta}{\Theta} \qquad (12.10)$$

Now we can deduce the optimal saving rate in such an economy. Note that gross investment is $\dot{K} + \delta K$. Therefore, the ratio of that investment to total output, equal to AK, must be the optimal savings rate, to be denoted by s. Hence:

$$s = \frac{\dot{K} + \delta K}{AK} = \frac{\dot{k}/k + n + \delta}{A} \qquad (12.11)$$

By substituting Equation (12.10) into Equation (12.11), we obtain:

$$s = \frac{1}{A}\left(\frac{A-\rho-\delta}{\Theta} + n + \delta\right) \qquad (12.12)$$

Two distinct types of individuals

Recent parliamentary elections in Poland, the former Czech Republic, Hungary and the Baltic Republics have become battlegrounds between those who emphasize solidarity and security, and those who place more emphasis on reforms and policies needed to promote employment and growth. The first group includes, above all, pensioners, while the second group includes the young generation, typically well-educated and often unemployed, as well as entrepreneurs of all ages. I shall denote these two groups with letters P, for pensioner, and Y, for young. The group P is interested less in long-term growth and, instead, wants higher social transfers and greater public spending on health. The group Y wishes to promote growth as a way to secure employment and long-term income. Individuals of that group want, above all, more investment in physical and human capital, as well as lower taxes on labour and profits.

In the model presented above, we have two parameters to express individual preferences: Θ, the elasticity of marginal utility and ρ, the time preferences rate. My key assumption is that the values of those two parameters differ between these two groups. The difference is likely to be particularly strong with respect to the time preference rate. This rate should be expected to be relatively high for type P individuals and low for type Y individuals. This difference would reflect the concern of P individuals with consumption over a short period, so they would heavily discount the consumption in the more distant future. On the other hand, the Y individuals also value the more distant consumption. Many of these individuals are typically well-off, or expect to be so. Hence, for them the marginal utility of consumption should be low compared to the average utility, or to fall with rising consumption. Individuals of the P type may be assumed to have relatively low income, so for them the marginal utility might be almost as high as the average utility, or to be almost unchanged with rising consumption. Although we have no precise estimates of Θ and ρ for these two groups, the two situations worth comparing are the following:

Situation I, in which Θ and ρ are the same for those two groups, and Situation II, in which Θ is the same for groups P and Y, while ρ is high for group P and low for group Y.

Implications for optimal growth strategies

Let us derive implications for savings and growth of these differences in preferences as between groups P and Y in situation II, which may be considered to be much closer to reality than situation I in the present circumstances of Central and Eastern Europe (CEE). The implications for growth and savings are tightly linked, since:

$$\frac{\dot{Y}}{Y} = \frac{\dot{K}}{K} = \frac{sY - \delta K}{K} = \frac{sAK}{K} - \delta = As - \delta \qquad (12.13)$$

Thus, the growth rate of output on the long-term optimal path is, in this model, strictly proportional to the optimal savings rate. In view of Equation (12.12), we have that:

$$\frac{\dot{Y}}{Y} = \frac{A - \rho - \delta}{\Theta} + n \qquad (12.14)$$

where the first term on the right-hand side is the growth rate of output per worker, to be denoted by $g_{Y/L}$. Let s^P and $g_{PY/L}$ be respectively the optimal savings rate and the optimal per capita growth rate from the point of view of P individuals, and let s^Y and $g^Y_{Y/L}$ be the corresponding rates for Y individuals. We can now derive the differences between s^Y and s^P, and between $g^Y_{Y/L}$ and $g_{PY/L}$, namely:

$$s^Y - s^P = \frac{\rho^P - \rho^Y}{A\Theta} \qquad (12.15)$$

and

$$g^Y_{Y/L} - g^P_{Y/L} = \frac{\rho^P - \rho^Y}{\Theta} \qquad (12.16)$$

It is instructive to give the parameters in Equations (12.15) and (12.16) specific values, so that the difference in policy preferences between the groups P and Y can be seen more clearly. Since Θ is between 0 and 1, let it be equal to ½. The coefficient A is the inverse of the capital/output ratio. For the countries of CEE, A may be taken to be ⅓. Hence:

$$s^Y - s^P = 6(\rho^P - \rho^Y) \qquad (12.17)$$

and

$$g^Y_{Y/L} - g^P_{Y/L} = 2(\rho^P - \rho^Y) \qquad (12.18)$$

A key role of the difference between time preference rates is thus revealed. To specify further, let this difference equal to (a) 2 per cent; (b) 5 per cent; and (c) 10 per cent. Even in the case (a) of a very moderate difference, there would be a significant difference in the optimal growth strategy between groups Y and P. In the possibly more realistic case (b), this difference would become quite large. It is therefore not surprising that election debates are, in the CEE, so confrontational.

Earlier in the chapter, I mentioned that the elasticity of the marginal utility, denoted above by Θ, might be lower for P individuals than for Y individuals. If this were the case, the P group would value investment in future consumption a little more. The intergenerational gap between economic policies would then be somewhat reduced. However, people of these two groups should not be expected to differ much with their utility functions. One can even take the view that there are no significant differences in Θ between individuals.

China versus CEE

The model above may be used to explain large differences in national savings and growth rate of output between China and most CEE countries. Simply put, in China and in some of the other countries of South-East Asia, the proportion of young people in the total population is much higher than in the CEE countries. Moreover, the solidarity and security syndromes in China might not be as highly developed as in Europe. Consequently, the growth strategies actually chosen in China reflect mainly the preferences of Y-type individuals, while in Poland and most of the CEE countries, they reflect to a much greater extent the preferences of P-type individuals. In particular, if there is a labour reserve, as in China, conditions as stated in Equations (12.13) and (12.14) imply that the strategy with a higher s is also capable of increasing the growth rate of employment.

Long-term risks

In an economy dominated by P-type individuals, economic policy would promote large social transfers and large public expenditures on consumption-related services such as health and housing. This, in turn, would require the imposition of higher taxes on workers and firms. Such a policy would limit the long-term growth of per capita consumption. As a result, in such an economy, Y-type individuals would be faced with the prospect of a permanently and significantly lower income than their own optimal policy would secure. In addition, in the medium term a disproportionately large proportion of them would be unemployed. The response of these individuals to this prospect might be to emigrate to the richer member countries of the European Union. A large emigration from Poland to the UK and Ireland since 2004 is such a response. This emigration, in turn, would lower the standard of living of future pensioners. Thus, the current generation of P individuals, by insisting on their short-term interests, could act against everyone's interests in the long term.

The optimal economic policy of a nation is one that takes into account the interests not only of those individuals who vote, but also those who do not vote yet, as well as, to some extent, the interests of the unborn. This is possibly recognized by many P-type individuals and certainly should be recognized by political leaders. The policy actually chosen is, as a result, a weighted combination of the two optimal policies discussed above, in which the weights reflect the strategic intergenerational compromise.

References

Barro, R.J. and Sala-i-Martin, X. (1995) *Economic Growth* (New York: McGraw-Hill).

Gomułka, S. (1990) *The Theory of Technological Change and Economic Growth* (London/New York: Routledge).

13
In Search of a Perfect Regulatory System

Ewa Freyberg

Introduction

Every contemporary economics textbook contains a chapter analyzing various forms of market imperfections and methods of addressing them by the government. Most textbooks also analyze cases where the government cannot control its own actions and fails in regulation. Such failures are believed to be much more harmful to economic development than the market imperfections that they seek to address. In such a situation, two solutions are possible: for the government to refrain from any regulatory activities based in the belief that the market has a built-in, efficient, self-regulatory mechanism or to take good care of the quality of regulation, limiting the incidence of failures to a minimum.

The first solution exists only in theory, as a model useful only to examine the ideal behaviour of markets. The second assumes that a certain level of market regulation is necessary and that improving the quality of regulation is a good way to speed up economic growth. Therefore, it is necessary to search for ways to improve regulatory systems. The regulatory reforms started in the 1990s follow that direction, trying to answer the question: How to achieve better regulation?

These reforms are accompanied by the increasingly common view among economists about a growing role for the institutional environment in the process of economic growth. Empirical research indicates that differences in regulatory systems might be helpful to explain why some countries develop faster than others. The analysis of such differences is increasingly used in discussions on how to reduce the distance between the US economy and those of the EU member states.

The US leads in rankings that rate the competitiveness of the economy, in part because it allocates a much larger portion of its revenue to scientific research than does Europe, US universities are more appealing for foreign students than are European schools. The US economy is more innovative and dynamic. All those and other examples of American superiority over Europe are commonly known and cited.[1] The EU's Lisbon Strategy was formulated in order to reduce the gap between Europe and the US. Its implementation, however, is seriously threatened. A question that arises is how important is it for Europe in this race with the US to remain consistent in reforming regulatory systems. Perhaps the utilization of American experience in that regard will prove an effective way to increase European competitiveness. It is not an issue of achieving convergence of legal regimes. Differences in those regimes are the result of different legal cultures, traditions, and systems of values on both sides of the Atlantic, which makes those differences permanent. What is worth following is the American model of regulatory reform management, and it seems that a number of that model's components could, and should, be transplanted to the regulatory reforms carried out within the EU.[2]

Upon its EU accession, Poland was incorporated into the process of transposing European legislation and reforming the EU regulatory system. At the same time, significant changes in the regulatory system have been taking place as a result of Poland's system transformation, starting in 1989, and applied to all economic sectors, including, in particular, capital markets, banking and privatization of state-owned enterprises.

The regulatory system currently in effect in Poland was thus emerging in very peculiar conditions: deep changes in legislation and the institutional environment had to be implemented within a relatively short period. The greatest time pressure was visible during the adjustment of Polish laws to Community legislation, and the distrust of private ownership inherited from the previous system, where an entrepreneur was treated as a burdensome applicant rather than a partner, and which encouraged overproduction or the inflation of provisions regulating the institutional environment of business. Insufficient numbers of well-prepared lawyers made the laws that were being written non-transparent and inconsistent. A further obstacle to drafting good legislation and implementing an efficient state model was the highly politicized law-making process.

There is no doubt that the reform of economic, social and administrative regulations is extremely important for Poland, and its progress will decide Poland's future development. Good implementation of regulatory reform means not only the introduction of appropriate formal rules and procedures, but also the ability to implement them. From that point of view, it is useful to borrow from the good experience of other countries.

Regulatory reform in the European Union

The Better Regulation legal regulation reform programme was introduced at the level of the European Commission and member states relatively late, in 2002, as a priority of the Lisbon Strategy.[3] Earlier, all 15 member states had taken part in a regulatory reform programme within the OECD (1995). The basic programme objective is to simplify Community and national regulations and to reduce administrative burdens, which are particularly onerous and costly to small and medium enterprises, as well as to improve the credibility of EU institutions among Community citizens. It is not the EU's intention to deregulate or limit previous efforts in the area of law-making.

In 2002–05, significant progress was achieved in implementing reform objectives. A number of documents were published concerning:

- Methods of regulatory impact assessment[4]
- Communication from the Commission on an EU common methodology for assessing administrative costs imposed by legislation[5]
- Communication from the Commission on the outcome of the screening of proposed laws pending before the legislators[6]
- Communication on a strategy for the simplification of the EU regulatory environment.[7]

The above documents are a good basis for the application of good regulatory principles, both at the level of the European Commission and the European Parliament and at the level of individual EU member states. What is worth noting is the fact that all the entities concerned took part in the preparation of these documents, and the number of consultations organized by the Commission has grown each year. For example, in 2005 there were 293 consultations in comparison with 37 in 2004. Increasingly, consultations are held via the Internet, which speeds up the collection of comments and facilitates the process of making them available to the public.

The EU Commission anticipates that as a result of the above efforts, begun in 2005, 222 legislative acts will undergo the simplification procedure, which will result in subsequent amendments of 1,400 related regulations.[8] To speed up the regulatory reform in member states, the EC suggested that the Better Regulation programme should form part of national reports on implementation of the Lisbon Strategy programme. According to the EC, the majority of member states has, and implements, their own programmes of regulatory reform. However, there is no information on the quality of such programmes, and, particularly, it is not known whether they are comprehensive and consistent, and actually improve the quality of legislation. Some of them probably only meet formal requirements that, for various reasons, are not put into practice.

Also, non-EU states, including the US, Canada, Australia and New Zealand, have their own regulatory reform programmes that have yielded relatively good results. Those countries also participate actively in the regulatory reform programme initiated in 1995 by the OECD and their successes have undoubtedly precipitated the European Commission's decision to set up the Better Regulation programme. Particularly important from the point of view of the implementation of the EU's Lisbon Strategy, is the US experience in carrying out regulatory reforms.

Progress of the regulatory reform in the US

Contrary to widespread popular belief, the US is not a country with a low degree of regulation. Every year, federal government agencies issue about 4,000 new regulations.[9] What sets the US apart from other countries is its different method of regulation, which is strongly linked to a pro-competitive approach to the economy, as well as providing for high transparency of the laws and regulations; most important is the high quality of the cost and benefit analyses and alternative scenarios prepared for all major regulatory proposals. What is important is that competent specialists draw up analyses and the law-making process is public. Thus regulatory reform enjoys the support of a well-developed civic society. As a result, public debate over legislative proposals has a truly public character. Also, the private sector exerts pressure to accelerate public sector reforms. In the US, the economy is more liberalized than in Europe, and the private sector is particularly sensitive to any malfunction of the administration that increases the cost of business operation. The private sector is also the source of innovative IT solutions and provides well-educated experts who are able to apply quantitative methods to analyze the impact of regulation.

The beginning of public sector reform in the US is usually regarded as having taken place in the 1980s, when the disproportion in the quality of services between the private sector and the public sector was particularly large. The oft-quoted example is that of Mother Theresa who, after two years of efforts to set up a shelter for the homeless in a New York district, had to give up due to excessive bureaucracy. The adage 'Even the patience of saints is not enough to overcome American bureaucracy' became a motto for the proponents of rapid changes.

Also in the 1980s, a strong effort to control the cost of administering government regulation began. The following measures proved particularly helpful:

- Measurement of the productivity of government expenses and application of a number of procedures supporting cost cuts
- Introduction of cost controls in the production of public goods and services
- Budgeting based on the performance of particular administrative units[10]
- Preserving flexibility in the use of funds in various accounts and strengthening ability to use savings where they occur
- Promotion of productivity
- Service quality management borrowed from the private sector, based on the concept of a one-stop shop to take care of all the formalities necessary to set up a business and broad collaboration with citizens, including social consultation mechanisms, citizens' participation in making decisions on some budgetary expenses, and so on.

Greater effectiveness of the public sector was also encouraged by cooperation between the central government administration and the local administrations and civic organizations. OECD research indicates that, as the economy grows, so does the number of local administrative officials. Central government administration seems to be burdened by bureaucracy while local officials such as teachers, providers of medical services, police and so on, have a more direct input in improving the quality of public sector services.

The positive effects of regulatory reforms in the US include a reduction of employment in administration. For example, during the Clinton administration, the number of government officials decreased by 17 per cent. The resulting savings were used, for example, to increase the number of policemen patrolling the streets. Such a strategy certainly increased popular support for the government, but it was also an important component of the programme to improve public safety.

The introduction of innovation in administration was accompanied by a belief that such innovation must be continuous, and not subject to interruptions caused by changes in the political party in power, and the experience of civil servants was treated as common public good. It is worth noting that innovation is usually brought about by middle-level employees and not by bosses. Creating incentives and organizational structures that gave all employees a sense of involvement in the cost reduction process helped innovation. Improvements in the quality of work of government employees were also encouraged by the application of a suitable promotion and remuneration system modelled on private sector practices. For example, in 1996 the State of Georgia introduced a civil service recruitment process based on the recruitment policies used by private corporations.[11]

A key role in overseeing the regulatory reform in the US is played by the Office of Management and Budget (OMB). It has relatively strong powers that allow it to effectively control and coordinate the operation of 60 regulatory agencies. The Office oversees all major types of regulations, except those that are excluded from the President's authority; that is, money supply regulation, safety of nuclear plants and certain elements of the anti-trust law. Annually, there are about 100 OMB-monitored regulations out of 4,500 new regulations adopted each year. Analysis of the impact of regulatory projects is the responsibility of a special OMB unit, the Office of Information and Regulatory Affairs (OIRA), with only 25 staff members who, however, are highly specialized in all areas and also use the assistance of external experts.

Adoption of new regulations in the US is governed by a set of integrated procedures. First, a draft of the regulation is published, together with a cost and benefit analysis and an alternative regulatory scenario in the Federal Register. This opens a public debate of 30–90 days. The regulation with any changes is published again in the Federal Register 30 days before the regulation comes into force, together with a written rationale for all the amendments of existing regulations, but this is done only after obtaining a positive opinion on the consistency of the proposed regulation with the government's economic policy. Finally, Congress must evaluate the regulation as well. What is important is that the procedures are applied in practice and continuously improved in cooperation with independent experts from research centres. The experts are required to report their income and professional ties to avoid any conflict of interest. The public is informed on an ongoing basis about the quality of information used in the evaluation of regulations.

The reason for entrusting regulatory reform to the OMB is, among other things, the high annual cost of regulation per household. In 2001, that cost was US$6,000. J.D. Graham, an OMB Director, calls it an invisible tax whose amount is approximately equal to the annual revenue from the income tax, $800 billion.[12] The cost of regulation has been estimated for the past 30 years by particular regulatory agencies and the OMB. Currently, the cost to the public arising from the obligation to apply new regulations is about $1.5 billion annually. During the Clinton administration it was $5.7 billion and under G.W. Bush, it was $8.5 billion.[13]

Despite the nearly 30-year history of concentrated efforts to reduce the regulatory burden, the principle of cost estimation has not always been followed. Among the 115,000 published regulations, the cost of only 20,000 have been verified prior to publication. In effect, only 1,100 regulations gained the status of being economically significant requiring formal cost-benefit analysis. This means, however, that a vast number of applicable regulations has still not been analyzed to justify their existence.[14]

In 2001, the Regulatory Right-to-Know Act introduced an obligation on the President to report annually to the Congress on the costs and benefits of regulations adopted by the US Federal government. Each successive report contains the estimated costs and benefits of regulations subject to OMB's review over the past 10 years. The 2006 report states that the annual benefits from adopting major regulations in 1995–2005 fell within the range of $94 billion to $449 billion, while the cost was between $37 billion and $44 billion. Over the past 25 years, the cost of introducing regulations increased by about $123 billion, therefore, the average annual increase was at $5 billion.[15] At the same time, benefits from regulations increased threefold.

This optimistic picture of the effectiveness of regulatory reform is also a favourable assessment of the American administration's operations in the area of regulations. Notwithstanding any reservations about the data presented in the report and the estimation methods used to measure cost and benefits, they constitute important information for economic policy-makers because they confirm the hypothesis that quality regulation need not damage the market economy. The most important feature of the entire process of putting regulations into force is the obligation to express costs and benefits in terms of money, and to propose alternative scenarios to a given regulation. The purpose is to maximize net benefits. Thus, the public sector is subject to the same rules of rational utilization of resources as the private sector.

The discussions regarding the evaluation of regulatory activities by government agencies placed a number of new demands on those agencies. Among the most important ones are: monitoring the work of officials responsible for particular regulations; publishing on the Internet the information on costs and benefits of a given regulation; standardization of the assumptions for calculating costs and benefits; improvement of the methods for incorporating uncertainty; limitation on agencies' ability to adopt economically non-viable regulations.[16] Most of these new obligations are set out in the 2002 Information Quality Law. The law requires federal regulatory agencies to apply certain standards in preparing and publicizing the results of their operations.

An interesting initiative in regulatory reform is the focus on the need to control the volume of not only legislative acts themselves, but also of the provisions explaining their application. Quite often, particular agencies produce instructions containing considerably more pages than the regulation concerned. Equally noteworthy is the programme initiated in the 1980s to simplify the language of regulations. Language that is hard to understand for an average citizen makes it difficult to observe law, increases the cost of law enforcement and exposes citizens to sanctions caused by not understanding the laws in effect. Unfortunately, the effectiveness of that programme is relatively low. Successive American presidents, starting with Nixon, have issued decrees to this effect, but their practical implementation still faces difficulties.

Cooperation between the US and the European Union

US cooperation with the European Union is based on the recommendations for cooperation in regulatory reform, negotiated under the Economic Transatlantic Partnership. Implementation of those recommendations has been satisfactory and much progress has been achieved in many disciplines. As a continuation of these efforts, a road map for future cooperation in regulatory reform was developed at the EU–US summit in 2005. The main elements of that agreement include: setting up a dialogue among higher-level officials on best regulatory practices; identifying methods to facilitate exchanges of experts; and developing sectoral initiatives. This cooperation has led to progress in harmonizing provisions, applicable standards and regulatory systems on both sides of the Atlantic, based on a comparative analysis.[17]

The European Commission's Better Regulation Programme received full support from the US.[18] The US regarded the initiative to develop a common legislative culture within the EU with the purpose of increasing the transparency. Greater transparency means lower costs of doing business for companies from both the EU and third countries. In principle, all the EU programme components are consistent with American regulatory reform, which bodes well for a good cooperation.

US experts, nevertheless, have some reservations about the absence of clearly formulated methods for implementing the proposed solutions, including, especially, the effectiveness of the open coordination method. Also evident is the lack of a sufficient precision in defining the consultation rules for particular reform stages or identifying the consultation participants. However, there is no doubt that adopting a number of solutions applied in the US – for example, extending the consultation period to 60 days – as well as the exchange of experiences will encourage development of best practices for the regulatory system, assisting the OECD efforts.

A certain discord in this optimistic picture of the US–EU relations is caused by the European Commission's activities in the area of competition. Due to different objectives and policies, a convergence in that area is relatively difficult. Although, in 1990, the European Commission and the US signed an agreement whose provisions, in the event of anti-trust proceedings, are binding on both parties, its text does not contribute anything new in terms of harmonization of laws. In effect, US and European enterprises pay a high cost and adjust their rules of conduct to complex and different regulations in force on both sides of the Atlantic.[19] The discrepancy exists mainly in the criteria for approval of mergers or acquisitions in all those situations where at least one company is from the EU area. The criteria applied by the European Commission are stricter than those used in the US, and the EC often uses the right of direct control, examining the records and operating procedures in companies participating in a merger. The purpose of such conduct is to prevent companies active in the European market from gaining the so-called 'dominant position', defined in terms of its share of sales in the global and European markets.

It seems that one of the reasons for the different approaches of the EC and the US to mergers and acquisitions is their differing views on markets and competition. In the US, there is a visibly high level of confidence in free market mechanisms, which is probably due to their market institutions being mature and very effective. The prevailing belief is that the market is not only capable of protecting competition but also of introducing new pro-competitive solutions.

A characteristic of the European approach is a strategy based on restricting the number of companies operating in a given market. Those differences account for the different formulation of requirements for mergers to be considered legal. In the EU, the Commission examines whether a planned merger will result in a dominant position threatening consumer interests. In the US, a planned merger is examined in terms of whether it will affect the level of competition. The test is thus less rigorous. Moreover, in the EU the threshold marking a dominant position is assumed to be a 40 per cent market share. In the conditions of the

US economy, such a threshold is believed to be absurdly low. Another difference is the rule adopted in American legislation whereby the burden of proving the illegality of a merger rests on the government, and courts render verdicts in such cases. In Europe, it is the companies planning a merger who have to prove the planned transaction to be consistent with applicable laws.

Barriers in regulatory convergence result in a relatively large number of cases where a merger or an acquisition passes successfully the US procedure but is deemed illegal under EU laws. A certain facilitation in the complicated process of seeking approval for a merger might be a planned amendment to the EC regulations, that would take into account a cost analysis in decision-making. The very act of attempting to measure the cost of rejecting or approving a merger and making that cost known to the public is very positive. It is certainly a step in the direction pursued by regulatory system reform and, simultaneously, a sign of the convergence of US and European procedures. An emphasis on measuring precisely the effects of regulation is a characteristic feature of regulatory reform in the US. A similarly positive response was provoked by the intention to incorporate expected changes in the technological progress into the analysis of regulatory effectiveness. Rapid changes in technology shorten the time within which a company gains a dominant market position. Another facilitation in the current procedures is the idea that companies seeking merger approvals, in particular EU member states, should be able to take care of all the formalities at a single institution within the EU.

Reform of the Polish regulatory system

There is no doubt that the most in-depth reform of the regulatory system in Poland took place during its transformation from a command economy to a market economy. The second phase of reforms included adjustment of Polish legislation to Community laws in connection with preparations for Poland's EU membership. Characteristics of those reforms were the following:

1 Unprecedented scope and rate of changes introduced;
2 Relatively low quality of the laws adopted, resulting both from the haste in implementing changes and from the absence of well-prepared specialists in various legal disciplines;
3 The lack of well-developed market economy institutions;

4 Use of both financial and advisory external assistance of international financial institutions and the European Commission, as well as the governments of particular countries, including the US. One the one hand, the assistance speeded up the necessary changes, but, on the other hand, it encouraged excessively superficial adoption of regulatory models and standards that were not always well suited to the Polish economic and social system;

5 Deficiency of strategic thinking among political elites, resulting mainly from immature democracy and the highly politicized process of making economic decisions;

6 The burden of experience gained in the planned economy showing a tendency to over-regulate, accompanied by distrust of market mechanisms and market institutions.

In sum, the period beginning in 1989 in Poland was marked by a growing volume of regulations to meet the needs of the emerging market economy and the requirements of EU membership and the criteria for obtaining international financial assistance. Much less attention was paid to the quality of regulations. Critical opinions in that regard were rare and dispersed, which limited their effectiveness.

The issue of caring for the quality of regulation was incorporated in the Polish government programme after Poland became an OECD member in 1996. The regulatory reform focused mainly on the formal aspect; that is, on creating appropriate institutions, and defining their procedures and scopes of authority. Thus, in September 2000, an inter-ministerial team for the quality of regulation was set up, a textbook was prepared on drafting the Regulatory Impact Assessment and provisions on coordination of reform efforts were introduced in the Prime Minister's Office Regulations.

In 2002, an OECD report evaluating the progress of the Polish regulatory reform was published.[20] After becoming an EU member in 2004, Poland was covered by the regulatory reform programme within the European Union. A new inter-ministerial team for modern regulation was set up in 2006, and the government approved the Regulatory Reform Programme for 2006–08. Poland is also participating in the joint OECD and EU Sigma programme for new EU members.

From a purely formal point of view, the implementation of reforms could be assessed as good. This is how the European Commission rated Poland in its Communication of 2005. The table showing categories of measures adopted by EU member states under the Better Regulation Programme lists Poland, together with Denmark and the UK, at the very top.[21] An assessment of the actual reforms is much worse. Major weaknesses of the Polish regulatory system include:

- Low operating effectiveness of the institutions responsible for the quality of regulation
- Inadequate coordination of those institutions' work, and no coordination of reform efforts at an appropriately high level makes it easier for ministries to pursue their own interests at the expense of the public interest
- Poor implementation of the most important aspects of the reform from the point of view of their quality – namely, the estimation of the costs and benefits of a given regulation; the lack of information on the effects of government regulatory activities makes it difficult to make rational decisions and renders the decision-making process itself more susceptible to political pressures
- Weak pressure from the private sector for reforming the legislative system
- Lack of a civil society, and thus weak pressure for improving the quality of regulations, especially social ones.[22]

Regulatory reform is a reform of the bureaucracy conducted by the bureaucracy. Its effects depend on how effectively the government is controlled but also on the extent to which the process is assisted by democratic state institutions. In this area there is much to be done in Poland to overcome the legacies of the previous system, the absence of a habit to respond continuously to all irregularities in government administration, and the inability to make changes favourable to the public interest.

There is no doubt that access to adequate information on the costs and benefits of legal regulations and on alternative methods of regulating a given issue has an important role in stimulating social activity that forces the state to attempt to provide a higher quality of regulations. The knowledge about the zlotys it costs – for example, for a business to adapt to specific regulations – in combination with information about the benefits in terms of zlotys to be enjoyed by the consumer from those regulations, facilitates rational choices about the utilization of available resources. There may, certainly, be reservations as to the selected method of estimating effects, the accuracy of data, the skills of people doing the calculations. It is obvious that, at all stages of such calculation, failures might occur, and that there is a strong temptation to manipulate data to obtain an outcome that would serve the interests of certain groups. However, for politician and citizen alike, the effect of a given regulation expressed in monetary terms, even if the estimate is imprecise or deliberately distorted, will always be better than no estimate at all.

Formally speaking, the procedures introduced in Poland in 2001 contain all the elements necessary to carry out a regulatory impact assessment in compliance with OECD and EU standards, to identify the entities that a given regulation affects and to assess its impact on public finances, the labour market, competitiveness and the situation of particular regions. A review of 163 major economic legislative drafts from 2002–04 indicates clearly that the entities responsible for assessing the impact of regulations do not carry out their duties well. Only 28 per cent of all assessments indicated the costs or benefits of a given regulation, even fewer, only 12 per cent, quantified the effects of regulations, limiting themselves only to analyzing their impact on the state budget. Numerous reservations are provoked by the methods used in computing effects, the selection or reliability of data, and the frequent practice of purposefully understating the costs or overstating the benefits.[23] Officials of the institutions drafting the bills, who lack specialized knowledge and appropriate economic and analytical skills, perform this work. They are also not motivated to improve their qualifications because nobody really evaluates the quality of the cost–benefit analyses prepared by them. The institution responsible to date for coordinating efforts in that area, the Government Legislation Centre, performed only formal verifications; that is, checking whether regulatory impact assessments contained all the elements enumerated in the relevant ordinance. However, the absence of sanctions for failure to submit a RIA (Regulatory Impact Assessment) or to include all its required elements means that the requirement of providing such an analysis has not been a barrier to setting in motion the legislative process.

All those poor solutions from the point of view of managing the law-making process are the cause of the above-mentioned weaknesses of the Polish legal system: inflation of laws and instability and inconsistency of regulations, which encourage corruption. Most important of all, however, they result in the waste of public resources. The public sector, whose objective should be to address market failures, by generating a poor product in the form of poor quality regulation, lowers the potential for economic growth.

Another important element of the quality of regulation is the method of implementing provisions and of enforcing the law. In that area, much is to be done in Poland, starting from a reform of the judiciary and ending with focusing attention on the quality of lower-tier regulations, such as ordinances and normative acts adopted by particular ministers. Very often such provisions are delayed, blocking the entry into force of a given statute.

In evaluating the quality of regulation in Poland, account must be taken of the quality of provisions passed by local government authorities. In 2000 only, local law publishing houses published 13,637 legal acts adopted by local government agencies.[24] In that situation, one can hardly speak of a transparency of laws or proper monitoring of the law-making process. Also clearly visible is the lack of good cooperation between the local and central government at the regional level, resulting partly from the unclear distribution of authority.

Regulatory Reform Programme for Poland, 2006–2008

In 2006, in response to the European Commission's recommendations, Poland presented the Regulatory Reform Programme 2006–2008, containing all the elements of the EU programme, together with a schedule of changes and identification of the institutions responsible for particular programme components. The programme promises a number of important innovations, major ones including:

1 Announcement of a future revision of the methods for preparing the regulatory impact assessment: that assessment should, according to the Ministry of Economy, who authored the programme, contain a thorough analysis of costs and benefits arising from regulatory activities;
2 Inclusion in the regulatory impact analysis of the estimated administrative burdens imposed on entities covered by a given regulation;
3 Empowering the Prime Minister's Office with the right to block draft legislation based on inaccurate regulatory impact assessments;
4 Creation of a central regulatory impact assessment database;
5 Identification of the legal acts to be simplified and initiation of the simplification procedure;
6 Improvement of the process of implementing EU directives.

Particularly important from the point of view of the quality of regulation is the initiative to estimate the cost of administrative burdens and the efforts toward limiting these costs, as well as the revision of the methods for compiling full regulatory impact assessments. According to recent analyses conducted by the Ministry of Economy, general information obligations are particularly burdensome for businesses. For example, in several Labour Law regulations there are 80 such obligations to provide information. This generates high costs on a nationwide scale. The annual cost of issuing an employment certificate by all the companies in Poland is about PLN 250 million. Hence, the proposal to reduce administrative burdens by at least cutting the frequency of reporting, exempting small and medium-sized businesses from that obligation, or a wider application of electronic communications should provide some relief.[25]

The very fact that a programme containing all the elements required by the EU programme has been prepared is obviously very good. However, Poland's experience with implementing regulatory reforms indicates that the main barriers in reforming the law lie in the highly politicized law-making process, poor coordination of the activities of government institutions, insufficient quality of social consultations and the lack of qualified specialists, especially in conducting quantitative analyses of regulatory impacts. Entrusting the oversight over the regulatory reform to the Minister of Economy does not guarantee smooth implementation of the programme.

The oversight and coordination of reform efforts should be situated at the highest possible level of government administration; that is, in the Prime Minister's Office. Unfortunately, the programme speaks little of any planned changes in the scopes of authority of particular institutions or the oversight over their efforts. This entails a risk that the Polish government's regulatory reform programme might share the fate of other unimplemented programmes. The winners will be particular political interests, the ambitions of high officials and the inability to apply modern impact assessment methods. The loser will be the belief in good laws and the fight against over regulation in the belief that they would invite excessive liberalism and loss of control over economic processes. In Poland, regulation is still believed to be the only effective control tool and an attribute of power. It is difficult to estimate presently to what extent the inflation of regulations in Poland is a legacy of the command management system and to what extent it results from the still unstable political system and ineffective government administration.

Future directions of change in the European regulatory system

Up to now, regulatory reform in Europe has been characterized by relatively highly dispersed activities carried out by individual states. Although there has been an exchange of experiences and dissemination of good practices, the coordination of those efforts has not been sufficiently strong.[26] The legal regimes of member states are collections of laws enacted at the Community level and national laws. The quality of the regulatory system is, therefore, decided by both the quality of the Community law and its effective transposition into the legal systems of member states, as well as by the quality of autonomous national regulations.

Community rules have been, and are, commonly criticized for their excessive detail, lack of transparency and burdensome administrative procedures. EU member states have so far had little influence on the quality of EU regulations. The view that the low quality of the EU regulatory system is one of the causes of the relatively low competitiveness of the EU economy is gaining more followers. That general opinion seems to have somehow forced the launch of reforms of the regulatory system at the EU level (European Commission 2002). Due to the short amount of time that has elapsed since the start of this initiative, it is still impossible to identify all its effects. Some of them are the simplification and reduction of the volume of regulations, as recorded in successive EC communications.

What is worth noting is the positive impact of the decision to place reform management at the level of the European Commission. Thus, the US has gained a partner in a single institution coordinating the activities of all 25 member states. This creates better conditions for cooperation in harmonizing provisions concerning, for example, product safety, protection of the natural environment or standards. One may expect this cooperation to result in the gradual convergence of some regulations, which would be beneficial from the point of view of the cost of economic activity.

On the other hand, a much slower pace, if any, will characterize convergence in the area of liberalizing competition rules, including the operation of product markets, and some aspects of the welfare state and the labour market, although there is no doubt that the differences in those areas are the main reasons for Europe's lower competitiveness in comparison with the US.[27]

Moreover, from the point of view of Poland, the active role of the European Commission in reforming laws entails an opportunity to rationalize the existing efforts to improve the quality of law. Lessons learned from the regulatory reform to date indicate that Poland needs an extremely radical change in its approach to reforms, so as to emphasize comprehensive, consistent and prompt actions at each law-making stage. What we are observing now is merely an 'adequate crawling' toward better government.

Doubtless, a form of shock therapy could be started by the reconstruction of the system of regulatory impact assessment. The politicians who make laws and the entities to which laws apply must have knowledge about the effects of proposed regulations. Presently, extremely important decisions, from the point of view of public finance and the cost of business operations, are made intuitively. One cannot help noticing how much room this leaves for errors and abuses. In transitioning from the 'crawling' stage to a quick-paced trot, more use should be made of the American experience in terms of calculation methods, selection of indicators facilitating a comparison of the impact of various types of regulations, econometric models that serve as the basis for appraising the effects of regulations. For unknown reasons, academic communities show little interest in that type of research.[28] What is needed, therefore, is better cooperation between research centres and the public administration and the private sector; here, again, the American experience could provide useful examples.[29]

The European Commission's commitment to regulatory reform is particularly important for new EU members. The transfer of reform management coordination to the level of the entire Community and the introduction of reform monitoring should speed up the process of improving the regulatory system, forcing not only the emergence of appropriate institutions and procedures, but also the creation of an appropriate climate for regulation reforms. The right climate means, for example, the transfer of the responsibility for reform coordination to the level of the decision-making centre of a given country[30] and dissemination of information on the benefits of reforming laws expressed in terms of money.

Notes

1   W. Bieńkowski (2006) 'Rosnąca rola gospodarki Stanów Zjednoczonych w świecie: przyczyny i kierunek zmian', in *Amerykański model rozwoju gospodarczego* (Warsaw: SGH).
2   The UE Better Regulation programme was adopted in 2002.
3   European Commission (2002) 'Action Plan "Simplifying and Improving the Regulatory Environment"', COM(2002) 278 final, Brussels.
4   European Commission (2005) 'Impact Assessment Guidelines', SEC(2005)791, Brussels.
5   European Commission (2005) 'Communication from the Commission on an EU Common Methodology for Assessing Administrative Costs Imposed by Legislation', COM(2005) 518 final, Brussels.
6   European Commission (2005) 'Outcome of the Screening of Legislative Proposals Pending before the Legislator', COM(2005) 462 final, Brussels.

7 European Commission (2005) 'Implementing the Community Lisbon Programme: A Strategy for the Simplification of the Regulatory Environment', COM(2005) 535 final, Brussels.

8 European Commission (2006) 'Report from the Commission "Better Lawmaking 2005"', SEC(2006) 737, Brussels.

9 US Chamber of Commerce (2006) 'Fighting for Your Business'.

10 Government Performance and Results Act (1993).

11 E.C. Karmack (2003) 'Government Innovation around the World', Ash Institute for Democratic Governance and Innovation, J.F. Kennedy School of Government, Harvard University.

12 Statement of J.D. Graham, Administrator of the Office of Information and Regulation Affairs before the Subcommittee on Small Business, United States House of Representatives, 28 April 2005.

13 James L. Gattuso (2004) 'Reining in the Regulators: How does President Bush Measure Up?', Heritage Foundation, 28 September 2004.

14 *Ibid.*

15 2006 Report to Congress on the Costs and Benefits of Federal Regulations and Unfunded Mandates on State, Local and Tribal Entities, January 2007.

16 R.W. Hahn (1998) 'Regulatory Reform: Assessing the Government's Numbers', Brookings Center for Regulatory Studies.

17 Draft Report to Congress on the Costs and Benefits of Federal Regulation 2005: 31–3.

18 US Mission to the European Union, Brussels, 31 July 2002.

19 S. Walus and D. Tompkins (2004) 'Impact of European Antitrust Regulations on Transatlantic Business', www.westga-edu/bquest/2004/europa.htm

20 OECD (2002) 'Reviews of Regulatory Reform. Poland. From Transition to New Regulatory Challenges' (Paris: OECD).

21 European Commission (2005) 'Better Regulation for Growth and Jobs in the European Union', SEC(2005) 175: 17.

22 According to OBOP surveys, only 12 per cent of Poles are affiliated with a non-governmental organization; there is still a strong mistrust in other people as well as institutions and organizations. OBOP 5–9 January on a sample of 1005 persons of 15 or older, *Gazeta Wyborcza*, 23 January 2007.

23 R. Zubek and K.H. Goetz (2006) 'Final Report on the Ernst & Young "Better Government" Programme', available on www.sprawnepanstwo.pl

24 OECD (2002) 'Reviews of Regulatory Reform. Poland. From Transition to New Regulatory Challenges' (Paris: OECD).

25 *Rzeczpospolita*, a daily newspaper, 2 January 2007.

26 Since 1995, the regulatory reform has been carried out within the OECD, an organization affiliating 30 well-developed countries. The OECD focuses on developing expert opinion recommendations for the governments of its member states.

27 M.J. Radło (2006) 'Economic Reform in the European Union: Will the Lisbon EU Catch Up with the US', in W. Bieńkowski, J.C. Brada and M.J. Radło (eds), *Reagonomics Goes Global. What Can the EU, Russia and Transition Countries Learn from the USA?* (Basingstoke, UK; New York: Palgrave Macmillan).

28 At least, according to the Ministry of Economy officials supervising implementation of the regulatory reform in Poland.

29   The significance of combining private and public funds in research financing in the US is pointed out by R. Rybarski (2006), 'Uniwersytety jako element amerykańskiego modelu gospodarczego', in *Amerykański Model Rozwoju Gospodarczego* (Warsaw: SGH): 66.

30   That view is shared by: R. Zubek and K.H. Goetz in 'Wpływ reguł legislacyjnych na jakość ustawodawstwa', *Prawo i podatki*, November 2005, stating that: 'Insufficient governmental control over the legislative process leads to an excessive growth of legislative activities and reduces consistency of the established law' and 'A weakness of the Polish legislative process is the absence of the Prime Minister's substantive intervention with the shape of legislative draft'.

Conclusions

Despite the recent apparent reversal of long-standing trends, with the EU's economic growth accelerating in 2005–07 and US economic growth slowing down in 2006 and 2007, the underlying problems causing our concern about most European countries' relatively poor performance vis-à-vis the United States remain intact. The recent trends have been too short in duration and reflect only aggregate data, not the structural problems of critical importance such as the capacity to innovate and the general flexibility of markets. Thus, despite the recent growth spurt, the EU countries have been unable to close the productivity and innovativeness differential or the 30 per cent GDP per capita gap that still exists between the two sides of the Atlantic.

But what really clouds the picture, over and above the new trends and economic data on Europe's economic acceleration and the US's slowing down, is another worrisome factor, that of a growing confusion among many members of European elites on what to do to make Europe competitive and not to fall further behind the United States. What is particularly worrisome is the fact that the political elites refuse to address the real issues of why Europe is losing the global competitiveness race and, instead, prefer to grasp for evidence to support second-best solutions, trumpeting findings on the relatively good performance of the Scandinavian countries or pointing at the relatively successful performance of some other countries that have started to scale down their large social programmes, to reduce income taxes or to direct more money for R&D and education and, as a result, begin to perform better that before or better than others. EU leaders continue to see the Scandinavian socio-economic model as a solution for reconciling what are, to them, the conflicting objectives of security and growth or as a compromise between growth and security, thus having their cake and eating it too.

We take a different view. Most of the authors contributing to this book strongly believe that the causes of Europe's relatively poor economic performance in the 1990s and after are the deeply rooted problems inherited in the socio-economic models that dominate most of the European countries, especially those of the big continental countries – Germany, France and Italy, but also including a 'model' country such as Sweden.[1]

Most of our contributors, and ourselves also, fully subscribe to what the Nobel laureate Edmund Phelps said in 2006; namely, that 'there are two economic systems in the West – two systems of economic institutions'. Free enterprise capitalism such as is in existence in the US, Canada or the UK is one system; the second, although also based on private ownership but modified by the introduction of institutions aimed at protecting the interest of 'stakeholders' and 'the social partners', can be found in operation mostly in Germany (the social market economy), France (social democracy) and in Italy (*concertazione*). What is critical however, as Phelps underlines, is that 'the two systems are not operationally equivalent, contrary to some neoclassical views. The free enterprise system is structured in such a way that it facilitates and stimulates dynamism while the Continent's system impedes and discourages it.'[2] The way to reconcile the two systems is very difficult to find, if not impossible.

This is why most of the authors contributing to this book advocate deep reforms in the European countries, both in old and new Europe, that would restructure the economic models of these countries in a way that would make their economic policies as close to the Anglo-Saxon model as possible. They all point to globalization, open and flexible markets, technological innovation and other factors that leave little room for an inflexible economic system seeking to secure the benefits of the past but unable to face the international competition of the present, not to mention the challenges to come. To survive and prosper, Europe must change dramatically, leaving cosmetic adjustments behind.

Notes

1 See Chapter 1 by Birgitta Swedenborg, in this volume.
2 Edmund S. Phelps, 'Lecture at the Honoris Causa Ceremony', Institut d'Etudes Politiques de Paris, Paris, 22 June 2006. See also http://economistsview.typepad.com/economistsview/2006/10/phelps_dynamic_.html

Index